CRY OF THE DRUMMER

☆ ☆ ☆ ☆ ☆ ☆ ☆ ☆ ☆ ☆ ☆ ☆ ☆ ☆ ☆ ☆

"MUCH OF 'CRY OF THE DRUMMER' HAS AN AUTHENTIC RING TO IT."

Stu Bykofsky,
Philadelphia Daily News

☆ ☆ ☆ ☆ ☆ ☆ ☆ ☆ ☆ ☆ ☆ ☆ ☆ ☆ ☆ ☆

"NOTHING WILL GET YOUR ATTENTION LIKE 'CRY OF THE DRUMMER'. THE LAST CHAPTER WILL MAKE YOU FEEL LIKE YOU ARE RIGHT THERE AMIDST THE EXCITEMENT... JOHNNY AND ROSANNA SHOW THE KIND OF LOVE WE ALL LONG FOR."

Patty Kitch,
Recording Artist

☆ ☆ ☆ ☆ ☆ ☆ ☆ ☆ ☆ ☆ ☆ ☆ ☆ ☆ ☆ ☆

John Michael Austin

S0-APY-552

CRY OF THE DRUMMER

☆ ☆ ☆ ☆ ☆ ☆ ☆ ☆ ☆ ☆ ☆ ☆ ☆ ☆ ☆ ☆

"AUSTIN'S KNOWLEDGE OF LIFE ON THE STREETS AND THE STRUGGLES AND HARDSHIPS OF THE STRANGE AND EXCITING WORLD OF ROCK'N'ROLL IS EXTRAORDINARY."

Zanne Miller,
King of Prussia Post

☆ ☆ ☆ ☆ ☆ ☆ ☆ ☆ ☆ ☆ ☆ ☆ ☆ ☆ ☆

"READERS WILL BE ADDICTED FROM BEGINNING TO END. LEAVING THEM WANTING TO READ IT AGAIN AND AGAIN."

Ray Kitch,
Recording Artist

☆ ☆ ☆ ☆ ☆ ☆ ☆ ☆ ☆ ☆ ☆ ☆ ☆ ☆ ☆ ☆

John Michael Austin

A WorldRock book by John Michael Austin

CRY OF THE DRUMMER

CRY OF THE DRUMMER

☆ ☆ ☆ ☆ ☆ ☆ ☆ ☆ ☆ ☆ ☆ ☆ ☆ ☆ ☆

JOHN MICHAEL AUSTIN

WORLDROCK PUBLISHERS
VALLEY FORGE

WR WORLDROCK PUBLISHERS

P.O. Box 80212, Valley Forge, PA 19484

Cover design by WorldRock Publishers

Library of Congress Catalog Card Number: 94-62207

ISBN: 0-964-51310-2

Printed in the United States Of America

First Printing 1995
Second Printing 1997

WR

WorldRock Books are published by WorldRock Publishers

AT

VALLEY FORGE

This novel is dedicated to all the people who gave me encouragement, showed me love and kept me in their prayers. The dream has become a reality.

Thank you sweet Jesus.

"In everyone's life there is someone special, and though they may be gone they will never be forgotten."

– John Michael Austin

But they that wait upon the Lord shall renew their strength; they shall mount up with wings as eagles; they shall run, and not be weary; and they shall walk, and not faint.

– ISAIAH 40:31

1

* * * * * * * * * * *

THE STREETS WERE CALM IN SOUTH PHILADELPHIA ON THAT SUNDAY
night in late March. There it stood on the corner: Harry's Bar. The
sign that hung from the building looked like it was about to fall
off. It was so dirty, it was beginning to look black instead of its
original color, white with red letters. The red brick was cracked in
many places, and the front door was peeling. It was a dull green,
and seemed it hadn't been painted in years.

Inside the bar were many of the neighborhood locals just
sitting at the bar and at the few tables in the corner. Many of them
just nursing their drinks, just trying to pass the time of the lonely
night. The drinking bar was brown, faded, and dingy. In back of
the bar was a big mirror, and a used display of all types of whiskey.
The wooden floor certainly could have been replaced, it was dusty
and worn.

The bar was a fairly good size, and supplied a stage off to
the right-hand corner about a foot high. It was about eight feet
wide and six feet long. It looked like it would crumble at any minute.
The bar generally supplied live music Friday, Saturday and Sunday night whenever they could get a band to come in and play.

On the old, dilapidated stage stood a three-piece band—bass,
guitar, and drums. Mickey Percaro, a thirty-five-year-old burnout
musician was trying to stay awake as he held his vintage black

Fender Precision bass, plucking at the big strings. His black hair was thinning as it covered his ears, and the circles under his eyes were beginning to match his hair. He was pale and needed a shave.

On the other side of the stage was Kenny Pascarelli. Kenny was pushing forty. He had played the nightclub circuit on a full-time basis for fifteen years. Finally, his wife told him she would leave him if he didn't get a steady job, so he decided to get a straight job, and just play music on weekends. Kenny's graying, stringy hair seemed to be pointing in all directions. He stood about six-foot-two and extremely thin. His long, pointed nose, and wire-rimmed glasses were just what his long face needed. Kenny was a funny-looking character as he held his vintage Gibson Les Paul guitar, stringing chords as the band played on.

Behind the drum kit sat a good-looking character. He had a face only a mother could love. His hair was pitch black and styled well, it was just over his ears on the side, and to the shoulders in the back. His frame was well built. He wore a black t-shirt and blue jeans. On his feet were black and white alligator boots. Like the other guys, he looked tired and beat. He was the youngest of the three at thirty-one years old. His name was Johnny Covini.

Johnny was a good drummer; one of the best in the tri-state area. His drums were shiny black and always polished to the hilt. His cymbals were so clean, they would blind you under the bright lights. Johnny loved his drums. There had been women in Johnny's life who wished he would have looked at them the way he looked at his drums. He always thought he would be in the recording industry, but because of drugs, alcohol, and fast women, he was never able to give 100% to his music. He was never married and didn't have a steady girl. He managed to pick up a gig or two on the weekends, and repaired and sold old drums as well as being a bookie for a neighborhood numbers king. He was just another frustrated musician going nowhere, but somehow he just kept believing he would someday make it to the big time.

The song they played had come to an end. A shout came

from in back of the bar. "Hey you guys, keep it down! Youse are playing too damn loud." It was Harry, the owner and operator of Harry's Bar. Harry was sixty years old and had operated the bar for over thirty years. He really didn't need the money, or any loud bands, he just kept the bar open so he wouldn't have to be around his wife all day.

As the band began to play an old standard, a few of the regular patrons shouted out, with a slur in their speech,

"Come on, liven it up a little! We're falling asleep."

A little man siting at a table alone, ready to pass out shouted, "You guys ought to retire—take up needlepoint!"

The guys were just too tired and burnt-out, they couldn't wait for the night to end. It was 1:30 A.M. and they finished the song, and Harry told them to cut it, he would soon be closing. Mickey Percaro and Kenny Pascarelli began packing up their equipment. Johnny Covini stood up from the drum throne. With his black hair, dark eyes, and tall, slender physique, he stood out from the others. He was six foot-one, and looked like a star. He seemed to be a bit angry that Sunday night, and pushed aside the cymbal stand. He walked off the stage, and headed for the bar.

An old pathetic drunk who Johnny had seen around many times shouted, "Hey Johnny, how about you guys play one more tune?" The drunk attempted to put his arm around Johnny. "Johnny, one more tune—how 'bout it kid?"

"Go home old man, and sleep it off." Johnny threw the man's arm off his shoulder and continued toward the bar. "Hey Harry, how about a nightcap? You know, one for the road."

"Sure Johnny, what will it be?"

"A cold one will do it."

Harry brought the glass of beer to Johnny. Harry stood about six-foot-two, totally bald on top. He was very husky, a bit over weight. He had bags under his eyes and a big, wide nose. His face was rugged-looking. He always wore a white, short sleeved shirt, and a white apron. Harry was from the old school. "Johnny, you guys were a bit loud tonight. Youse keep it up, youse won't play here no more."

"Yeah sure, Harry, I'll talk to them." Johnny barely acknowledged Harry, but still held a lot of respect for him. He had been going to his bar for over seven years, and took Harry's bets. As Johnny lifted the cold glass to his mouth, a hand clutched his forearm before the glass reached his lips. He tried to turn to see who had the nerve to annoy him at this time of night, but before he completed the turn, he heard a voice.

A very pretty girl with long black hair and big dark eyes said, "Hey boy, I just love drummers." Her complexion was immaculate. She stood about five-foot-five. She was built well and big-busted. Her face and nose were just perfect, and she had the sweetest lips. It was Penny Delulla, an old girlfriend of Johnny's.

He was stunned. "Penny, what the hell are you doing here?"

"That's a fine way to treat an old girlfriend!"

"Yeah, I think it is." Johnny reached over and tried to hug her.

Penny stiffened her body. "Well you know where you can go. I'm not going to let you talk to me like that." She turned and started walking away.

Johnny shouted, "Hey Penny, I'm sorry."

"Hey Johnny, I don't need your attitude. I thought you would have changed by now."

"Come on, have a drink. Hey Harry, how 'bout one for the lady?"

Penny walked back and leaned across the bar reluctantly. "Can you spare it?" she asked.

"For you, anytime."

Penny finally sported a smile toward Johnny. "Thank you," she said.

"Hey Penny, things just ain't been goin' too well lately, you know what I mean? I didn't mean to talk to you the way that I did. I heard you were dancing at the Eastside Club." He looked at her with curiosity.

"With two kids and no husband, a girl's gotta do something, I mean, I just can't make it working nine to five, somebody's got to feed them kids. Hey, have you heard from any of the guys from the old band?"

"No, I haven't seen or heard from any of them in eight years, and I hope I don't for another eight."

Mickey Percaro interrupted, "Hey Johnny, you going to help us with equipment or what?

"Hey Mickey, my back's been bothering me, how about givin' me a break tonight?"

"I should've known better than to even ask. I'll give you a call during the week, I'll see if I can get us a gig for next weekend."

"OK, Mickey, thanks." Mickey started to leave. "Oh, and Mickey, sorry about the equipment... and be careful with my drums."

"Yeah, yeah, yeah—same old story."

Penny continued, "Johnny are you still holding a grudge towards the guys in the other band? It's not healthy to hold grudges, you know."

"Look, we gonna talk about anything worthwhile?" Johnny was getting angry.

"OK, I'm sorry. I didn't mean to hit your soft-spot."

"It's not a soft-spot." He slammed his glass on the bar. "It's all over, you hear? It's all over."

The remaining crowd looked over to Johnny. Suddenly quiet came over the barroom. Johnny stared at the mirror in back of the bar. He looked at a lonely man at thirty-one years, no wife, no kids, and no one to turn to. He felt as though the music business had destroyed him. He turned and looked at Penny and fondly remembered the evening that they met, years ago. God, he thought, how her beauty stood out in the crowd that night. It was a very long time ago, at the beginning of his career. Things back then were less complicated, and Penny came into his life at the perfect time. Where were those simple days?

"I'm sorry Penny, I'm really sorry."

"It's OK. Johnny, don't worry, everything will be all right."

Johnny grinned, "Yeah, everything will be all right."

"Johnny, were you getting ready to leave? I know it's late, but I haven't seen you in almost ten years. I'd like to hear what you've been doing, and I hope you'd like to hear where I've been too. Could we spend a little time together? I know I came here unexpected, but I'd like to talk with you. What do you say, can we go somewhere else and talk?"

"Well I'm beat, but you look great, and we do have history together. Let's go now, before I change my mind." Johnny finished his beer and placed the empty glass on the counter.

Harry looked up from his newspaper. "Johnny, when you guys coming back here?"

"I don't know Harry, I gotta talk to Mickey. I'll see ya tomorrow Harry."

"OK, see ya tomorrow kid." Harry remembered Johnny when he was just a little runt in the neighborhood. He took a liking to Johnny from the first day that Johnny asked him if he could shine his shoes. Johnny always went to Harry's with his homemade shoe box when he was just a kid.

Penny and Johnny walked toward the door of the bar together. Johnny put his arm around her and felt a sense of warmth between them. It had been a long night and he was genuinely happy to see a familiar face. His car was parked in front of the bar. He wished for a second the car he was about to drive were a brand new Cadillac. But instead, there stood his 1972 Pontiac Grand Prix, black, dented, and dirty. He wondered if Penny was expecting anything more elaborate from him. No, she knew what he was like, and she knew that he had not grown up even in the last ten years. Penny had left him because he was stubborn and not progressing with his career.

"Here's my car. Wait, I'll get the door for you."

Penny looked at him with no expression. She had loved him so much at one time. She thought he looked tired and aged. She had so many questions to ask him, she didn't even know where to start. "Thanks Johnny. Where are we going?"

"There's a diner not too far from here—let's go get some breakfast." Johnny got into the car and made himself comfortable. He quickly started the car and drove away. "This place we're going to, I think you'll remember. You'll be surprised when you see it."

"What else have you been doing, besides playing drums on weekends, Johnny?"

"I'm taking some bets at my workshop, while I'm making some money buying and selling used drums."

"What about a steady job? Have you had any jobs that lasted a long time? Johnny, you really don't look that great. Have you been taking care of yourself? Tell me, is there someone special in your life? Have you fallen in love with anyone? Is anyone taking care of you?"

"You're asking too many questions, don't you think? Let's just go have some breakfast and have a few laughs." Johnny pulled into the parking lot of the diner and turned towards Penny. "Look, do you remember this place? Does it look the same to you?"

Penny opened her car door and began to get out. She looked up. "Isn't this the Rock Stop? Johnny—isn't this the Rock Stop?!"

"Not anymore it isn't. It's just another diner with a new name and new sign. You won't find any rock'n'roll musicians here like we used to. Let's go in and eat." Johnny held the door open for Penny as they both went inside. It was almost empty and one of the juke boxes was playing an oldie. A chubby blonde hostess picked up two menus and showed them where to sit.

"Johnny, I can still feel the old times here. This is where all the musicians came after the gigs."

"Yeah, all the groupies too."

"We had a ball here, didn't we?"

"They were the times of our life."

Penny looked around the diner. Nothing had changed. The walls were the same color and the booths were in the same place. All of a sudden she felt very old and very sad. She turned back to look at Johnny again. Johnny looked very old and very sad too. "Johnny what's troubling you?"

"Penny I could always be straight with you and confide in you. I can tell you're full of questions and you want answers from me. I really don't have anyone to talk to these days." Penny placed her hand over Johnny's to make him feel at ease. "I'm pushing thirty-two years old. I've invested half my life in music, lugging equipment, one-nighters, Philadelphia, Jersey, New York, fifteen freakin' different bands, up, downs—never on a steady course. You know what I mean?" He began to fill up with tears. "I'm like some kind of wandering star—some kind of drifter. I feel like a bum, a loser."

For a moment there was silence. Johnny looked around the old diner. Everything looked the same. The brown walls, the brown booths, even the rug looked the same, but spotted all over. Johnny looked back at Penny. "Can you believe it? This place used to be the Rock Stop, it used to have class. I can't believe it, now they call it Ray's Diner. It looks like a damn dump." Johnny shook his head in disgust. He wished he could have taken Penny somewhere that had a little class.

Penny still held on to Johnny's hand. She suddenly felt sorry for him. She knew he was hurting.

"I'm sorry Penny. I guess you just happened to be around when I needed a shoulder to cry on."

"Johnny you're not a loser. You're a good musician and a damn good drummer. You and everyone around the tri-state area knows it too."

"Yeah, what good is it doing me? Look at the damn life-style I'm living. I thought I'd be at least part of one album by now."

"It's not the music Johnny, it's your damn stubborn nature. Everything has to go your way, or it's no way. And what about the things I hear about you at the East Side Club? I hear you're still drinking too much, snorting coke, and running around with every girl that gives you the eye. You have to change your life-style before it's too late."

The waitress returned to the table. She let out a sigh and waited patiently for some response. Johnny looked over at Penny and said, "What do you want to eat?"

"Two eggs over light, some bacon and toast will be fine. One decaf."

"I'll have the same, thanks." Johnny decided to lighten the conversation. "Penny, where have you been staying?"

"I'm over in Jersey now. I have a nice apartment, nice car, beautiful clothes, but I can't find a man."

"Maybe we should have taken your car, instead of the piece of junk I drove you over in." Penny grinned. "Penny, I'm really sorry for all the bad times, you know I didn't mean to treat you the way I did at times, it's just that I got a big head when the band got on stage and the music got started. It's always been like another world to me."

"You really love it, don't you Johnny?"

"Yeah, I really love this craziness." Ten minutes had passed and the waitress appeared with their food, and Johnny was relieved. He didn't want to discuss his life any longer. He had lost it for a moment. Penny had a way of bringing out things in him like no one else ever could. There were long periods of silence as they both ate their food quickly. When the waitress returned with the check, Penny tried to grab it, but there was no way Johnny was going to let a woman pay for his meal at this point in his life. It was getting late—close to three A.M., and he had had enough of hearing of himself and his problems. They finished their food and left the diner.

As they rode back to the bar where Penny's car was parked, she continued to question him about his future. Johnny finally answered her.

"I don't know where I'm going. I may continue on like this for the rest of my life. I just don't have the answers. It seems like I don't know where I'm going from one day to the next." It was not a long ride from the diner to the bar, and the remainder of the ride was in silence.

Johnny pulled into the parking lot and stopped the car. Penny seemed to be waiting for something to happen, just something more than silence. Johnny rubbed his hands through his hair at that moment. He felt tired and frustrated and wanted to go home to bed.

"Penny, what brought you out so late tonight anyway?"

"I was visiting my sister in center city. When I left I started thinking about you. I saw Tommy Heart Saturday, and he told me you were playing Harry's Bar for the weekend."

"Tommy Heart, what's he doing these days?"

"He's a car salesman. He sells Buicks."

"Doesn't play the keyboards anymore?"

"No. He gave that up, but he still likes to talk about musicians and find out where everybody's playing gigs."

"Listen Penny, thanks a lot, you've been a big help, I can always depend on you to talk to me."

"Just do me one favor."

"What?"

"When you make it big, don't forget me Johnny."

"I won't forget you, I won't ever forget you." Johnny leaned over and kissed Penny gently. Her lips were so soft, he thought, but it wasn't like before. It didn't feel the same.

Penny looked disappointed, but she knew there was no longer anything between them. She said her good-byes, and handed him a slip of paper with her number. "I know you won't call, but keep it just in case."

"Good-bye Penny, take care of yourself."

Penny said good-bye, and got out of the car. She just stood there and waved as Johnny drove away. Tears filled her eyes. Johnny never waited till Penny got her car started. He thought it best to just drive away.

As he started on the road to his apartment, he began to have flashbacks of the past run crazily through his mind. The good times, the bad times, the hurts, and the sorrows. His mind was going a mile a minute. He covered so many events so quickly, that he became overwhelmed with anxiety. He pulled into a spot in front of his apartment, ran up the steps, opened the door, and collapsed onto his bed. He didn't even take off his clothes, just passed out.

2

* * * * * * * * * *

ANOTHER MONDAY MORNING HAD ARRIVED. JOHNNY DREADED MONday mornings after playing three nights in a row. He rolled over at the same time the phone rang.

"Hello," he said, with a groggy voice.

"Johnny, ain't you supposed to be working today?" It was Frankie Benelli, Johnny's numbers boss. Frankie had grown up in South Philadelphia and spent his life on the streets. He learned early in life about the rackets. He was thirty years old, and never married. He had more women than he knew what to do with. He always had two bodyguards, and was usually seen in a black Mercedes. Most of the people in South Philadelphia hated Frankie. He was self-centered, ruthless, and had a naturally angry disposition. And, his bodyguards were dangerous men. No one got in his way.

"I just got a call from three of your customers," said Frankie, "let's go man, there are too many guys out there looking for work."

"OK, OK Frankie, I'll get there in the next twenty minutes." Johnny slammed the phone down and looked at the clock on his dresser. "Oh shit! It's already eleven," he shouted, "no wonder Frankie's pissed off at me."

Johnny jumped out of bed. He stared in the mirror above his dresser. Johnny opened his eyes and laughed to himself, thinking, yeah—hurry off to your career. You have a real good career as a bookmaker. Johnny was feeling sorry for himself. He headed to the kitchen for a glass of juice. The clothing that he had slept in all night was all wrinkly. He didn't even take off his boots.

As he got near the entrance of the tiny kitchen, he began to feel slightly dizzy, and reached for the refrigerator door for support. A feeling of fear rushed through his body. He had felt a lot of highs and lows, but never a feeling like this. Grabbing a bottle of orange juice, he forgot about using a glass, and headed back to the bedroom. His head was pounding, but he managed to take a swig of juice, hoping this would make the feeling disappear. He sat down on the edge of the bed and set the bottle down on the floor. "Oh my God," he said, "what's happening to me?" He laid his body down on the bed, and within a few minutes, the feeling subsided.

Johnny waited for a few minutes to pass, even though it seemed much longer. He had to get up and get started. Slowly he lifted his body from the bed, and prayed that the feeling would go away. He was scared. Perhaps all the years of partying, drugs, and alcohol were finally catching up with him, not to mention the women. Finally, the dizziness stopped. Johnny got himself together, did a quick change of clothes, and threw some cold water on his face. He grabbed his leather jacket and left the apartment.

As he locked his apartment door, a little boy about ten years old, fair complected with blond hair hanging over his ears, and the biggest bright blue eyes approached Johnny. He was holding a chrome snare drum on his shoulder. It was little Joey Cunningham. He was the son of the young couple who had moved into the apartment building around the same time Johnny did. Johnny had taken a liking to Joey, and gave him his first used set of drums. He let him keep them in the garage that Johnny rented in the back of the apartments, where Johnny generally kept his drums also. If Johnny didn't get any gigs for a few weeks, he would set his drums up in the garage and practice. Joey looked up to Johnny as a big brother. Johnny became friends with Joey's parents. He had even helped them out financially when Joey's father had been out of work at one time. That was before Johnny became addicted to cocaine and had quite a bit of money, but now he was broke, and living day to day. Cocaine and alcohol were absorbing all his funds.

"Hey Joey, how you doin' kid, what's up?"

"Hey Johnny, I broke my snare drum head, can you fix it for me?"

"Sure kid, let me take it to my shop, I have plenty of drum heads there. I'll have it done for you tonight."

"Gee thanks Johnny."

"Joey, why ain't you in school today? Do your parents know you're home?"

"I didn't feel good today Johnny." Joey looked down to the floor, and then looked up again at Johnny.

"You mean you didn't feel like going to school today."

"Well… sort of."

"Joey, listen to me, stay in school, and don't be a fool." They both laughed. Johnny rubbed his hand on Joey's head. "You still practicing them snare drum rudiments?"

"Well I forgot last night."

"Well, you need a night off once in a while. Gotta run." He lifted the drum from the floor into his arms and ran down the steps. "See ya later kid," he shouted.

"See ya Johnny."

Johnny reached the bottom of the steps and headed toward his car. Thank God it was out front, he thought. Sometimes he forgot where he parked his car if he had a bad night before. Looking away from his car for a moment, he noticed a guy stumbling toward him. He couldn't quite make out the face, but the guy looked familiar to him.

"Tom Cat, is that you?" Johnny extended his hand to welcome an old friend. He had worked with Tom Cat in his first band. Tom Cat had played a mean guitar. He and Johnny always had good times together. Tom Cat was a little guy about five-foot-five.

He was wearing a long dirty tan cashmere coat. He needed a shave badly and his eyes had the darkest circles under them. His hair was long and greasy. He was wearing a yellow shirt underneath which had been all wrinkled. His jeans were faded and dirty. He wore high-top white sneakers that were turning black from all the dirt. He looked pathetic.

The memories with Tom Cat were clear in Johnny's head, and he had not seen him in years. "What's wrong Tom Cat? You look tired and run down. Are you sick?" Johnny was shaking his hand at that point.

"Johnny, since you seen me last, I been married, divorced, strung out on dope, and now I'm a drunk."

Johnny felt so badly for him. They had been good friends and shared a lot of good times together. The guy looked frightening.

"You know, Johnny, I tried for almost ten years to get a recording contract with that freakin' band, you know—The Cats. Can you believe we never caught a break? I invested ten good years in that band. I could have sworn we were going to make it. I lost my wife, my two kids, and now I'm too sick to work anymore. I had a nervous breakdown you know, Johnny. I drove that damn furniture truck six days a week to support my family, then I played four nights a week in the local bars, trying to get some exposure for the music we wrote. You know what I think Johnny? I think we had poor management. What do you think Johnny, what do you think it could have been? Maybe it was the band, huh Johnny? Maybe it was the players. I keep thinkin' and wondering what the hell it could have been. It's drivin' me nuts. You know what Johnny? I think I'm insane. I think I cracked up. I feel like a real wacko."

Johnny knew at that point that Tom Cat was a sick man. He couldn't believe how he kept rambling on and criticizing himself. He didn't know what to say. "Yeah, it's a tough business Tom Cat."

"Tough? It's sending me to an early grave. As a matter of fact, I'm already dead. What are you doing Johnny?"

"Me and Mickey Percaro and Kenny Pascarelli, we pick up a few gigs here and there. I buy and sell drums, and I take bets for a local numbers boss."

"Sounds like you're doin' pretty good, Johnny."

"Well, to tell you the truth Tom Cat, I'm addicted to cocaine and alcohol. That's where all my money's going. I'm not much better off than you are, believe me. Hey Tom Cat I gotta go—I'm running late."

"Hey Johnny, just one more thing—my cousin Poodie, he works down at Far Out Studios. Why don't you give me your number. I'm usually down there a couple hours a day. I clean up the place and he gives me a few dollars. I can give him your number and maybe he can turn you on to something good musically. I know you're one of the best drummers around."

"Why not?" He reached in his pocket and gave Tom Cat a card.

"Still using business cards, huh Johnny," Tom Cat laughed.

"Hey Tom Cat, you take it easy."

Tom Cat said good-bye and started walking away. Johnny walked to the driver's side of the car, put his hand on the door handle and looked at Tom Cat walking down the street. He couldn't believe how bad off Tom Cat appeared. What the hell was happening here? First Penny last night, and now Tom Cat today. Was someone trying to tell him something?

He opened the door, lifted the seat forward, and threw the drum into the back. Climbing into the car, he looked down at his watch and realized that Frankie would kill him. It was 11:30, and he still was not at work. He should have been there at ten. He sped off and drove to his workshop.

JOHNNY PULLED INTO A BACK ALLEY AND PULLED ALONGSIDE OF HIS WORK-shop, a garage. It was an old red brick garage with a big green door, and little windows. To the right of the big door was a little door. Johnny tried to keep the place in good condition, but it needed lots of plaster work and paint. He jumped out of the car and entered the garage quickly, carrying Joey's drum on his shoulder.

Inside was an old orange rug lying on the cement floor. The garage was about twelve feet by eighteen feet. There was an old work bench in the corner where Johnny repaired old drums. On the other side was a desk, a phone and an adding machine; that's where Johnny did his bookmaking.

Frankie had installed a heating system in the garage for Johnny. He used to like Johnny a lot, and could always depend on him, but he was beginning to get sick of Johnny's tardiness and his ignorance. He knew Johnny was plagued by drugs. Frankie was beginning to get fed up.

There were drums and drum accessories all over the place. The desk was brown and very old. It was covered with dust and papers. The workbench looked like it had been there since the garage was built. Inside was red brick also, and the ceiling was cracking, but Johnny enjoyed it just the same, it served the purpose. As long as there were drums inside, he was happy. The telephone rang. He placed the drum on the floor quickly and ran to the phone.

"Yeah, who is it?"

"Johnny, where you been man? I been tryin' to reach you for over an hour." It was Jimmy (The Blimp) Deligada, a steady customer of Johnny's who bet the numbers and horses very heavily.

"Come on Jimmy, it's Monday morning—you know what I mean. Give me a break. What do you got for me Jimmy?" Johnny grabbed a pencil and paper quickly.

"Let me give you the horse bets first." Johnny started writing everything down. Listening very carefully, he did not want to make any mistakes. He had done that a few times and it cost Frankie Benelli a lot of money. Jimmy began to put his horse bets in.

Johnny responded, "OK—Who's Who in the fifth, Ziggy's Choice in the eighth, and Time Traveler in the ninth."

"That's it for the horses Johnny, you got it?"

"I got it."

"Here's the numbers."

Johnny repeated as Jimmy rapped off the numbers, "OK—433 straight and boxed for five, 502 straight and boxed for five, 747 straight and boxed for ten, 445 straight and boxed for ten, and 551 straight and boxed for ten."

"OK, Johnny, that's it."

"OK. Gotcha Jimmy, talk to you tomorrow morning." He hung up the phone and walked over to the workbench in the corner.

He pushed some old drum accessories aside and cleared the bench. He turned and walked to Joey's drum and brought it back to the bench. He picked up a drum key and began to loosen the lugs. He wanted to get Joey's drum done before he got too busy on the phone. He didn't want to disappoint the kid. Johnny enjoyed repairing drums. It was the time he allowed himself to fantasize.

As he began taking the lugs off the drum, he pictured himself on a big stage in a giant concert hall playing a drum solo. There were at least ten thousand fans watching him play. The phone rang and startled him back to reality. Oh well, he thought, I'll get back to that one.

When he picked up the phone he heard the familiar voice from earlier that morning. It was Tom Cat. "Johnny, how's it goin'?"

"Tom Cat, I haven't seen you for years, and now I get to talk to you twice in one day."

"Listen Johnny, there might be an opening for a drummer with a local band. They're going to go out on their first tour soon. I'm talking about a shot at the bigs, man—do you hear me? Johnny, are you there?"

Johnny just held the phone in his hand. Suddenly, he was speechless. How could Tom Cat—a guy so messed up—turn him on to something that could be the big time? "Who's the band?"

"The Angels. You remember them, don't you?"

"Them guys still around?"

"Yeah, and they're bigger than ever. Look man, I already gave your name and number to my cousin Poodie down at Far Out Studios. If I can't get it together to become something big, maybe you can Johnny. You can do it. Just go to Far Out Studios on Wednesday, say about seven o'clock, and ask for Poodie. He may even give you a call before then. Don't forget to bring your drumsticks, and you may want to bring your own snare drum. He will tell you exactly what is happening just before audition time."

"Hey Tom Cat, thanks a lot."

"Good luck Johnny."

Johnny hung up the phone and wandered over to the window, hoping that no one would call for a while. Johnny was feeling anxious and insecure. He had never had a chance like this with a touring band, and he was scared. Just the thought of it made him fearful. He stared out the window and began to think to himself, it's only an audition—no big deal. He walked over to the tool cabinet where he always kept a bottle of whiskey tucked away. He took a glass and poured himself a drink.

Leaning back on the table, he wondered if he could pull this off. Down went a gulp of whiskey. He cringed. I'm nothing but a washed out nightclub musician, he thought, who the hell am I kidding anyway? He poured himself another drink and gulped it down. Suddenly he became enraged, mad at himself for being so fearful. He was angry because he knew he really wasn't ready for this type of challenge. All he ever knew was the nightclub circuit. He held the bottle tightly. He began to pour another drink, then suddenly threw the glass to the floor. "Damn!" he said, "I'm never gonna make it." He raised his right hand and threw the bottle of whiskey clear across the room, into the brick wall. Broken glass and whiskey splattered everywhere.

Suddenly there was silence. Johnny couldn't move for a moment, and then the phone rang. He shuffled across the room and answered. It was Tony (The Horse) DiJavante calling to place bets. When Tony finished placing his bets, Johnny walked back to the tool cabinet where he always kept a couple bags of cocaine. Even though the drug was controlling his life, he could always depend on its effects to make him feel better in troubled times.

He neatly placed a line on the top of the tool cabinet. He snorted the line of coke and instantly felt like a new man, like he could conquer the world. Johnny loved cocaine and was a severe addict.

Johnny finished fixing Joey's drum and continued to take bets through the afternoon. He was glad to be busy that afternoon, so he wouldn't be burdened with the fear of the audition on Wednesday night.

5:00 P.M. came quickly and Johnny was on his way. He clutched Joey's drum at his side, carefully locked the garage door, and jumped in his beat up car. He headed directly for Harry's Bar. He hadn't had a thing to eat and was starving. As he pulled up in front of the bar, he noticed some friends walking inside. It was Buddy Santangelo and Sal Morello. They were also bookmakers for Frankie Benelli.

The two walked inside and took a table near the stage. Johnny followed. As Johnny entered the bar, Buddy shouted, "Hey Johnny, how 'bout a drum solo?" He tapped Sal on the shoulder. They both laughed as they began to tease Johnny.

"You're a rock star, aren't you?" They were both still laughing. They knew the trouble that Johnny had in the music business, and knew how he was screwing up his job with Frankie.

Johnny wasn't laughing. The bar was full of patrons. It was Happy Hour. Johnny was embarrassed and a bit pissed off. As Johnny reached the bar, he shouted, "Why don't you guys shut up, before I play a drum solo on your head?"

"Aww, what's the matter—did Frankie give you a tough time today?" Sal asked.

Johnny never did like either of those guys. Buddy Santangelo was a little guy about 5' 6". He had a funny looking nose and squinted eyes. He always needed a shave, and always dressed like a bum. He was a real snake, no one ever knew he was well off financially. He would use his scrawny appearance to cover-up his illegal doings. He even drove an old 1975 Buick that looked like it was ready to fall apart. He and Sal covered a much bigger area of bets than Johnny did. Sal and he worked together and were two of Frankie's best employees. They didn't take drugs, and they weren't alcoholics. They were both married with children, and took good care of their families. They made good money with Frankie and didn't have a need to work in a factory. They always reminded Johnny of two rats, and they always teased him, even when they were in grade school.

Johnny felt bad because Frankie barely gave him enough money to live, but he knew he really wasn't dependable and could understand why Frankie couldn't do better for him. The two continued to make remarks at Johnny. He had had enough. He gulped down a shot of whiskey, took a sip of beer, and walked over to the table where the two idiots were sitting.

Johnny grabbed Buddy by the neck and started choking him. "I had enough of you—you hear? I had enough of your stupidity! Now you're going to die."

Sal jumped up and grabbed Johnny's wrists. "Johnny, what are you doing! Are you crazy?" He continued to choke Buddy. Sal couldn't pull his hands off Buddy's throat. Suddenly Harry and the patrons saw what was happening.

Harry ran to the table, grabbed Johnny around the waist, and raised him off the floor about six inches. He started pulling him away, but Johnny wouldn't let go. He pulled Buddy right off the chair. Buddy was turning blue in the face. His eyes were twice as big as normal. Finally, Sal bit into Johnny's left hand. Johnny let go.

Buddy fell to the floor. "Johnny, what the hell's wrong with you?!" yelled Harry.

Johnny was in shock. He couldn't believe what he'd just done. Harry let go of his waist. Sal helped Buddy up and sat him on a chair. Johnny turned to Harry, "I'm sorry, Harry. I went blank for a moment." He then walked toward Buddy and Sal.

"I'm sorry Buddy, I don't know what happened to me."

Buddy was gasping for air. "It's OK, Johnny, maybe I had it comin'."

Sal looked to Johnny. "Johnny, you got problems? You need money?"

"Nah. I'm OK, Sal. Guess I've been a little under the weather lately." Johnny looked back at Harry. "Harry, is it OK if I stay?"

"Yeah sure." Harry took a deep breath.

Sal sat there in his black blazer and turtleneck sweater. He wore tan shoes and gray pants. Sal was affiliated with a legal business and used it as a front, and for tax purposes. He was part owner in a pizza shop in South Philadelphia which did a good business. He was about the same height as Buddy, but much better looking. Sal was fair complected and had pitch black hair. He was always well groomed, and never worried about who would notice him and where he got his money from. He always dressed well and bought a new Cadillac every two years. He just sat and shook his head. "Poor Johnny," he said, "I think he's crackin' up."

Johnny walked back to the bar and Harry gave him another drink. "Johnny, what's bothering you? You in some kind of trouble?"

"Nah, it's not that Harry, I just got a few things on my mind. You know how it is."

"You know kid I shouldn't say this, 'cause it could be bad for business, but maybe you should stay off the booze for a while. You know it's good to get away from anything once in a while."

"Maybe you're right Harry." Johnny's mood had changed. He turned around and looked at the pool table setting in the right hand corner. "Eh—anybody want to shoot a game of pool?"

He spent the next few hours shooting eight ball with anyone who would take him on and managed to take in a couple beef sandwiches in between. He was a decent pool player and usually managed to have the other pool player buy him his booze. He had consumed several shots and beers, and was feeling no pain when he finally made his way to the door to leave.

IT WAS A MIRACLE THAT HE HAD DRIVEN HOME IN ONE PIECE. AS JOHNNY climbed the steps of the old apartment building, he had Joey's drum on his shoulder and was singing an old rock'n'roll tune out loud. Little Joey heard the racket and opened the door. "Johnny, you fixed my snare drum!"

When Johnny reached the top of the steps, Joey shouted to his mother in the kitchen, "Hey Mom, I'll be right back, I want to get my drum from Johnny."

"Yeah it's all fixed kid—just like new." Johnny handed him the drum.

"Gee, I can't believe it, a brand new drum head. Gee thanks Johnny."

"It's OK kid, anything for a friend."

"Hey Johnny, this guy Mickey Percaro was here."

"Oh yeah, what did he want?"

"He wanted to leave your drums off."

"Why? What's up?"

"He said he wouldn't be able to work with you and this guy named Kenny anymore."

"And what else did he say Joey?"

"He told me to tell you he joined a band playing weddings. He said it's more money and less aggravation. So I opened the garage in the back, and I set your drums up for you."

"That's great. Now I don't have a band. It's the same old bologna."

"Hey Johnny, how about we go down to the garage so you can play a drum solo."

"Sure kid, let's go raise some hell." Johnny was slurring over his words. He'd definitely had too much to drink. The two walked to the garage together, down the steps and around the building to the alley. Joey was carrying his drum over his shoulder just like Johnny did. Some of Joey's friends were playing and looked at Joey with surprise.

"Hey guys, this is Johnny—the guy I always tell you about. He's the best drummer in the world."

"Yeah sure, I bet."

"Yeah sure, I'd like to see how good he really is," shouted another of Joey's friends.

"Can they come in and watch, Johnny, can they?"

"Sure kid, bring the whole damn neighborhood in if you want."

Johnny, Joey, and about ten other kids entered the garage. Johnny sat on the drum stool and the kids looked on intensely. Joey took a seat off to the side where he always sat when Johnny would teach him drum techniques.

"OK, let's get this snare drum tuned up a bit, and we're ready to rock'n'roll. Looks like you've learned well how to set my drums up Joey. When I go on tour some day you can be my roadie."

Little Joey smiled and felt embarrassed. He felt like a real big shot in front of his friends when Johnny was around.

Johnny picked up the sticks that were laying on the bass drum. He started playing with a tricky syncopated beat that sounded fantastic. Then he came in with a double bass drum style that sounded like sweet thunder. He began to play the tom tom drums. His hands were moving quickly and with power. The kids were looking on in amazement. The sound he was producing was spellbinding. He played as though he never wanted to stop. He was full of vigor and excitement. He felt like he was on stage. Johnny's solo lasted five minutes with a very exciting climax. He lifted himself off the drum stool and walked in front of the drums. He leaned over and took a bow. The kids were going wild. Several of them came rushing up to him, full of praise. It was though he had just finished a drum solo in a well-known auditorium, and he had been the star.

"Hey man, can I have your autograph?"

"Sure kid." Johnny reached in his shirt pocket for a pen and paper. He scribbled his signature quickly. Joey made his way through the crowd to Johnny.

"Man that was great, Johnny! I knew you were good, but not that good."

Several of the kids were shouting at Johnny and asking him if he would teach them to play like that. Johnny thanked them all for listening and told them that maybe some night he would hold a drum clinic. He turned away from the kids and left the garage with Joey. Joey felt proud to be with Johnny. They walked around the building and up the steps.

Joey had his drum on his shoulder as usual. "Johnny, I have to go in and do some homework, thanks for the drum solo! Oh, and Johnny—"

"What's that kid?"

"You think you'll ever be a big rock'n'roll star?"

"I don't know Joey, sometimes I just don't know."

"See ya tomorrow Johnny."

"Yeah, see ya tomorrow kid." Johnny entered his apartment. He was proud of his drum solo. He walked directly to the mirror and took a good long look at himself. Out loud he said, "Yeah Johnny, you think you'll ever be a rock'n'roll star. Do you?" He placed his hands on the dresser and sighed. He walked over to the bed and jumped on top. He rubbed his hand through his hair and quickly fell off to sleep. It must have been nine o'clock.

3

* * * * * * * * * * *

THE NEXT MORNING HAD ONCE AGAIN COME QUICKLY. JOHNNY WAS AWAKE but had a difficult time getting out of bed. The alcohol had taken its toll on his body. Slowly he placed his feet on the floor, and again he felt that dizzy feeling he experienced the previous morning. His heart was pounding loudly and his stomach began to cramp up. It felt like someone was pulling his stomach up into his chest. He cried out, "Oh my God, don't let this happen to me."

He lay back down on the bed, hoping to relieve the pain. The dizziness was getting worse, not better. His heart seemed to be beating faster. Fear was overwhelming him like never before. He wanted to get to the refrigerator to get a swig of orange juice. He figured that would make him feel better. He tried to crawl off the bed and onto the floor. He didn't want to try and stand, for fear he would get dizzy again and maybe pass out.

He made his way to the refrigerator, and as he began to stand up, the pain became unbearable. He managed to open the door and reach in for the juice. He was a sad sight and was thankful no one was there with him. He took a drink of juice and sat down on the floor. He appeared as a hopeless invalid. A few minutes had passed and he was starting to feel a little better. He took a deep breath and slowly raised himself up. He walked over to the bed and got back on top and relaxed his muscles.

Some time had passed. He must have dozed off for a few minutes. He carefully lifted himself off the bed again. He looked at his watch and it was close to eleven. The phone rang and as he expected, it was Frankie. He reluctantly picked up the receiver.

"Hello," he said in a groggy voice.

"Hey Johnny, what the hell you doing man? That's twice this week! Come on, do you want to work or not?"

"OK, OK, I'm on my way."

"Now look, this is it. This is your last chance. You screw me up once more, and you're gone. Is that clear?"

Johnny didn't speak.

"Is that clear!?"

"Yeah OK, OK it's clear."

Frankie slammed the phone down. It took Johnny a half hour to shower and get into some fresh clothes. He was feeling too badly to rush. The hell with Frankie Benelli, he thought. He finished dressing and left the apartment. He drove slowly to the garage.

When he finally arrived, it was 12:00, and the phone was continually ringing. This was a really bad day for Johnny. He had missed over three thousand dollars in bets. Tuesdays were generally an early day, and he should have been there at 9:30. Johnny continued taking bets, and at 1:30, the phone rang once again, but this time it was from Far Out Studios.

"Hello, is this Johnny Covini?"

"Yeah, this is Johnny."

"This is Jerome, Poodie's assistant. Hey listen, the audition's tonight. They got you down on the list for tomorrow, but things have changed. Poodie's going out of town tomorrow, and he wants everybody here tonight."

Johnny was silent for a moment.

"This is Johnny Covini, isn't it—Tom Cat's friend?"

"Yeah this is me, OK I'll be there."

"OK be here at 8:00, and don't be late, Poodie doesn't like to wait for people, he's a really prompt guy. Trust me, if this means anything to you, you'll be here on time."

Johnny hung up the phone. The phone immediately rang and continued at an almost steady pace until five o'clock. He didn't have too much time to dwell on the evening that was ahead of him. When he checked his watch, it was 5:00 and he decided his day was over.

He left the garage and stopped at Ninth and Passyunk for a cheese steak, and then drove directly home. When he arrived at the apartment he looked toward the corner where his drum pad was set up. He thought about practicing for a minute, but first he needed a drink and a snort of coke.

He tried to remember where he'd left the bottle of whiskey he kept around the apartment. Johnny had a three room apartment. The bedroom walls were light blue and had stains all over them. The ceiling was cracking. There was no rug on the floor and he had one dresser. There was a mirror about six feet high fixed to the wall. He was generally too lazy to clean, or too drunk. The closet was a mess.

He managed to keep the kitchen fairly clean around the sink area, but then again, he never really cooked or had to wash any dishes. The floor had black tile that was aged and scuffed. The kitchen table was beginning to rust on the legs, and the four chairs were weak and tearing. There was little cabinet space under the sink and over top. His refrigerator was about the newest appliance in the apartment. He had finally convinced the landlord to replace it after begging him for almost a year. The acoustic ceiling had water stains from the roof leaking when it would rain, even the wall in back of the table had a big stain from water seeping into it. The kitchen walls were white and needed paint badly.

There was a very small living room which contained only a recliner chair, a small portable TV, and an old gray rug. Johnny never took an interest in his living quarters, and the place was a bit empty. He had managed to keep the bathroom clean, he couldn't stand a dirty bathroom.

He remembered leaving the bottle underneath the sink and went into the kitchen to check. He located the bottle, grabbed a glass, and sat down at the kitchen table. He poured the whiskey in a glass and gulped it down. He then went to the bedroom and grabbed a bag of coke out of his top dresser drawer. He returned to the kitchen, prepared the line, and snorted the cocaine. Johnny was feeling better, but his insides were getting eaten away.

He picked up the glass and the bottle, and went into the corner of the living room and sat down at his practice drum pad. He always kept his drum pad and a folding chair in the living room. They were the only two other things beside the recliner and TV. He would usually watch TV while he would practice on his drum pad, but today was different and he wanted to get serious for the audition. He placed the bottle and glass on the radiator next to him and picked up the drumsticks off the floor.

He wanted to get himself prepared, so he tried some paradiddles for a beginner. He played for a while, trying some regular exercises, and even threw in a difficult pattern. He stopped after each exercise to take a bit of whiskey. Johnny had practiced for over an hour. One more swig of whiskey before he jumped into the shower. He had finished half the bottle.

After a good shower, he picked out his clean jeans, a black pullover top, and his snakeskin boots. He picked up his snare drum from alongside the dresser, grabbed his leather jacket, and out the door he went. He always took his own snare drum to an audition so he could accomplish the exact sound he needed from the drum.

Johnny jumped in his car and pulled away quickly. He turned on the radio to a high volume. The song being played was one of his favorites, so he turned up the sound full blast, and began tapping on the steering wheel with his fingers, keeping time with the beat. As he turned a corner, he noticed a girl walking to the left. He took his eyes off the road just long enough to see her face. He smiled at her, and when he looked back in front of him, a car was stopped at the light ahead. He slammed on his brakes and barely missed hitting the guy in front of him. He took a deep breath and lowered the radio.

The light changed and he decided to stop at Harry's for a drink. He hurried down the street and was glad there wasn't too much traffic. It was 7:30, and he knew he shouldn't have stopped off, but he felt the need to be in a familiar place before going to the audition.

Upon entering the bar, he waved to some of the regular guys. There sat this hunched old man with a long black coat and black hat at the bar. He must have been seventy years old. His wrinkled, pale face showed every sign of a tired old man. It was Lefty. He had been a friend of Johnny's for years and taught him a lot about bookmaking and a lot of the facets of street life. Lefty was one of the only people he trusted.

Johnny leaned over Lefty's shoulder and whispered in his ear, "What's a good number for tomorrow?"

Lefty turned toward Johnny and laughed. "Hey Johnny, forget the numbers, go to work and earn an honest living kid. Sit down next to me here, and let me buy you a drink. Hey Harry, give my young protege a drink."

Harry placed the shot and beer in front of Johnny. "Johnny, how you doin'?" he asked.

"I'm OK Harry, feelin' better tonight."

Lefty looked toward Johnny, staring him right in the eye. Lefty was feeling a bit drunk. "Don't you ever forget I gave you your first job running numbers."

"How could I ever forget, Lefty? They were the good ole days." Johnny took his shot of whiskey and patted Lefty on the back. He shouted loudly, "We had it made then, didn't we?" He quieted down quickly after that, and again he repeated softly, "Yeah, we had it made, didn't we. Hey Lefty, thanks for the drink. Where've you been the last few days, I missed you? I tried to call your place to check up on you, but you haven't answered for days. How did your trip to the doctor's go? Lefty you don't look too good."

"I've been busy going from doctor to doctor, we'll talk about it another time. You look like you're all keyed up." Lefty wanted to change the subject. "Johnny, I heard you've been drinking quite a bit. Why do you look like you can't sit still?"

"I can't stay around to talk with you Lefty, I have to be somewhere soon." He didn't want to tell Lefty or anyone for that matter, where he was going. Why should he tell anyone anything, just in case things didn't work out for him.

"Sure kid, I understand." He knew Johnny for a long time, and he knew him really well. Johnny must have been close to seventeen when they first met. Lefty had been a pool hustler at Babe's Pool Hall on top of Demarco's Pizza Shop. Johnny was a neighborhood kid who liked to come in and watch the older guys play. Lefty would send him out for sandwiches, and always tip him well. He had dropped some money on the floor one day after a big score, and Johnny had picked it up and gave it back to him. Any of the other kids would have run off with the money, but for some reason, Johnny was honest and returned it to him.

Lefty took a liking to him after that incident, and learned that Johnny was a loner. He himself had no family in the area. Johnny was an only child and had very few friends. He spent a lot of time at the pool hall. Lefty took Johnny along with him to other pool halls. He taught him how to play and how to hustle. Sometimes he sent Johnny ahead of him to check out the other players, so he would know what the place was like. Johnny felt important being with an older pool player, and he had a companion, someone he could trust. Lefty looked after Johnny and treated him like a son. He watched him grow and change over the years. He really worried about the way Johnny drank too much, maybe he had taught him that too.

Lefty stared into the mirror behind the bar. He smiled and remembered the days of pool hustling. They were fun times for him, but now he was sick with cancer. He hadn't told Johnny that the last visits to the three different doctors weren't very encouraging. They all had agreed he didn't have long to live. He thought he would tell Johnny another time when he didn't look so rushed. There probably would never be a right time to tell him, but this was definitely the wrong time—Johnny looked frazzled.

Johnny said good-bye to Lefty and dashed out of the bar. It was getting near the time of his audition. He had about ten minutes to get there. He was so preoccupied with his own needs at that moment, he hadn't taken the time to really tell Lefty about how he felt. If he had, he would have noticed how pathetic the old fellow really looked. But he didn't, he was more concerned about getting to the studio and what might be his first real break. Maybe his time had finally come, and he could get on with becoming somebody big. He knew he was a good drummer, but was he good enough for the big leagues?

IN FRONT OF FAR OUT STUDIOS THERE WAS A LARGE BLINKING RED SIGN. The name Far Out Studios must have been at least eight feet long. It was big and bold, but very professional-looking. This was considered the big time in the recording business. There were other studios in the city, but none with the reputation of this one. Some of the biggest acts had walked through those doors. This studio had been there for over thirty years, and many Philadelphia based musicians had recorded there and became successful through the effort of the quality production. The building appeared to be freshly painted in a stark hospital-like white. Johnny had driven past this place probably a million times, but he had never been inside.

As he walked up to the front door carrying his snare drum over his shoulder, he stopped and took a deep breath. He checked his watch and it was ten after eight—he was already ten minutes late. He opened the door reluctantly and entered. A woman was dusting and wiping up the front lounge.

The furniture in the area where she was cleaning was very modern, and the leather was as red as the letters in the sign outside.

There were too black tables and two black chairs, also in leather. What a place, Johnny thought. He reached over and rubbed the sofa with his fingertips; it was the softest leather he had ever touched. He looked around for someone else besides the cleaning woman to get directions. He had no idea where to go. There was no one. He waited for a minute and then walked over to the woman and asked her if she knew where he could find Poodie.

The little old black woman pointed her finger. "Go through the doors over there." She had such a miserable look on her face. Maybe she hated her job, he thought. He thanked her anyway, and started towards the doors.

The only doors he found were double swinging ones. He looked through the glass windows and saw two men at the big, forty-eight track mixing board. Johnny opened the doors and asked where he could find Poodie.

The one man shouted, "This is the recording room, Poodie's in the rehearsal room."

"Well where's the rehearsal room?"

"Man, we're getting ready for a session. Just go out the doors, you'll find it."

Johnny just turned and walked out of the room. He was really getting off to a great start, he thought. He was nervous enough and now he didn't even know where to go. He walked out of the room and just decided to walk to the left and then found a hallway off to the right. Finally he saw a door marked "Rehearsal Room," and let out a sigh of relief. Clutching his drum, he entered the rehearsal room with six drumsticks sticking out of his back left pocket.

Upon entering the large rehearsal room, there must have been at least twenty-five guys hanging around waiting for a shot to join the Angels. Who would get the job? Johnny could feel the tension. Everyone was talking and laughing, they all must have known one another at one time. Just about every drummer there held his own snare drum, however, Johnny was puzzled as to why there were lots of long haired rock'n'rollers holding guitars in their hands and practicing quietly with no amplification. He thought for a minute then asked a few of them if they knew who Poodie was. No one knew. He spotted an old buddy, Stevie Roselli, standing alone off to the side, holding a purple guitar in his hands.

Stevie was in his late twenties, and he looked much younger. He had always managed to take good care of himself throughout his musical career. He was never involved in drugs or heavy drinking, and generally always had a steady girlfriend. He was always fussy about the women he went out with. Stevie always lived a clean life, and was well respected by all the musicians for his unique style of guitar playing. Stevie stood about 5'9". He always kept his dark brown hair styled well, as it almost covered his ears, and long in the back. He was always well known in the nightclub circuit for his good looks and charisma. He had big brown and mysterious eyes. He was fair complected and had a bit of a narrow face. As a musician, he was never out of work, but just like the rest of the guys in the room, he wanted a job with a recording band—a shot at the big time.

"Hey Stevie, how you doin'?" Johnny asked.

"Johnny Covini! How the hell are you?" Stevie immediately extended his hand. He was happy to see Johnny, and had always respected him for his talented drumming.

"I'm just kickin' around, still hoping to make the big time."

"Yeah. You and me both. By the looks of it, you're here for the audition."

"Yeah, you remember Tom Cat, don't you?"

"Sure, how could I forget that guy?"

"He got me an audition with the Angels through his cousin Poodie."

"Yeah, well lots of luck. I hear Poodie just got fired. You'll have to see Schemer, and he's a real son-of-a-bitch."

"Well, I came down here for an audition, and that's just what I'm going to get. Will you do me a favor and watch this drum for me?

"OK, Johnny, you got it."

Johnny walked to the front of the room. He asked one of the members of the Angels who was tuning his guitar where he would find Schemer. The guy pointed to the back of the room. "He just walked in the door," he said.

Johnny waited patiently till Schemer got to the front of the room. A short, thin man maybe in his early thirties with very little hair began to speak. He was impeccably dressed and looked like a real smooth guy. He was calling out to the musicians to get lined up in separate groups. "OK, listen up." Johnny couldn't seem to get a word in. "I'm only going to say this one time, guitar players on one side, drummers on the other. According to this sheet I hold in my hand, we have thirteen drummers and fifteen guitar players. Of course, the Angels only need one of each." Everyone laughed. "No kidding," everyone shouted. "Hey, that was real good Schemer," Johnny tried to introduce himself to Schemer.

"Hey man, you a drummer or guitar player?"

"I'm a drummer."

"Then get with the others, you'll get your chance."

Johnny just frowned and joined the other drummers.

"This is how it works; I'm going to call each person in alphabetical order. A drummer and guitar player will audition at the same time. The Angels plan to have their new members by the end of the evening. We didn't plan to have quite this many this evening, so if there is anyone who did not sign up, it's too late, you may as well go home. As for the rest of you, you can stay in the room and watch people audition or go sit in the lounge until we call your name."

Johnny shouted out with an angry voice, "Hey man, wait a minute, I didn't know you had to sign up. Nobody told me anything about signing up."

Schemer replied, "Sorry man you missed the boat, better luck next time." Schemer turned to talk with one of the band members to discuss one of the songs they would use in the audition. Johnny was furious. He couldn't believe what was going down. He walked toward Schemer and shoved him in the left shoulder.

"Look man, I came down here for an audition. Who the hell do you think you are, you rotten bastard!"

"Hey, I told you it's too late. Hit the road before I have you thrown out of here."

He didn't hear a word Schemer had said. He hauled off and punched him right in the nose, dead center. Schemer fell right into the drum set that was setting behind him. Blood was all over his face. Cymbals went crashing and drums were bouncing all over the floor. The keyboard and bass player for the Angels, who were good friends of Schemer's, immediately left their instruments and went after Johnny. They began to beat on him and then the lead singer joined in to help them.

Johnny tried to fight back but there were three of them, and they were just too much for him. They continued to punch him as he fell to the floor. Some of the other guys standing around rushed over and pulled the band members off of Johnny. "OK man, that's enough," one guy yelled out.

Johnny was on the floor holding his head. He was badly hurt. He touched his lip and there was blood. He looked down at his clothes and there was blood on his t-shirt and jeans. His nose was bleeding. He reached up to touch his right eye and felt it carefully. It felt huge. He had obviously taken a shot to the eye too. He tried to stand at that point, but could hardly catch his breath. He wiped the blood from his lower lip onto his arm. Stevie Roselli walked over to him, carrying Johnny's drum. He then picked up the drumsticks that had fallen out of Johnny's pocket. He and some other guys helped Johnny up and Stevie started to walk him to the men's room. Johnny was holding his side; someone must have punched him in the ribs.

"Johnny come on, let me help get you cleaned up."

"I'll be OK Stevie, I'll be OK. You just stay here and get

your audition."

"Johnny, will you make it home OK?"

"Yeah just give me my drum and sticks and I'll be fine." Johnny looked a mess, but he wanted everyone in the room to know he could walk out of there on his own. He felt so embarrassed.

"You better go home Johnny, you're hurt pretty bad."

Johnny took the drum and sticks from Stevie and slowly walked out of the room. Many of the musicians standing around were asking one another who the hell that guy was. Most of them were recording musicians who were from out of town and never knew Johnny Covini.

By now, Schemer was back on his feet and was being escorted out of the room by one of the recording engineers who had entered upon hearing all the racket. He suggested that Schemer let him drive him to the hospital. His nose appeared to be broken. The Angels would have to conduct the audition without him.

Schemer mumbled to the engineer, "That guy hits pretty hard, that bum broke my nose."

Johnny barely made his way to the car. He was bleeding and hurting pretty badly. Somehow he managed to get himself together enough to drive home. The drive home was a shaky one. Fortunately, he did not get stopped by the police. He really should have driven to the hospital.

As he pulled up in front of the apartment building, he was relieved he had made it home in one piece. He dragged himself out of the car, reached into the back for the drum and sticks, and as he was about to kick the door closed, he noticed some blood on the front seat where he had been sitting. It must have dripped down from his face, he thought. He wiped his mouth with the sleeve of his leather jacket. He stumbled over his own feet to the curb and climbed the steps of the building slowly. He held his sticks and drum in his left hand, and his ribs in his right.

As he approached the door of his apartment, he heard someone calling from down at the bottom of the steps. He set his drum and sticks on the floor and turned slowly. It was Penny. As she reached the top of the steps, she cried out, "Johnny what happened to you! You're a total mess."

Johnny looked her right in the face and collapsed.

Penny was stunned. She immediately dropped her handbag and reached down to the floor to see if Johnny was conscious. She shoved him, but he didn't respond. She thought for a moment, I'll have to pick him up, somehow I'll have to get him into his apartment—and quick.

She noticed Johnny's keys in his left hand. She quickly grabbed them and tried about three or four keys before she found the right one. Her hands shook as she tried each key in the lock. Finally, the key went into the lock. She was relieved and let out a gasp of air. She opened the door wide and pulled the key out of the lock. She stooped down and grabbed him under his arms. She began to pull him into the apartment.

Johnny was 165 pounds of dead weight. Penny was struggling. As she continued to pull his limp body Johnny's right foot accidentally kicked the snare drum he had placed on the floor. There was only four feet between the top of the stairs and Johnny's apartment door. The drum rolled to the step's edge and tumbled down the whole flight. "Oh no!" Penny screamed. I better get him inside and then I will go get the drum, she thought.

Around the banister catacorner to Johnny's door another apartment door opened. The stillness of the evening was broken by the drum's crashing sound. Joey and his parents looked out the door. The three saw Johnny's door open and walked over. They saw Penny dragging Johnny toward the bedroom. Joey's father rushed in.

"Here, let me help you," he said to Penny. Joey's father was a big man and had no trouble getting Johnny to the bed. Little Joey felt so badly for Johnny. He turned to his mother and asked, "Mom, what's wrong with Johnny? Why is he bleeding like that? Did he fall? Did someone hurt him?"

"I don't know Joey. I don't know what happened to Johnny."

"I better go get the drum downstairs," said Penny.

"I'll get it, I'll get it," shouted Joey.

As Joey's dad placed Johnny on the bed, Johnny gained consciousness and began moaning. Penny and Joey's mother were looking on. "I don't know, maybe I should get him to the hospital," said Joey's father.

Johnny understood him. "No hospital Charlie," he mumbled. Johnny recognized the tall, blond haired man watching over him. He then looked to the pretty blond headed women. "Nancy, I'm sorry you have to see me like this." Johnny recognized Penny and felt relieved. He was so happy to see her. "Penny—can you stay?"

"Sure baby, I'll stay with you."

Suddenly Joey rushed in. "Mom, I got Johnny's drum. Here lady, your pocketbook was outside the door. Is Johnny OK Dad?" Joey walked slowly to the bed and saw Johnny's bloody face. "Johnny, what happened to you?"

Johnny mumbled, "Joey, sometimes the music business can really get tough. You know how it is, you're a musician. Hey, where'd you get the drum?"

"It's yours Johnny, it fell down the steps. I got your sticks for you too. They were on the floor outside of your door."

Joey's father turned to Penny. "Will you be alright here with him?"

"I'll be OK, I'll get him cleaned up and make him something to eat."

The three started to leave and Johnny thanked them. "Hey Joey," he said, "See ya tomorrow kid."

"See ya tomorrow Johnny."

Penny immediately began to take Johnny's jacket off. She then proceeded to take his other clothing off. She was very gentle. She knew Johnny was hurting. She piled his clothes on the chair next to his bed, then got him under the covers. She went to the kitchen and filled a pan with water. She got a clean towel and went back to the room and began to clean Johnny up very carefully.

As she cleaned him she asked, "Johnny, what happened to you?"

"Well I'll tell you Penny, all I wanted was an audition. You know what I mean, a simple audition, and I get this." He was trying to tell her what had happened.

"What do you mean, Johnny, what audition?" She had no idea what he was talking about.

"Penny, could you do me a favor?"

"What?"

"Could you go get me the bottle of whiskey in the living room, I left it there earlier today. There's some clean glasses in the kitchen. Let's have a drink, I could sure use one."

As she cleaned around his swollen eye, she said, "Yeah, so can I."

"Ouch! Careful around the eye area."

"Sorry. Give me a minute, I'll get us a drink." Penny walked into the kitchen and found two glasses. She then went to the living room and got the bottle of whiskey, and returned to the bedroom. She placed the two glasses on the dresser and poured them both a drink. She handed Johnny a glass and sat at the edge of the bed. Johnny had managed to sit up a bit. He rested his head against the headboard. They both took a swig of their drinks. Penny placed her glass on the floor and pulled the covers down over Johnny's belly.

"I noticed you had a big bruise on your stomach. You know, you could have a couple broken ribs."

"Well, if this pain don't go away in a few days, I'll get to the hospital."

"I don't know, it looks pretty bad Johnny."

"Look don't worry, I'll be OK, just get me another drink."

Penny pulled the covers back over him, went to the dresser and got the bottle. She poured him another drink, and herself one as well. "Now, would you please tell me what happened tonight?"

"I went down to Far Out Studios. This friend of mine, Tom Cat, hooked me up with an audition. Must have been about twenty-five guys there, half of them were drummers. I got there about fifteen minutes late. There was this guy, Schemer—he said anybody that didn't sign up, it was too late. I tried to explain, but he wouldn't listen. He was a real ignorant mother. He even looked like a weasel. Anyway, I punched him in the nose. He went down and a couple of his friends from the band—I don't know, two or three of them—they did a number on me."

"Johnny I wonder about you sometimes. I wish you would clean up your act and get your crazy life together."

"What are you doing here anyway?"

"I stopped by to say goodbye."

"Goodbye? Where you goin'?"

"I got a new job in L.A., and I'm leaving Thursday."

"Thursday? That's only a couple days from now."

"I know it's sudden, but it could be the best thing that's happened to me in a long time. I wanted to say goodbye to you in person."

Johnny took Penny's hand and looked her in the face. "Penny, stay with me tonight. I don't want to be alone. You know what I mean, don't you? Will you stay with me tonight?" Johnny was practically begging her.

"Yeah, I know what you mean. I think I need to be with someone tonight too. I mean, someone who understands. I guess I really don't have anyone either, Johnny. I'll stay with you."

Johnny smiled. He was so happy she was there. Johnny continued to hold her hand. He thought for a minute and said, "Just like old times, you and me after the show."

Penny loosened her hand from his grip and poured another drink for them. She made a toast. She smiled at him. "Here's to your music."

"Here's to your dance career." He lifted up his glass and toasted. The two took their last drinks, and Penny set the glasses on the floor alongside the bottle.

"Well," she said, "if I'm going to stay, I better go call the babysitter, and then I'll call my sister. I'll tell her the babysitter will be dropping the kids off at her house for the night. Penny made her calls and came back to the bedroom and disrobed, only leaving her bra and panties on.

Johnny looked at her. "You still have a beautiful body," he said. Penny slowly climbed onto the bed alongside of Johnny and rested her head gently on his chest.

Johnny rubbed his hand along her back. "You still have soft skin, Penny, I never knew anyone who had skin so soft."

Penny smiled and took a deep breath. Johnny was exhausted and fell asleep, and Penny followed.

AT 8:00 A.M., THE SUN WAS SHINING THROUGH THE BEDROOM WINDOW on that March day. In one week, spring would arrive. Penny opened her eyes slowly. She felt so comfortable next to Johnny. It was as though they'd never parted. I can't believe it, she thought, I'm lying here again with Johnny Covini. She slowly raised herself out of bed. She didn't want to disturb Johnny, he looked so peaceful. She went to the bathroom and took a warm shower. She came back to the bedroom and got dressed. She didn't bother to put any makeup on, just combed her hair, and decided to make some breakfast for Johnny and her.

She opened the refrigerator door and mumbled to herself, "Johnny, you'll never change. Refrigerator's empty as usual. Orange juice and milk—that's all you ever had, orange juice and milk." Penny grabbed her jacket and handbag and rushed to a nearby store for some food. She returned to the apartment with two bags full of groceries. She wanted Johnny to have some food around the house while he healed from his beating. She put everything away neatly and then began to prepare breakfast.

The aroma of bacon, eggs, and hot coffee throughout the

small apartment was enough to waken Johnny. She walked in to check on him for a second. He was lying there with his eyes open. "Well don't tell me you finally decided to wake up."

Johnny could barely see out of his swollen left eye. He tried to sit up, and immediately held his ribs.

"Here, let me help you," she said.

"I feel like a truck hit me. What time is it?"

"It's 9:30."

"Well, whatever you're cooking sure smells good."

Penny put her arms under Johnny and helped him off the bed.

"Penny, could you get me that black robe in the closet?"

While Penny was getting Johnny's robe Johnny took a look in the mirror above the dresser. "Oh my God! Looks like somebody took a razor to my face. And my eye! Look at my lip. I look like a monster." Penny approached Johnny with the robe and helped him to put it on. "Penny, how did you sleep alongside this ugly face?"

"You took a pretty bad beating, Johnny." Johnny grabbed his rib as a sharp pain ran across his side. "Here, let me help you to the kitchen." Penny walked him slowly to the kitchen and sat him down gently. She returned to the stove and finished cooking and put breakfast on the table. She poured Johnny some hot coffee.

"Penny this looks great. I haven't had a good breakfast in weeks. You always come around at the perfect time." Penny took a seat across from Johnny. Johnny looked at her seated across from him and smiled. "Thanks for staying the night."

Her eyes began to fill up. She knew she would be leaving the next day and would soon have to be leaving Johnny to go home and pack. It was a long way to L.A. and she would be driving with two little kids.

The two began to eat breakfast. Johnny was eating a bit fast. He was starved. With his mouth full, he asked, "How long you think you'll be in L.A.?"

"As long as the money is rolling in. They're starting me out with $750 a week and a furnished apartment."

"$750 a week?! Where's this place at?"

"It's a well-known place. It's called the Palace, it sits right in the heart of Los Angeles. It's a classy place Johnny. I won't be dancing in bars anymore, I'll be doing shows with other people."

Johnny reached across the table and took her hand. "I'm really happy for you Penny, I'm sure going to miss you. You know, even though we've been broke up all these years, I have to admit I've thought about you every day."

Penny, still teary-eyed, with her lip quivering said, "Johnny please, don't make this any harder for me."

"Well listen, before you go today, I'll give you my number and my address. You know, don't forget to call or write."

When they were just about finished breakfast, Penny looked at the clock on the wall. "Johnny, it's almost ten o'clock. I better get cleaned up here, and then I have to go. I have a lot of last minute things to do here today, and then I have to leave at six o'clock tomorrow morning."

They finished breakfast and Penny gathered the dishes and took them to the sink. She then cleaned the table and proceeded to wash the dishes. As she continued to wash the dishes, she was standing almost sideways talking to Johnny. Johnny was sitting there in a sort of daze.

"What about you, Johnny? What are you going to do? Are you going to continue to buy and sell drums and take bets, and play music whenever you can get work?"

"Hey, it's a living."

"Yeah, it's a living—it's a living, big deal. With us it just can't be a living. We have to be in the limelight. Wake up Johnny, you're a professional. A professional. You'll never be happy with a living." At that point, she caught herself starting to lecture Johnny. "I'm sorry Johnny, maybe this is none of my business."

"It's your business, it's your business."

Penny finished washing the dishes and then cleaned the table. "Johnny, I have to go."

"Come on, stay a few more minutes."

"I'm sorry Johnny, I can't." Penny went to the bedroom and got her coat and pocketbook. Johnny got off the chair slowly. Penny entered the kitchen and immediately Johnny walked toward her. They put their arms around one another tightly. As Penny's head laid on Johnny's shoulder, her eyes began to tear and her lip quivered. "I love you Johnny, I'll always love you, but for now it just wouldn't work out. Please, I have to go now." She wanted to get out of there before she really broke down.

"So long Penny." As she reached the door, he said, "Penny, thanks for everything last night."

"You gonna be OK?"

"Yeah, I'll be fine."

She opened the door and left quickly. He wanted to go after her, but he was too weak to even try. He turned and headed back to the kitchen table and sat down. He then banged the table with a fisted hand and yelled, "Damn! Damn!"

Johnny spent the rest of the day sleeping on and off, only waking once to a wrong number. He desperately needed rest. His body was in really bad shape from the booze and the beating he had taken.

4

* * * * * * * * * *

THE FOLLOWING MORNING JOHNNY LEFT FOR THE GARAGE, AFTER SPEND-
ing most of the early morning cleaning himself up. He was pretty
stiff and sore, but managed to grab a hot shower.

When he arrived at the garage, another one of Johnny's old
musician buddies, Sonny Terrillo, was driving by in front of the
garage in his pickup truck. Sonny was considering buying some
real estate and was in the area looking at the back of the homes he
was interested in. Sonny beeped the horn and yelled out the window, "Hey, Johnny Covini—how's the music business?"

"Sonny—Sonny Terrillo," he looked at him with surprise.

"Yeah it's me Johnny—the one and only."

"Where the hell you been man?"

"I've been busy. Got myself a little scrap business, a wife,
kids and a home."

"Gee that's great Sonny, I'm really glad for you. What the
hell you doing driving down the alley?"

"I'm thinkin' about buying some homes on the block, I want
to see what they look like from the back."

"Man, you're really doing good for yourself, aren't you
Sonny?"

"Yeah, it beats playing guitar for $50 a night. Can you imag-
ine me Johnny—with a home and a family!"

"Well, that is hard to believe. What'd you do with all them girlfriends you had?"

"My wife took care of that Johnny."

Johnny shook his head and laughed. He then grabbed his side because of the pain of the possible broken rib.

"Johnny, you OK? What happened to you? How come your eye is all busted up and you're holding your side?"

"Eh, had a little problem last night—no big deal."

"You know Johnny, I'm really happy. For the first time in years, I'm really happy. Once I was so low I thought I'd never get up. The music business almost destroyed me—drugs, women, drinking, up all night-sleep all day. What about you Johnny, what are you doing these days?"

"You know, just kickin' around."

"Well what are you doing in this alley?"

"I rent this garage here—I buy and sell used drum equipment."

"Still playing music?"

"Yeah, whenever I can get work on the weekend—nothing steady."

"I hear you been working for Benelli."

"Yeah, I take a few bets."

"Well if you ever decide to leave that creep, come and see me. Here's my card."

Johnny reached in the truck for Sonny's card and thanked him.

"Hey Johnny, you know anybody kickin' around the neighborhood lookin' to make some extra cash? I just bought a couple homes over on the Boulevard and I need somebody to clean up the rooms a little bit.

Johnny thought for a moment, "Yeah, I might know somebody. You remember Tom Cat, don't you—he could use some extra cash. Sonny looked down at the steering wheel and waited for a moment. He turned back to Johnny with a scary look and tried to find the right words to tell him some bad news. There were no easy words.

"Tom Cat is dead, Johnny." Sonny Terrillo was a pretty husky guy, must have weighed 180 pounds at five-foot-eight. With his dark brown hair and pointed face, one would think he was one mean character, but when Sonny was saddened, you knew it. Johnny looked at him in shock. He was stunned.

"Tom Cat is what?"

"He's dead, Johnny."

"He can't be dead—I just saw him a few days ago. How did it happen?"

"Suicide. He hitched a ride. When the driver got to the Walt Whitman toll booth, Tom Cat jumped out and ran to the center of the bridge. They say he let out a loud scream something like, "I love you Mom, please forgive me," and he jumped. Sonny looked down at his watch and realized he had to be on his way. "Johnny, I have to go, I'm real sorry man. I know you and Tom Cat were good friends at one time." Sonny drove away slowly.

Johnny just stood there and stared up at the sky with his hands on his hips. He took a deep breath and wondered if he should go on any longer. The music business was beginning to kill him and everyone around him. He and all his friends seemed to have been getting more and more disappointed as they headed toward middle age. Maybe they were just getting too old for the business and would have to face the music and just realize it was all over for them. They missed the big time, and now it was just too late. What the hell is going on here, he thought, something bad seems to be happening everyday.

Johnny walked slowly to the garage and upon entering headed straight for the cabinet where he kept his bottle of whiskey. He took a drink right from the bottle. He gulped it quickly and began to work on one of the broken drums. The phone hardly rang. His customers were going elsewhere because of his poor attitude and behavior.

One of the lugs on the drum he was repairing was stripped. He got frustrated and threw the key across the room and reached for another, he then noticed an iron bar on the table and reached for it. He began to beat the drum with the iron bar, and each time the bar hit the drum, he let out a loud scream that sounded like a wounded animal. He was in such pain, mentally and physically.

After he had totally destroyed the drum with his continual banging, he started to cry. He was sobbing at this point, and crying harder than he could ever remember. He threw the iron bar through the window and dropped to the floor. He held his face in his hands and continued to cry aloud. What the hell is going on with my life, he thought. His friend Tom Cat died, Sonny had given up the music business to find happiness, Penny was gone, and he had screwed up his first big audition. Here he was in an old garage taking bets and fixing drums. What had he done that was really good? His life seemed to be going on a down hill swing. Things were worse for him now than ever before. As he sat on the floor of the garage, he ignored a ringing phone. He didn't care about taking any bets. He felt lost, alone, and terrified.

Finally, enough time had passed and he wiped his eyes on his shirt. He decided to leave the garage and head for Harry's bar. He wondered if anyone at Harry's knew about Tom Cat. When he arrived at the bar, there weren't many customers at that time of the afternoon.

"Johnny, what the hell happened to your face?" asked Harry.

"No problem Harry, just a little misunderstanding."

"What'll you have Johnny?"

"I think I'll have a double shot today Harry, and a cold one." Johnny threw his money on the bar; he felt miserable.

As Johnny waited for his drink, sitting about four bar stools down was a handsome-looking character with mid-length blond, curly hair. He must have been about 5'11". He was well-dressed: three-piece gray pin-striped suit, white shirt, and burgundy tie. He even had a burgundy handkerchief in his suit pocket. His shoes were black and polished to the hilt. It was Danny Rosco. He was one of Johnny's best friends at one time. He was a bass player and played in a band with Johnny in the early seventies. He knew Johnny was standing there, but wanted to surprise him.

Harry placed Johnny's whiskey and beer on the bar. "Here take it out of here, bartender," shouted Danny.

Johnny looked over at the guy in surprise. "Danny! Danny Rosco—is it really you?"

"In the flesh man, in the flesh. How you been, Johnny?"

"I'm not doin' too bad for a guy with a busted eye."

"Yeah man, what happened?"

"Let's not worry about that, where the hell have you been?" Johnny got his beer and whiskey and moved a few stools over to Danny. He was really happy to see him. The two shook hands and gave one another a hug. "So tell me Danny what's going on—what are you doing in Philadelphia? The last I heard you were out in L.A. doing session work."

"I got a job in New York selling shoes for Sigway."

"You? Sell shoes?"

"Yeah, as a matter of fact, I just had an interview right here in Philly at 13th and Market for a manager position. I knew you used to hang out here at this bar, so I thought maybe I would find you here."

"Yeah? Well here I am."

"Johnny I miss you man. You're the best drummer in the world as far as I'm concerned."

"Yeah I'm the best all right—I'm the best failure in the world."

"Come on man, you're not a failure, you're just nuts. Remember, you're a musician. So tell me, Johnny, what have you been doing?"

"Going crazy man, I'm really going crazy."

"Hey, things can't be that bad."

"You'd be surprised. I went down for an audition two days

ago at Far Out Studios—I couldn't even get a shot to play. Instead, I got beat up. Then just this morning, I found out that Tom Cat committed suicide."

"Tom Cat from that crazy band the Cats?"

"Yeah, Tom Cat. He was a sick dude man, really screwed up."

Danny started asking Johnny more questions. Johnny took a sip of his beer and started staring into space, not paying attention to his friend at that minute. He was day dreaming about nothing.

Suddenly three men entered the bar. Danny turned to see who they were as he heard them talking. Johnny was still day dreaming. It was Johnny's numbers boss Frankie Benelli and his two bodyguards. Frankie was very angry. Johnny had left the garage early that day and didn't even show up the day before. He walked up to Johnny with his two bodyguards behind him—they were bruisers. Johnny was in big trouble. Frankie was nobody to mess with. The few customers who were there when Johnny came in had left. The only people there were Johnny and Danny, Harry the bartender, Benelli and his men.

Harry was at the end of the bar reading his paper. As he turned and began to walk toward the customers, he immediately recognized Frankie Benelli and the two rugged men who worked for him.

Frankie grabbed Johnny by the shoulder, swung him around and looked him straight in the eyes. "You're through, man, you hear? You're through!"

Johnny was taken by surprise. Danny didn't know what the hell was happening. Suddenly Harry shouted, "Look Benelli, I don't want no trouble in here!"

One of Frankie's bodyguards shouted, "Shut up old man before I throw you out of your own bar!" Harry froze. Harry never kept a gun in the bar, and knew if he tried anything, he would get his arms broken, or maybe even shot at. He kept silent.

"You lost over five thousand dollars in bets between yesterday and today," shouted Frankie, "you're a loser. Some of my regular guys took their action to someone else. I knew you were there, because people on the street told me they seen your car in the alley. My customers said they were tired of letting the phone ring and getting no answer."

"Hey come on Frankie, we'll make it up tomorrow."

"You bastard!" shouted Frankie. He reached forward and landed his fist on Johnny's jaw. He then began to swing wildly at Johnny. Danny Rosco threw back his bar stool and tried to stop Frankie. He saw that Johnny was in no condition to defend himself. This guy was coming down on Johnny quick and hard. One of Frankie's bodyguards immediately grabbed Danny by the back of the collar and the seat of his pants, picked him up over his head, and threw him over the bar into the display of whiskey bottles in front of the mirror. Danny and the bottles went crashing to the floor. Danny was helpless.

As Frankie continued to beat on Johnny, Johnny knew he had to do something quickly. As Frankie was swinging wildly, Johnny managed to block most of his punches, he then grabbed Frankie's throat with his right hand and jumped off the barstool. With all his strength, he kicked Frankie in the balls with his right knee. Frankie began to crumble and fell to his knees.

Johnny took his hand off Frankie's throat, pulled his right arm back, and was ready to swing down on Frankie's face. Johnny's face was wide open and in seconds flat, one of Frankie's bodyguards punched Johnny square in the jaw. He hit him so hard you could hear Johnny's neck snap from the impact.

By this time Frankie had hit the floor with his two hands between his legs, and moaning from the pain. The big man began to punch Johnny in his chest and abdomen with devastating force. Johnny felt like he was being attacked by some kind of wild animal. Each time he got hit, he would let out a fearful groan.

Harry shouted out, "Stop it! You're going to kill him!", as the man began to throw forceful punches to Johnny's face and jaw.

The other bodyguard reached across the bar and smashed Harry in the face with his right fist. Harry fell helplessly behind the bar, banging his head on the refrigerator under the bar. The bodyguard then joined his friend, and the two began to brutally beat Johnny to the floor. Johnny's face was a bloody mess, and there was blood all over his clothes. Ribs were definitely broken. Johnny fell helplessly to the floor.

By now Frankie was holding onto the bar, pulling himself up. "OK fellas, that's enough," he moaned. Johnny wasn't moving. He appeared to be a dead man as the men stopped beating on him. "Let's get out of here," said Frankie. Before they left the bar, Frankie held onto the top of the bar and forcefully kicked Johnny in the side of the head as he lay there unconscious. "I should have never hired this scumbag," he said. The three men exited the barroom.

Forty minutes had passed, and no one had come into the bar, it was a slow time of day. Suddenly a moan and a rattle of glass came from behind the bar. Danny Rosco was regaining consciousness slowly. By now, Harry was also coming to. Danny Rosco could barely move, he felt like he had a broken back.

Finally an old man who was a regular at the bar made his daily stop. He immediately saw Johnny's body lying on the floor. Fear gripped his face as he saw the battered body lying there. Not knowing how to react to the situation, he could only think of running to the phone and calling the police. Within minutes, the police arrived. By now Harry had managed to get back on his feet. Danny Rosco couldn't move off the floor, his back was in extreme pain.

The two officers that arrived were Officers Monahan and Danko. Monahan had been on the force for twenty years, and knew the neighborhood well, and was good friends with Harry. Officer Danko was just a rookie and didn't mind the excitement one bit. "Harry, what the hell happened here?" Monahan asked.

"We got visited by a few rats," replied Harry. Monahan and Danko immediately ran over to Johnny's bloody body.

"Danko, get to the phone. We need an ambulance down here real quick. Tell them to send the coroner also, this guy looks dead." Monahan immediately checked for a carotid pulse. He felt nothing. He then administered two breaths to Johnny's mouth. Johnny didn't respond, so Monahan began CPR. He quickly opened Johnny's shirt and began chest compressions and then ordered Danko to apply one breath to Johnny after every five compressions. There was absolutely no response. Monahan looked to Harry. He asked him how long ago the incident had happened. Harry was holding onto the bar and looked at the clock on the wall.

"From what I can remember, Johnny came in about 2:15 and within five minutes, he was getting beat up."

"Forget it Danko," said Monahan, "he's been here too long. He's probably been dead for the last forty-five minutes or so."

From the back of the bar, Danny Rosco moaned, "Somebody help me up, I can't move."

"Who's that Harry?" asked Monahan.

"It's one of Johnny's friends."

"Johnny? I knew this guy looked familiar. This is Johnny Covini. I've known this guy for years. He was a musician, wasn't he? Danko, go see what you can do until the ambulance gets here." Officer Danko made Danny feel as comfortable as possible.

Suddenly the paramedics and two more police officers entered the bar. Monahan ordered them to not let anyone in the bar. The sidewalk was getting crowded with onlookers. The old man who had entered the bar sat at a corner table shaking nervously. Harry also took a seat at a nearby table. He was feeling very dizzy, and probably had a concussion. Monahan told the paramedics Johnny had been beaten up about 50 minutes ago, and that he had administered CPR, but got no vital signs. The paramedics did their routine check for vitals on the body, and concluded that it was too late for any further aid. The coroner soon arrived and pronounced Johnny dead.

Johnny's bloody and battered body was placed in a body

bag and taken to the hospital. Harry and Danny Rosco were also taken to the hospital for treatment, and the bar was closed down for the day. The crowd outside the bar soon dispersed. No one was sure what had taken place or who was in the body bag. An old man was leaning up against the front of the bar. It was Lefty, Johnny's old friend. He had absolutely no idea that his young protege was now a dead man.

THE PARAMEDICS ARRIVED AT CENTER CITY MEDICAL CENTER WITH Johnny's body. They carried the body bag inside and placed it on a stretcher in the hallway. They were advised to wheel the body to a nearby room; there the body would be prepared for an autopsy. They took the bag from the stretcher and placed it on the table. The on duty nurse entered and they gave her some last minute information and signed the necessary paperwork. She thanked them and told them she would take care of things from there. All of them had witnessed this type of situation before, and to them it was just another day's work.

When the men left, the woman began writing something on the clipboard she held in her hand. The room was quiet, and as she wrote, she thought she heard a slight noise. Probably nothing, she thought. Again she heard the noise. I know I'm not cracking up, she thought. She looked to the top of the body bag where Johnny's head was. She thought she was going crazy—the top of the bag was moving in and out slightly. She gasped and froze. She broke out in a sweat, but quickly gathered her thoughts and realized the first thing to do was unzipped the bag.

She unzipped the bag and found inside a man with a bloody face and swollen eyes. She put her ear to his mouth and detected breathing. She quickly reached for the phone on the wall and called the emergency room team. She just stood there watching the face until they arrived, and then explained what had transpired. They had determined that the man's body had been in a state of shock, and his pulse had been too low to be detected. This was not the first time they had witnessed such a miracle. A physician instructed the team to prepare an injection of atropine, get an I.V. started immediately, and hook up a heart monitor. "This man is in bad shape," he said, "his jaw may be broken, his eyes are swollen shut, his nose doesn't appear to be broken—that's a miracle, he has several cuts, the one over the right eye looks pretty serious." A nurse quickly began to strip Johnny of his garments, and the doctor felt around the rib area, determining Johnny had several broken ribs and was bleeding internally. "Nurse, please get in touch with Dr. Barnes and Dr. Goldstein for me." The nurse called the hospital operator and had her page the other doctors.

After a few minutes, Dr. Barnes arrived. "My God, what happened to this man?" he asked.

"According to the paramedics, he was brutally beaten," replied Dr. Martinez. Dr. Goldstein rushed into the room at that minute. He had been affiliated with the medical center for over twenty years, and was very well liked and respected by his peers. He and Dr. Barnes often operated together. With the assistance of Nurse Collins, each of the doctors performed the necessary tests to diagnose Johnny Covini and prep him for the operating room.

SEVERAL HOURS HAD GONE BY, AND THE TEAM OF DOCTORS AND NURSES had stitched Johnny in several areas, and managed to stop all internal bleeding with the necessary surgery. Johnny had four broken ribs that would have to be treated in a few days. "This man must be made of iron," said Dr. Goldstein, "how he didn't die from this beating, I'll never know."

Johnny was wheeled to the intensive care unit where he was carefully monitored and treated for the next week. Harry was released the day of the incident. Danny Rosco spent three days in the hospital for cuts and bruises and a minor back injury, he also had a severe concussion.

5

* * * * * * * * * *

ON SATURDAY, MARCH 24TH, IT WAS A BEAUTIFUL SPRING DAY, AND Johnny was moved out of I.C.U. and into a semiprivate room on the third floor. He would now be allowed visitors. The nurse, who was a very pretty light-skinned black woman in her mid-thirties, entered the room.

"Good morning, I'm Chera. And how are you feeling this morning Mr. Covini?"

Johnny was laying there in a daze. "I'm in a little bit of pain, but other than that, I feel plain miserable." Johnny's voice was hoarse. His eyes were no longer swollen, just black underneath. The stitches above his right eye and inside his upper lip were removed just before leaving intensive care. His jaw and forehead were slightly swollen and still black and blue. His insides were feeling much better, and his broken ribs were now healing with the help of the wrapping around his body. He still couldn't move too well because of the stiffness and pain he was experiencing.

"I'm going to give you something for the pain," said the nurse.

"How long have I been in here anyway?"

"A little over a week," she replied.

Johnny just looked away toward the window in disgust.

"I'm going to lift your bed a little, Mr. Covini, and then I want you to take these pills." After she lifted the bed, she handed Johnny the little cup.

"Ow!" Johnny could barely lift his arm due to the pain in his right shoulder. He placed the pills in his mouth, and then she handed him a cup of water. "When do I get something to eat?" he asked, "I'm starving."

"I will have someone send some breakfast up to you shortly. Dr. Barnes will be in to see you in a couple of hours." Johnny nodded at her and looked up at the ceiling for a second. He closed his eyes and dozed off. The nurse checked the man in the other bed and left the room.

Johnny's sleep was disturbed by a nurse bringing his breakfast. After he ate, he felt very tired and went back to sleep. At 11:30, Johnny woke up. At 11:45 a tall, handsome red-haired man walked in the room. It was Dr. Barnes. "Good morning Mr. Covini, I'm Dr. Barnes. How are you feeling?"

"I'm miserable Doc', I feel miserable." He began checking Johnny's ribs and other bruises on his face and jaw area. "Hey Doc', let's have it—am I going to be OK? I feel like I've been killed and gone to hell."

"Well almost, but you beat it."

"Beat what? What are you talking about?"

"You were brought in here in a body bag."

"Look, what are you telling me?"

"You're a lucky man, Mr. Covini, you were taken for dead. Your body was in shock. It wasn't responding to CPR, we couldn't get a pulse. Your heart was barely pumping."

A look of fear came over Johnny's face. Johnny started asking lots of questions as he began to get frantic.

"Take it easy Mr. Covini, you must remain calm," the doctor replied.

"Look Doc', I can't stay here. I'll go crazy. Don't keep me here, I've got to go home."

Dr. Barnes placed his hand on Johnny's forehead and said,

"Settle down man, it's going to be OK." He then leaned over and pushed the buzzer on the table to get the nurse to come in. The nurse entered the room within seconds and asked Dr. Barnes what he needed. "Mr. Covini is beginning to get very anxious." He prescribed a sedative and the nurse immediately went to get the medication. Dr. Barnes continued to talk to Johnny, trying to reassure him that he was going to be OK.

Johnny tried to sit up, but the pain was far too great. He began to scream at the doctor about how he had to get out of there and go home. He kept telling him he would go nuts in the hospital if they kept him there. Finally, the nurse arrived with the sedative and Dr. Barnes administered it into Johnny's arm.

In the hallway were a couple of patients and some hospital personnel peering into the room. The sedative took effect quickly, and Johnny settled.

"I wonder what frightened him," said Dr. Barnes to the nurse.

"I have no idea," she replied.

"He's probably still in shock from the beating." Dr. Barnes gave instructions to the nurse to take a blood test and check for traces of drugs and alcohol. He told her he could possibly be having withdrawal symptoms. "I'll be back later on to check on him," he said.

By now Johnny was pretty calm. He was still babbling on about getting out of the hospital, but he was no longer screaming. The patient in the bed next to him just kept staring over, but he never said a word.

A couple hours had gone by and it was 1:15 in the afternoon. Johnny had managed to sleep for an hour. The nurse returned to check on him and saw that he was awake.

"How are you doing, Mr. Covini?"

"I'll let you know when I wake up." He sounded very groggy.

"I'm going to check your blood pressure, and then you can have something to eat—that should make you feel much better."

Johnny just nodded his head at her. The nurse left the room

and soon after Johnny's lunch was brought in. The orderly placed it on the table and swung it over in front of Johnny. He tried to reach for the roll, but he knocked it over onto the floor. "Shit!" he yelled. He was so weak and sore, he could barely get the food to his mouth. He didn't really eat much at breakfast and he was starving. He tried to sit up a little. He pulled his body up and leaned himself across the table. And with his face about two inches from the plate, he picked up the fork and began shoveling the food into his mouth. There was no way he was calling some nurse in to feed him.

After he had consumed almost everything on the tray, the nurse walked into the room and saw him with his face lying close to the plate. She smiled, "Hey, slow down-you'll get sick. Why didn't you call me if you couldn't do it yourself?" The nurse picked up his face and wiped the food from his nose and cheeks with the napkin on the tray. He looks so pathetic, she thought. She moved the bed up, put the food tray away, and helped him lay back on the pillow.

Johnny laid back on the pillow and looked up at the TV. The man in the next bed must have paid for it. He realized that the music station was on. He watched and listened to a band perform. He recognized the guitar player on the left-hand side of the screen. It was someone he had worked with a long while back. He thought for a moment, "I'll be damned," he said, "I can't believe it, it's Davey Hunter." Johnny had worked with this guy for a period of six months when he was in his early twenties. He and Davey had had a lot of laughs and good times. Johnny thought to himself how lucky this guy was to be with a top name band and playing on TV.

The nurse who had just cleaned him up a few minutes before returned. Excited to see her, he said, "Hey nurse, you see that guitar player up there? I worked with him, and I know him real well."

She looked up at the TV and then back toward Johnny. "You mean the one with the long hair?"

"Yeah, that's the one. Man, he sure can play guitar."

"How did those guys get such beautiful hair?"

"It goes with the job," he laughed. Suddenly Johnny noticed a figure in the doorway. It was Danny Rosco.

As Danny entered, he said, "Hey Johnny, can't ever turn the music off, can you?"

"Danny! How the hell are you?"

"Well I feel like a train hit me, but other than that, I'm OK. I can still play a bass guitar. I even got a few weeks off from work, which I don't mind at all."

The nurse interrupted. "If you need anything Mr. Covini, just call—I'll see you later."

"OK, thanks nurse."

"Hey Johnny, she ain't bad! Don't you think you should be calling her by her first name instead of nurse?"

"Still got girls on your mind all the time, don't you?"

"Can you think of anything better to think about?"

"Yeah."

"What?"

"Getting the hell out of here."

"Hey Johnny, I'm sorry I didn't get up here to see you sooner, but I had to stay in the hospital three days myself. And then they told me to get home right away and rest. Drivin' back to New York with a sore back was a real bitch."

"What about the job at Sigway Shoes?"

"I called the district manager and told him what happened, so I had an interview yesterday. I got the job."

"Hey, congratulations Danny! At least somebody's doin' somethin' right with his life."

"Yeah, but I still wish I could play music for a living, but there's just not enough money in it."

"Yeah, tell me about it!"

"Well maybe someday you and me, Johnny, we'll make the big time."

"Yeah, well I don't know about you, but I forgot about that.

I'm beginning to think the music business is for crazy people."

Danny just laughed and sat on the chair near Johnny's bed.

"Hey Danny, I'm sorry I got you mixed up in all this."

"Man, who were those guys anyway? When I hit that wall, I felt like I was hit by a truck. Those guys were strong."

"I was booking numbers on the side for Frankie Benelli—you know, the guy I kicked in the balls."

"Yeah, I heard him say that you lost a few thousand dollars in bets."

"Yeah, well I hope he feels like he's gotten enough revenge, I was brought into this damn place in a bodybag."

Suddenly Danny couldn't speak, he sat there with his mouth open.

"Hey Danny, you OK?"

Finally, Danny spoke. "A bodybag? But... but Johnny, when they bring somebody in in a bodybag that means they're dead."

"Do I look dead?"

"But I don't understand it."

"They couldn't get a pulse. They tried CPR, but it just didn't do any good. I guess when they got me here they detected breathing. Now don't ask me if I saw any bright lights when I was dead."

For a moment there was silence. The two men were thinking the same thing. Suddenly Danny asked, "Johnny—"

"What?"

"Did you?"

"Did I what?"

"Did you see any bright lights?"

Johnny took a deep breath. "Look Danny, I didn't tell anybody else this, so please don't you tell anybody else."

"You can trust me Johnny." Danny was burning with curiosity.

"Well, I didn't see any bright lights, but I'll tell you what I did see. I saw policemen trying to revive my body, I also saw an ambulance pulling away from Harry's bar. I know this sounds crazy."

"No Johnny, I've heard about these things, and I've read about them. People claim that the same thing happened to them, as though their spirits left their bodies momentarily and then reentered."

"Look Danny, maybe we better talk about something else. I don't think I want to think about this right now."

"Sorry man, I shouldn't have been so curious." Suddenly the two heard footsteps. It was Dr. Barnes making a second check on Johnny.

"Feeling better, I see."

"Hey Doc', sorry I got a little crazy earlier."

"It's OK, that's to be expected. Did you have something to eat?"

"Yeah, the food's not bad in here."

Danny interrupted, "Hey Johnny, I'm going to go grab a soda, I'll be back in five or ten minutes."

"Yeah sure Danny, see you in a bit." As the doctor checked Johnny's face and ribs, Johnny asked, "Doc', was I dead? I mean, I'm alive now. Look Doc', I'm a bit confused about all this."

"Don't be confused Mr. Covini, and don't let it scare you. You're not the first person this happened to, and you probably won't be the last. I think at this point you should just be grateful to be alive, and think about getting well and starting a new life for yourself."

"What do you mean Doc'?"

"I mean people don't get beat up like this for no reason."

"Maybe you're right Doc'."

"I'm having some blood tests run today and we should have the results tomorrow morning. Why don't we talk further then about your condition? I'll check with you in the morning. Have a nice day and get all the sleep you can. You know Mr. Covini, you're a real lucky guy. I'll see you tomorrow."

Danny soon returned and the two spoke for over an hour. Johnny was glad Danny had come to see him. They spoke a lot about their past and what lay ahead in the future. Danny helped Johnny to release a lot of tension and get a lot off his mind. Danny left about 3:30 and Johnny spent the remainder of the afternoon and evening in and out of sleep. He was extremely sore and didn't feel like watching TV all night, mostly because he didn't care for the stations the guy in the next bed was choosing. He didn't really want to think about anything in particular, so sleep was the only safe thing for him to do. About the only thing that interested him was dinner.

SUNDAY MORNING HAD ARRIVED. JOHNNY HAD BREAKFAST AND BY 11:00 A.M., Dr. Barnes was in to see him. "Mr. Covini, how are you today?"

"I feel pretty good, Doc'." He spoke in a low voice. "I know one thing, I want to go home."

"Well you won't be going home today. You're going to be here for at least another week."

"A week? Doc' you gotta be kidding me."

"You've taken a bad beating. You're going to need medical attention for a while, and when you do get home, I strongly advise you rest for at least two weeks. No physical activity."

"You mean I can't even..."

"No, you can't even have sex. I have to tell you, we found traces of drugs in your system."

"So what. What's that supposed to mean?" He looked puzzled.

The doctor began to check Johnny's lower abdomen and made sure the stitches were holding up. He looked up at Johnny and said, "These stitches can come out tomorrow."

"What about this thing around my ribs?"

"It will take a while, your ribs have to heal. Tell me Mr. Covini, do you drink a lot of alcohol?"

"Hey Doc', what the hell is this? First it's drugs, now it's alcohol. How 'bout letting me worry about that."

"Mr. Covini I would like to help you, please don't get defensive."

"Look Doc', all I want to do is get the hell out of here. Let me be the one to worry about my habits." Johnny was getting annoyed.

"Look I only thought it was fair and my responsibility to try to help you. I can recommend a good counselor, maybe even some time in a rehabilitation center."

"Look Doc', I don't think I want to hear any more of this. How 'bout leaving me alone?"

Dr. Barnes took a deep breath. "OK Mr. Covini, have it your way." Dr. Barnes had seen guys like this before, and they always returned in worse shape. He doubted very much if this one would be any different than all the others. He turned away from Johnny and didn't even say good-bye.

Johnny turned toward the door and spoke in a loud enough voice for the doctor to hear him, "Hey Doc', thanks a lot—really." Dr. Barnes turned around and looked surprised. Maybe I'm wrong about this guy, he thought, maybe I did get something across to him. He gave him a quick acknowledgment and said, "Good-bye Mr. Covini, see you tomorrow."

It was getting close to lunchtime and Johnny was able to sit up a little straighter on the bed. Soon Johnny's lunch was brought in. He ate and then watched TV for a couple hours.

At 2:00 P.M. two men appeared at the door. They entered the room making all sorts of noise and commotion and started banging on the table near Johnny. It was Bobby Roedelli and Sal Morello. They were a couple of musicians who knew Johnny well and played local bars in South Philadelphia. Bobby started to sing to Johnny in a loud, shrieky voice. His voice was raspy—designed for clubs, not hospitals. The two men were pale and needed a shave. They were dressed very casually in jeans and lightweight black jackets. They both had long black hair and looked very tired. Bobby continued to sing and Johnny began laughing. The more he laughed, the more Bobby kept singing. Sal was pretending to play the guitar with the drumsticks he had brought to Johnny as a gift. The sticks were painted bright yellow with a balloon on the end.

As Bobby continued to sing, a petite brunette nurse came rushing in the door. She had huge brown eyes and she looked angry. "Guys, keep the noise down in here," she yelled, "this is a hospital, not a circus. This man was resting and the man in the other bed is also not here on vacation. If you want to stay, you'll have to stop the noise and calm down."

Sal turned toward the nurse. He liked what he saw. "Hey Johnny, what have we here? This must be the place to be—no wonder you got beat up."

Johnny smiled and replied, "Don't bet on it, it's murder in here."

"There's going to be a murder in this room if you guys don't keep it down. Do I make myself clear?" the nurse said. She waited for a second and walked out.

"What the hell brings you guys up here?" Johnny asked. He was happy to have company.

"Johnny I'm real sorry to hear you got busted up the way you did, it's too bad," Sal said as he placed the drumsticks on the bed.

"Yeah, we really feel bad about this Johnny," said Bobby, "I always told you not to get hooked up with that snake Benelli."

"How did you know Benelli did this?"

"Hey Johnny, the word gets around."

"Where the hell did you guys get these yellow drumsticks?"

"They're comin' out with all kinds of crazy stuff down at that music store—you know, the one on Cottman Avenue. So Johnny, how you feelin', when you getting out of here?"

"The doctor told me about a week. I can't wait till I get the hell out of this nut house."

"Don't worry Johnny, you'll be out before you know it. Hey

listen, we came to see you and tell you we're putting a new band together and we want you to be the drummer."

Johnny listened as Bobby and Sal started rambling on about this new group they were forming. They were so excited they kept going on and on about their plans. He waited until they were almost out of air and finally he interrupted them. "Guys, thanks for thinking of me, but I have a feeling it's time to hang it up, you know, grow up. Do you know what I mean? It's all over man. I think I've finally had enough. I have to face it, I missed the bigs and that's the way it goes. I'll just have to accept it."

Sal looked at Bobby with a strange face. "What's this guy talking about? Do you know what he's saying? You know Johnny, I think they stuck too many needles in your arm."

"No Sal, it's true. Since I've been in here, I've had a lot of time to think, and I just can't go through with any more of this craziness. It's making me sick. It's tearing up my brain. If I don't watch it, I'll end up like Tom Cat and take the bridge."

"Come on Johnny, you're just feeling sorry for yourself. You won't feel this way in a few days. You're a musician and you'll never be anything else. Sal, I'm thirty-one years old, and what do I have to show for it? I'm broke, I'm a coke addict, I drink too much, and now I almost lost my life working for that screwball Benelli." Johnny took a deep breath. "It's a joke, a real joke. It's all over Sal, I'm going to get a straight job. Eight hours a day—steady income. No more smoke-filled nightclubs, no more alcohol, and I'm sick of the one-night stands with them trashy women. And most of all, I'm not taking no more beatings. I'm gonna find a pretty and normal woman who will make me happy—someone that will take me out of this tragedy. I feel like I'm in some bad dream that never ends." He continued to pour his heart out, shaking his head back and forth looking at Sal and Bobby standing on opposite sides of the bed. "I never thought I'd end up like this— what a waste," he said with a total look of disgust on his face.

Sal waited to see if he was finished. When he was sure he

had ended his speech, he started his. "Well Johnny, when you decide to stop coming down on yourself, give one of us a call. There's no way you'll ever stop being a drummer. There's just no way you'll give up what's in your blood. You're a musician and that's that. Stop talking like a crazy person and think about what Bobby and I said before. We're starting a new group, and you'll be with us, OK?" He paused for a second. "Listen we're going to go now, you probably need some rest from all the bullshit you just told us." He started to laugh and gave Bobby a look that they should leave.

"Guys, thanks for coming," said Johnny. Bobby and Sal started to sing again as they walked toward the door to leave. They said good-bye while they were still singing, and as they walked out, Johnny could hear the nurse in the hall yelling at them to keep it down. They were two funny, crazy guys, and he really liked both of them a lot.

Johnny spent the rest of the day thinking about the future. He got a phone call from Harry and spoke to him for a while. Harry was feeling a lot better and he told Johnny he had his car towed to a nearby parking lot where it would be safe. Harry's friend owned the lot.

Johnny stayed up till one o'clock in the morning watching the music station on TV. He wished he could be on television, but he was truly beginning to believe what he had told Sal and Bobby; the music business was all over for him. Johnny finally fell asleep watching TV and the nurse had to turn it off.

THE FOLLOWING MORNING JOHNNY WAS AWAKENED BY A NURSE AT 7:00 A.M. She checked his blood pressure and temperature, and by 8:00, he was having breakfast. The sun was shining on that bright Monday morning in springtime. Johnny was feeling much better and the withdrawal symptoms from the alcohol and drugs were subsiding.

As Johnny was finishing his breakfast, the nurse entered the room. "Hey nurse," he asked.

"Mr. Covini you can call me by my first name you know."

"OK, what's your first name?"

"Janet."

"Nice meeting you Janet."

"Nice meeting you Mr. Covini."

"Since I call you Janet, how 'bout calling me Johnny?"

"OK Johnny. Now what's your question?"

"When am I going to get the hell out of this bed and start walking?"

"Well according to this chart, we will get you on your feet starting today."

"Man I can't believe it—finally." As the nurse began to check Johnny's abdomen, Johnny looked at her. She was very pretty. She had short blond hair and the cutest smile. He thought to himself, she's not built bad either. He hadn't been with a woman in quite a while, and was beginning to get hungry for some lovin'. She sensed him drooling over her and looked up and smiled. Johnny was embarrassed.

"These stitches will have to come out today, but we'll have to check with the doctor first. About 11:00 we'll get you on your feet, and start you walking around today. I will be back in a little while to check up on you. The doctor should be here about 12:00 today." As the nurse left the room, Johnny couldn't keep his eyes off her. Man, she's got beautiful legs, he thought.

Johnny ate breakfast and spent the next couple of hours daydreaming. He had so much to think about; how he would take care of himself when he got home, who he would get to pick him up from the hospital when he was discharged, and where he would find a decent job.

At 11:30 Dr. Barnes entered the room. "Good morning Mr. Covini," he said, "I hope you're feeling better today."

"Actually I feel pretty miserable, Doc'. I want to go home."

"You probably won't be going home till Friday, maybe Saturday, so you might as well make yourself comfortable for the next five days." Dr. Barnes picked up the chart at the foot of Johnny's bed. "Well here's something positive, you may start walking around today. Also, you'll be getting the stitches out today. Before you know it, you'll be home and well again—just be patient." Dr. Barnes rang the buzzer for the nurse.

"OK, OK, I'll try to be patient."

When nurse Janet entered, Johnny smiled and said hello. The nurse smiled back.

"Yes, you're definitely starting to get better," said Dr. Barnes. "OK, Nurse, we're going to gently get Mr. Covini out of the bed and start him walking."

"What about the stitches, Doctor?"

"I'll make arrangements to get them out this afternoon." The nurse and Dr. Barnes gently helped Johnny off the bed.

"I can't believe it," he said, "I was beginning to think I wouldn't be able to walk anymore." Carefully, they pulled Johnny up and he stood on his feet.

"Are you OK Johnny?" Janet asked.

"A little wobbly and a little stiff, but I think I'm OK." Johnny began walking to the door with the nurse and the doctor on either side of him. As they reached the room entrance, Dr. Barnes asked, "Would you like to try to walk without our assistance now?"

"Yeah, I think I'll be all right Doc, it's like riding a bike— you never forget." Suddenly they left go of Johnny's arms, and slowly he began walking on his own. He looked like an old man. He had lost ten pounds, and he was a bit hunched. He began rubbing the back of his neck and rolling his head around. His neck was very sore from lying in bed. Now that he could walk, he would get rid of a lot of the stiffness in his body. I hope I never have to go through this again, he thought to himself. Dr. Barnes and the nurse just looked on.

Most of the afternoon Johnny got himself acquainted with some of the staff and some patients also. Johnny was a talker and loved to socialize. He managed to meet an older gentleman who was in the hospital for prostate trouble. It turned out the man was a jazz drummer. He and Johnny had quite a lot to talk about. The man's name was John Bruford, and Johnny had told him that he had heard some of his music on a popular jazz station in Philadelphia. The old black man really enjoyed Johnny's company and invited him down to the FaRone Hotel to maybe sit-in for a couple of tunes when they both got well. Bruford's band had a six-month stay there. They used a fill-in drummer until Bruford recuperated.

Johnny was so happy to meet someone who was in the music business. When he began talking with the older gentleman, he forgot all about what he said about quitting the business. Maybe I can still do it as a hobby, he thought to himself.

At 3:30 that afternoon, Janet entered Johnny's room. She had to notify him that he was to get his stitches out at 4:00. He wasn't in his room, but she heard his voice two rooms down. I hope I don't have to go hunting him down all week, she thought. Johnny was so glad to be walking around and talking with everybody. He was beginning to feel like a human being again. He hadn't had any drugs or alcohol in over a week, and was beginning to feel like a new person.

Janet entered the other room. "Johnny, I'm sorry to disturb you, but we have to get those stitches out now."

"Aw come on, can't we wait till tomorrow?"

"No. The doctor said today. He wants you downstairs now. The stitches come out in a half an hour." Johnny looked at his friend Mike who was in the hospital to get his gall bladder removed.

"Well Mike, looks like we have to break up this conversation."

Johnny went downstairs and the doctor removed his stitches. The wrapping around his ribs barely got in the way. The incision was low enough to where it didn't interfere. Johnny returned to his room and had dinner. At 7:00 P.M., an old friend came to visit Johnny. Johnny looked to the door and saw the old gentleman walking toward him slowly. "Lefty—I can't believe it. I almost forgot you."

"Well believe it kid, I'm here." The old gentleman spoke with a raspy voice.

"Have a seat Lefty, take a load off." Johnny quickly sat up on the bed. He was very happy to see his old friend. Lefty took off his coat and hat, sat in the chair, and took a deep breath.

"So how you feelin' Lefty?"

"I think I should be asking you that question, Johnny."

"How did you know I was in here Lefty?"

"Harry told me the whole story."

"Well I guess you heard then, huh."

"You mean about you dying?"

"Yeah, what do you think about that?"

"You want to hear something funny kid?"

"What?"

"I saw them taking you away in that bodybag."

"You mean you knew that I was killed, or I mean beat up—you know, almost dead or whatever?"

"No Johnny, to tell you the truth, I didn't know who it was at the time, I thought there was just some trouble at Harry's Bar and someone got killed. It's probably better I didn't know it was you."

"And what's that supposed to mean?"

"I probably would have head a heart attack."

Johnny grinned. "So tell me Lefty, how are you feeling?"

"I'm no good Johnny."

"What do you mean you're no good, you're healthy as a rock."

"I got emphysema. I can hardly breathe anymore. By the way, can I smoke in here?"

"Lefty, this is 1980, you can't smoke in a hospital no more." Johnny laughed, "Lefty you're a nut! You have emphysema and you want to smoke."

"Hey Johnny, I'm an old man, it doesn't matter anymore."

"Look Lefty, don't talk that way. I want to see you around for a while."

"You know, you're the one in the hospital and we're talking about me and my troubles."

"Hey Lefty, it's OK." There sat Johnny and Lefty, one was young and the other old. They were both ailing, both without any family, and basically nowhere to go. Just the same, they were good company for one another, and Lefty stayed until visiting hours were over. They talked continually.

Johnny spent the next three days walking around, socializing, watching the music station on TV, he had another visit from Danny Rosco, a visit from Harry, and even got a phone call from his little friend Joey Cunningham. Joey's parents visited Johnny Wednesday night. On Thursday afternoon, he got a visit from his musician friends Mickey Percaro and Kenny Pascarelli; they also had tried to convince Johnny to form a permanent band with them, but there was no way Johnny could be persuaded. He enjoyed their company just the same, and was very happy that they had visited him.

Thursday night Johnny got a visit from Dr. Barnes who told him he would be able to go home on Friday. He would come in the following morning to give him some instructions before releasing him from the hospital. Johnny was so excited he could hardly sleep that night, and by 7:00 A.M., he was wide awake. At 9:00 A.M. Dr. Barnes entered his room. "Good morning Mr. Covini, how are you?"

"I feel great Doc', I'm ready to go. I am going home today, right?"

"Yes, you can go home today."

"Well I guess I better get dressed."

"Not so fast pal. Let me check those ribs." After checking the wrapping around Johnny's ribs, Dr. Barnes told him that he would arrange an appointment at his office, and he would soon be getting the wrapping off. "You know Mr. Covini, you're really going to have to take it easy for a while."

Dr. Barnes took a seat in the chair beside the bed. He began to speak in a quiet, caring voice. Johnny sat quietly and listened. "I suggest that you rest a lot; no alcohol, no drugs, and try to stay away from sex for the next couple weeks. Do you have a steady relationship?"

"No."

"You know Johnny—can I call you Johnny?"

"Sure Doc'."

"Maybe you should find yourself a good girl and think about getting married. Were you ever married?"

"Never had time."

"Do you have someone that can come and get you today? I definitely don't want you driving for at least two weeks. And you really should have someone around to help you for a while."

"I think I'll be OK Doc', I feel pretty good."

"I have a number here I want you to call." The doctor gave Johnny the piece of paper with the phone number.

Johnny noticed the name on the paper and asked, "Who's Mr. Schatz—"

"He's a trained counselor. He can help you get back on the right track. I'm sorry if I'm getting too personal with you, but I have to be honest, we found you with low blood pressure and anemia."

"What's anemia?"

"You're lacking iron in your blood and it's making you very weak. You have to start to rebuild your body. You're getting older now and you have to slow down. You're not a teenager, and let's not forget about your drug and alcohol problem. Who is your family doctor?"

"I don't know. I forget his name, as a matter of fact, I haven't seen a doctor since they almost tried to draft me into the army."

"I'm going to recommend you to a doctor who can also help

you."

"You're a doctor, why can't you be my family doctor?"

"I'm an Internist, you need a family doctor. There's one other thing I want you to know, I believe you're an intelligent young man and you must help yourself. And please, don't get yourself beat up again."

"I won't Doc', that you can count on. I don't ever want to experience this again."

"I'll be back in an hour to say good-bye."

"Hey Doc', listen—thanks a lot for all your concern."

"It's OK, just take care of yourself."

It made Johnny feel good to know the doctor took the time to talk to him. Dr. Barnes was fifty years old and for a few minutes, Johnny felt like he had a father. His father had died when he was just a young man. He drank himself to death and never had time to spend with Johnny, let alone talk to him.

The doctor left the room and Johnny thought for a second about who he should call. Harry, he thought. Harry would know someone. He quickly picked up the phone and dialed Harry's Bar. Harry answered the phone.

"Hey Harry, it's Johnny."

"Johnny how you feelin', when you coming home?"

"That's why I'm calling Harry, I need a ride, and somehow I want to get my car home. Can you help me?"

"Sure kid, no problem. I'll have Ramone get your car and he'll be there to pick you up. What room you in again?"

"335. Harry can you make it about 11:00? I have to wait until the doctor comes to release me in about an hour."

"Sure, no problem Johnny, but there's one more thing."

"What?"

"Your car didn't have any keys in it, you obviously have them."

"There's a spare set underneath the left fender in a little magnetic box. Just tell Ramone they're under the wheel well of the front left fender."

"OK Johnny, Ramone will be there at 11:00."

"Thanks Harry, maybe I'll get down to see you in a week or so. I really have to stay home and take it easy for a while."

"OK, Johnny, see you soon."

Johnny hung up the phone and walked to the closet to get his clothes. The closet was empty. Where the hell's my clothes, he thought. The only things there were his alligator skin boots. "Where the hell's my clothes?" he mumbled to himself.

Suddenly Janet the nurse walked into the room. She was carrying a big package. Johnny turned to her. "Janet, where the hell's my clothes at?"

"Your clothes are in the trash, Johnny."

"What are you talking about?"

"Johnny your clothes were a bloody mess, and we had to practically cut them off you."

"So what am I going to do—go home naked?"

Janet laughed.

"Oh, so it's funny."

She couldn't help herself, the thought of him going home naked made her crack up. "Come here, I have something to show you." Janet laid the package on Johnny's bed. She began to pull out clothing: new jeans, a beautiful red shirt, and a jean jacket. She also pulled out new underwear and socks. Johnny couldn't believe it.

"Where did you get the new clothes?" he asked.

"Downtown," she replied.

"You mean you bought these clothes."

"Yes I bought them."

"Hey Janet, you didn't have to do this."

"I wanted to do it."

"But why?"

"Please Johnny, don't ask me questions. Just accept them in good faith."

"How did you know what size to get me?"

"Girls look at guys bodies too, you know."

Johnny smiled and shook his head. "You're something else, you know that?" He leaned over and kissed her on the cheek. "No, wait a minute," he said. He turned her toward him and kissed her on the lips. Janet and Johnny had gotten very friendly in the hospital, and she obviously had a crush on him. She was young and single and really liked Johnny's looks and personality.

"Hey Janet, I really don't know what to say, I mean thanks a lot for the clothes. I mean, you hardly know me—I don't know how to thank you."

"How would you like a visiting nurse?"

"It's a deal, I'll give you the address before I leave."

"OK, I have to get busy, I'll see you in a bit."

Johnny quickly got dressed and waited for Dr. Barnes to return. He checked Johnny's blood pressure and wished him the best of luck. He gave him the number of a family physician and a prescription for a mild pain killer.

"Don't take anything other than I prescribed for you," said Dr. Barnes. "You're going to do what I said, right? If you start taking your own drugs, I'll be looking at you in this bed again before you know it. You need to get well. Make sure you call and see both of these guys I recommended. They are good men and they will help you. My office will contact you sometime next week for a visit. Can you find someone to pick you up?"

"There's someone coming shortly, Doc'." The doctor shook Johnny's hand. He smiled and said, good-bye. "Thanks a lot Doc'." Johnny went to the bathroom and rinsed his face off and quickly combed his hair. He had taken a shower the night before and felt pretty fresh. As he walked out of the bathroom, Janet entered the room.

"Well Johnny, I guess this is it."

Johnny looked at her. "I'm really going to miss you Janet, I didn't know nurses were so nice. I want to see you again. Let me write down my address. What you said about a visiting nurse sounds real good. I don't have a family or a steady relationship. I can use a woman's touch for the next couple of weeks around my apartment. Maybe you could stop by once or twice." Johnny wrote down his address and gave it to Janet.

At that point a medium-height, dark complected man with pitch black hair entered the room. Johnny looked over at him and wondered who he was.

"Hey men, you Johnny Covini?"

For a second, Johnny got nervous. He thought Benelli had sent someone up to finish the job. "Yeah, I'm Covini."

"I'm Ramone. Harry sent me to pick you up."

"Eh Ramone, man I'm glad to see you." Johnny extended his hand and shook hands with Ramone. "Ramone, where you parked?"

"I'm downstairs at the main entrance." Suddenly an elderly man who was a volunteer at the hospital walked into the room pushing a wheelchair. Johnny looked at Janet and said, "What's with the wheelchair?"

"Everyone has to leave in a wheelchair, Johnny, it's hospital regulations."

"Geez, I feel like an old cripple or something."

"Johnny please, just get in the chair."

"Hey man, I'll see you downstairs."

"Thanks Ramone." Johnny got in the wheelchair. Janet leaned over and kissed him.

"I'll come to see you next week," she said.

"Call first to make sure I'm there."

"You better be there—remember what the doctor said."

"Bye Janet."

"Bye Johnny."

Soon enough Johnny was in the lobby and the old man wheeled him out the doors to the car. Ramone was leaning on the car, waiting with his arms folded. Ramone did odd jobs around the bar for Harry. He was a really nice guy—very strong, but harmless. When Johnny and the old man reached the car, Ramone said, "Johnny how you feeling man?"

"I'm OK Ramone. Just a little blinded by the sun. I haven't been outside in two weeks."

Ramone opened the passenger side door and gently helped Johnny into the car. When he shut the door Johnny thanked the old man. Ramone walked to the driver's side, got in the car, and off they went.

"I hope I never see that place again. Take me home, Ramone." Johnny and Ramone got acquainted on their ride to his apartment. When they pulled up in front of the building, Johnny's little friend Joey was playing out front. He looked up into the car window and saw Johnny's black and blue marks around his eye and jaw. He looked scared for a second.

Ramone shut the engine off and walked around to the passenger side of the car. Ramone opened the door and slowly helped Johnny out. As Johnny got out of the car, he shouted, "Ow! These damn ribs. When the hell they gonna stop hurting?"

When Johnny stood up straight Joey asked, "Johnny where have you been? I got a new snare drum and I wanted to show it to you, but I haven't seen you in a while."

"OK Joey, just give me a few minutes to get upstairs, and we can check it out."

"Johnny what happened to your face?"

"Oh just a little accident Joey, no big deal." He didn't want to frighten his little friend. Most of all he didn't want to have to explain the reason for his bruises. "Ramone, can you help me up to my apartment? I'll give you some money to take a cab back to Harry's."

"No need for that Johnny, I think I'll just walk back."

"Well can I give you something for all your help?"

"Hey man, we're on Harry's time—he's paying me for this. All he told me is to take good care of you."

Ramone carefully helped Johnny up the steps to his apartment. Joey followed right behind his pal. He was wondering why Johnny was holding his ribs and why Ramone had to help him. The little kid was curious and puzzled. He had never seen Ramone before, nor had he ever seen Johnny in this condition. Finally, they reached the top of the steps. When they entered the apartment, Johnny could hardly catch his breath and his ribs were hurting pretty badly. He immediately took a seat at the kitchen table.

"Johnny, man you gonna be OK?" Ramone asked. Joey just stood quietly by the table.

"Yeah I'll be fine Ramone, I just gotta catch my breath. Have a seat Joey." Joey was glad Johnny wanted him to stay.

"Are you going to need anything before I leave?" asked Ramone.

"No, everything's fine. Tell Harry I'll see him soon."

"OK man, see ya."

"Oh and uh Ramone, thanks man."

"Hey no problem."

"Johnny how come you were in the hospital and why do you look the way you do?" Joey asked.

Johnny looked at Joey and grinned. He was very tired and really didn't feel like talking. He tried to think of something to tell Joey, but he didn't want to hurt his feelings by asking him to leave. "Hey Joey listen, I'm not feelin' too well kid, I gotta get some rest. How about tomorrow morning you stop on over with your new snare drum and I can check it out. Tomorrow's Saturday—you won't have to go to school, we can hang out for a while."

The little kid felt kind of hurt, but he also felt sorry for Johnny. "OK Johnny, I'll be back tomorrow morning. You get some sleep. If you need anything, just call over and I'll get it for you."

"Thanks kid, I'll do that."

6

* * * * * * * * * *

On Saturday morning Johnny woke up very early. It must have been 7:00 A.M. He just laid there and stared at the ceiling. He wanted to sleep longer, but for some reason he couldn't. He had been through a hell of a lot in the last few weeks. He was glad to be in his own place and not in the hospital. But now what was he going to do with himself for the next couple of weeks? He thought about all the things he had told Sal Morello and Bobby Roedelli the other day when they came to see him. No more music, no more drugs, no more alcohol. Can I really give all this stuff up, he thought to himself. It seemed to him that someone or something was trying to give him a message to get his act together. Jesus, he thought, I almost died a couple of weeks ago, or was I dead? What more of a warning did he need? He would have to find a regular job, and clean up his act. He continued to jump back and forth with his thoughts and finally dozed off.

At 8:00, he woke again and got out of bed slowly. Johnny wasted no time getting washed up and dressed. For a moment he had to gather his thoughts. He was so used to getting up and running out of the house, but now he would have to stay cool for a while and take it easy. He made his way to the kitchen and reached for a pot in the cabinet to put some tea on. I'll make myself some tea, he thought. He went to the refrigerator and fortunately found some eggs and butter. Bread, he thought, where's the freakin' bread? Guess I'll have to ask Joey to go down to the store.

Suddenly he heard a knock on the door. When he opened the door, sure enough it was little Joey with his new snare drum over his shoulder. He was grinning from ear to ear. The little boy was so excited, he was very proud of his new drum.

"Hey buddy, come on in and let me see what you've got there."

Joey rushed to the kitchen and placed the new drum down on the table. Johnny just laughed and shook his head. When Johnny reached the kitchen he said, "Hey Joey, this is some drum you have!" The drum was jet black and had really classy looking gold hardware. "Man, where did you get this thing?"

"My father bought it for me down at the percussion shop near where he works. It's a birthday present. I'm ten you know."

"Sure I know, I have your present being delivered later on today." Johnny tried to think fast. He didn't want to disappoint the young boy. He remembered the drumsticks Sal and Bobby brought him in the hospital. When little Joey would leave, he would call the hospital and see if they were still in the room. How the hell did I forget them sticks, he thought, they would have been a perfect gift for the kid.

"Joey how 'bout doin' me a favor?"

"Sure Johnny."

"I'd like you to run down to the store and get a few things for me. I'll write some things down on the paper and you can just hand it to the man down at Agostino's Deli." When the little kid left the apartment, Johnny quickly called the hospital.

He was transferred to the nurses' station and to his surprise, Janet took the call. "Hello, can I help you?"

"Hello, this is Johnny Covini."

"Johnny!"

"Janet, is that you?"

"Yes it's me Johnny, I didn't expect you to be calling here

today. I mean, I'm glad—oh you know what I mean."

"Yeah I know what you mean, how you doin'?"

"I'm fine, how are you?"

"My ribs are killing me."

"Were you able to get your prescription filled?"

"No not yet, I'll have to find somebody from the neighborhood or maybe a friend."

"Johnny listen, why don't I stop by after work and pick up the prescription, I'll be glad to get it filled for you."

"You're sure you don't mind?"

"Of course I don't mind, and besides, I would like to see you."

"Look Janet, the reason I called is that I think I left a pair of drumsticks in my room."

"You mean those bright yellow ones with the balloon at the end?"

"Yeah, they're the ones."

"They're here at the nurses' station. I believe someone was going to notify you today."

"Well listen, do you think you could bring them over tonight also?"

"Sure, I'll be glad to. Listen, I have to go now, someone's ringing for me."

"OK, see you tonight."

Shortly after Johnny hung up the phone, Joey was back with the groceries. Joey placed the groceries on the kitchen table.

"Joey, you're a good man. How would you like some tea and cookies, or better still, how about breakfast?"

"Nah, I had breakfast, but I will have some cookies and milk."

"Oh that's right, you younger guys need your milk. How about you get some dishes out on the table while I fix breakfast." Joey moved around the kitchen, following all of Johnny's requests. He then poured himself some milk and opened up the bag of cookies.

"Johnny, when you're finished breakfast, could you tune my drum up?"

"Sure Joey, I think we can do that today." When Johnny finished cooking breakfast, Joey watched him slowly lower himself onto the chair. He wanted to ask Johnny what had happened or if he wanted to talk about it, but he waited. Joey began to munch on the cookies while Johnny started to eat his breakfast. The little kid felt so bad for his friend, he looked so weak.

"Johnny—"

"What?"

"Whenever I have a problem my dad always says, 'Do you want to talk about it with me?'"

"Oh yeah?" For a few seconds, there was silence.

"Well, do you want to talk about it?"

"Nah, it's OK kid, but thanks anyway." He raised his right pointer finger and waved it at the young boy. "However, I would like to tell you a story about a certain drummer, so when you grow up and become a big star, hopefully you won't have to go through the hard times and bad things that being a musician can bring."

Little Joey positioned himself, and his eyes opened wide. He always liked whenever Johnny would tell him a story.

"Once there was this kid who wanted to be a drummer. He saw this band on TV, I think it was the Ed Sullivan Show. The drummer in the band was this guy with a funny haircut, as a matter of fact, they all had funny haircuts. Anyway, he saw this drummer having lots of fun. There were all these girls screaming and crying over this band and the drummer. Well this kid knew from that moment, this was the kind of fun he wanted to have for himself. He was fascinated and knew immediately this was what he wanted to do. That very evening after the show, he asked his mom and dad to buy him a set of drums. 'Drums,' his dad said, 'so you can do what them crazy guys were doing on TV?' he yelled, 'Forget it. Go to school and learn a trade.'"

"Well," Johnny said, "the next day he went out into the garage and spotted some old trash cans. He got a couple of sticks from the wood pile and started wailing away on the cans. From that day on, you couldn't stop him."

Little Joey was listening intently. "Every chance he got, he would bang away on the trash cans. Finally, he persuaded his dad to buy him a drum set. This kid was good. He practiced every day-one, two, sometimes three hours. Now, when he turned eighteen, he got in a band and began to have some real fun. He met lots of people and he got to be one of the best drummers around. This guy was hot. There was no way anyone was going to stop him from being a star.

One night, he was playing at this party and everyone was having a real good time. When the band took a break, a pretty young girl approached him and asked him if he wanted to have some fun. 'Sure, why not,' he said. When he finished playing that night. He packed up his drums and he and the girl left the party together. She drove him to a big house where there must have been a couple of hundred people, and man were they partying! After they had been at this party for a while, she left him for a few minutes to go and talk to a friend. As he waited for her to return, someone passed him this funny-looking pipe. Everyone seemed to be laughing and their eyes were real squinted and shiny. It seemed as though they could barely see out of them. Someone handed him the pipe and told him to take a toke—you know, a puff. He took the pipe, and after he smoked some of it, he began to choke."

Little Joey interrupted, "Is that the stuff my mom and dad told me about—pot, marijuana?"

"Yeah that's it kid, I can see your parents care about you. Anyway, because of marijuana, this guy started taking pills, alcohol, and finally the big time—cocaine."

"Cocaine—bad stuff!"

"Right. Not to mention the bad girls."

"You mean ones they call whores?"

"You got it kid. You know lots more than I knew when I was

your age. The bottom line is, keep practicing your drumming, stay away from drugs, and when you get older, find a girl you can love and trust, and remember, if you want to be a drummer, do it with all your heart, and you'll make it to the top."

Joey waited for a minute to see if Johnny was finished. "Johnny, this guy that you were telling the story about, was **it** you?"

"What do you think?"

"Do you still take drugs Johnny?"

Johnny laughed. "You're a good listener Joey, no more drugs for me. Me and you are two drug free guys."

Joey laughed. "Yeah," he said, "two drug free guys."

Johnny extended his hand, and he and his young friend shook hands and continued laughing.

AT 4:00 THAT AFTERNOON, JANET CAME TO JOHNNY'S APARTMENT. SHE gave him the drumsticks and then went to get his prescription and returned in forty-five minutes. Johnny had asked her if she would pick up some Chinese food and eat with him at the apartment. She agreed.

As they sat at the small kitchen table, Johnny said, "Janet this Chinese food is great."

"I know," she said, "I haven't had any Chinese food for the last few months, I'm glad you suggested it."

"Yeah, so am I, I mean I'm really glad you're here."

Janet just smiled, "Yeah, so am I. So tell me, how long have you been living in South Philadelphia?"

"Actually all my life. As a matter of fact, I was born and raised just a few blocks from here."

"God, you must like it."

"Ah, you know, where am I gonna go? Everybody I know is around here. I mean you know South Philadelphia, it's like a world of its own."

"Do you work close to here?"

"Janet, do you know why I was in the hospital?"

"Well, you apparently took a good beating."

"Well do you know who beat me?"

"No, I don't even know why you were beat up. Look Johnny, wait a minute, maybe this is none of my business."

"No, it's OK, I'll tell you. I was working for this numbers boss, I got a little screwed up and he lost five thousand dollars in bets because of me. He got really pissed off, and his bodyguards did a number on me."

"Gee I'm sorry Johnny, I had no idea."

"Eh, it's OK, maybe it happened for the best."

"But I don't understand, aren't you a drummer?"

"Well I don't know about a drummer, a frustrated musician maybe."

"So what you're saying is you don't have a steady job."

"I heard that."

"So what's the next move?"

"The next move is that you and I get better acquainted."

"Oh really?"

"Oh really. What are you doing tonight? Tell me, do you have a boyfriend? How old are you anyway?"

"I'm not doing anything tonight, the guy I've been dating is away for the weekend, and I'm twenty-five. Any more questions Mr. Covini?"

"No, but I think you should stay for the evening."

"I don't know, I really should get home and get cleaned up, and then maybe I could stop by later on."

"Hey Janet, look you can take a shower here, my bathroom is clean you know and I have this beautiful black robe that would look great on you. It would really match that beautiful blond hair of yours, and those big blue eyes."

"Johnny stop it, you're embarrassing me. Just the same, you talked me into it."

"Great! Somehow I thought you'd see things my way."

"You're pretty sure of yourself, aren't you?"

"No, I just got lucky tonight."

Janet just smiled and said, "Let me get this table cleaned up for you, and then I can get a shower." Janet got up off the chair and began cleaning off the table. As the two spoke, Johnny was continually looking at her body. God, she turns me on, he thought to himself, and then he thought, I can't believe this, I've got this beautiful woman here and I can hardly move.

"So Janet, what do you want to do tonight?"

"Well we can't go out, that's for sure. Johnny when's the last time you cleaned your kitchen floor?"

"I don't know, maybe six, seven months. And why can't we go out?"

"Get serious. You just came out of the hospital yesterday, you know what the doctor told you."

"He doesn't really think I'm going to stay in this apartment for the next couple weeks, does he?"

"Well you should stay in for the next few days, and then maybe you can go out a little bit. You know you're really going to have to take care of yourself, and be sure and take your medication."

"Hey Janet, you're not on duty now, I get the message."

"How long has this trash been in this can here?"

"I don't know, maybe a few weeks. Are you forgetting I haven't been here? Hey, what's with the kitchen floor and the trash? I guess next you'll be telling me how untidy my bedroom is."

"Oh really? I didn't expect to see your bedroom this evening."

"Oh. Actually, I was kind of hoping I could persuade you to rub my back for me."

"Are you forgetting, I'm not on duty now."

Johnny laughed, "Hey, that was good Janet."

"Listen, if you're good, I'll rub your back for you."

"In the bedroom?"

"Yes Johnny, in the bedroom, but please don't get any ideas.

You're in no condition for anything more."

"What are you talking about?"

"Oh stop it Johnny, I see the way you've been looking at me. Even the other nurses in the hospital saw you staring at me all the time."

"Boy, you're pretty conceited, aren't you? I mean I know you've got a great body, and I guess you know it too."

"Look, I'm just as physically attracted to you as you are to me."

"Well why did you come over here? I hope you didn't come here just to tease me."

"No, I came over here because I care about you."

"You care about me?"

"Yes. I mean I think you're a nice guy."

"Hey, I think you're nice too." As Janet began wiping off the table, Johnny grabbed her hand. "Wait," he slowly lifted himself off the chair, "come here," he said. He pulled her to him and put his arms around her. Janet then put her arms around Johnny. The two kissed. Suddenly Johnny began to get aroused by Janet's soft lips and her large breasts. He began kissing her with more passion all over her neck.

"Johnny wait, you're too hungry. Please, take it easy."

"I'm sorry, you just feel so damn good, and I am hungry."

Janet backed up, "Johnny don't make this hard for me. When you feel better, we can get together, but for now I know your condition. Your insides are still a little tender, and don't forget your broken ribs."

"OK, I'll take it easy, maybe you're right." Johnny held her in his arms again. "Hey Janet," he said, "I want you to know you really made me feel happy by coming over. I mean I just feel so damn alone." Janet held him close as she rested her chin on his shoulder.

"Don't worry," she said, "I'll help you as much as I can. I know you're going through some bad times now, mentally and physically, maybe I can help you work it all out."

Suddenly there was a knock at the door. "I'll get it," said Janet. When Janet opened the door, there stood little Joey and his parents.

"Hi, is Johnny in?" asked Mr. Cunningham.

"Johnny, there's a Mr. Cunningham to see you."

"Let him in. Hey, Charlie, Nancy, come on in. Hey little Joey, what's happening?"

"Here Johnny, I baked you a chocolate cake," said Nancy.

"Chocolate cake? I can't believe it. I knew there was something I was wishing for, but I couldn't pinpoint it. Thanks Nancy, I really appreciate it."

Johnny placed the cake on the kitchen table. He looked at little Joey and said, "Joey, chocolate cake is my favorite, how about you?"

"Yeah, me too Johnny."

"Guess what Joey, in honor of your birthday we're going to put some candles on this cake and have a little party for you right here. Charlie, Nancy, have a seat. And I'd like you to meet Janet." Charlie and Nancy shook Janet's hand and took a seat at the table.

"Johnny, you really don't have to do this, you know," said Charlie.

"Hey no problem Charlie, glad you stopped over. And besides, I got something for Joey. I'll just put some tea on, get the candles, and we'll have a nice little party for Joey."

"Johnny, you just sit down and talk to your little friend, I'll make the tea and set the table," said Janet.

"Joey, I forgot to introduce you to Janet. Janet, meet Joey, another musician."

Janet extended her hand. "Hi Joey, nice to meet you."

Joey extended his hand and began to blush. Nancy and Charlie laughed.

"Here, I'll help you set the table Janet," said Nancy.

Little Joey looked to Johnny, "Hey Johnny," he said, "she's

pretty! Does she have any younger sisters?"

"Take it easy son," said Charlie, "there will be plenty of time for that."

"Joey, just sit tight, I got something for you," said Johnny. Johnny went to get the yellow drumsticks for Joey. When he returned, Joey couldn't believe it. When he saw the bright, big, yellow drumsticks with a big red balloon at the end, his eyes opened wide. "Here you are Joey, happy birthday!"

"Wow! Where did you get these drumsticks at?"

"They're yours kid, now you can be the flashiest drummer in the neighborhood."

"They're a little heavy Johnny, must be 5-B's."

"You got it kid, perfect for rock'n'roll."

"Gee thanks Johnny, yellow drumsticks—these are fantastic." Everyone looked toward the boy and laughed. Soon they sang happy birthday to Joey and he blew out the ten candles with no problem. He was very excited. Johnny could always bring out the best in his little friend.

AT 10:00 P.M., JOHNNY WAS LYING COMFORTABLY ON HIS STOMACH AS Janet gently massaged his naked body. She had taken a nice warm shower and looked just fine in Johnny's black robe. She felt very comfortable with Johnny.

"Janet, I really wasn't expecting a body massage."

"I know you weren't, as a matter of fact, I'm surprised."

"At what?"

"You're really behaving."

"I'm only doing it for you, if you only knew the fantasies that were going on in my mind."

"When you get better, I want you to make love to me, not get crazy."

"Janet, have you ever been married?"

"Almost."

"What happened?"

"I like my career. The guy I was going with owned four car dealerships. He was thirty-five and one of those guys that didn't think a woman should have a career. He said when we got married he didn't want me to work anymore, just have his children and be a good wife. And on top of that, he was very jealous. I mean, he was just crowding me."

"You gave up a lot of wealth, your career must mean a lot to you."

"It does. I like helping people."

"Yeah, you give good massages too."

"Have you ever been married?"

"Married! Who the hell would want me?"

" What do you mean?"

"Janet, I ain't got nothing."

"You mean because you don't have anything nobody would want you?"

"You know what I mean."

"No I don't."

"I'm a frustrated musician, I don't have a steady job, you know things like that."

"Johnny, you can get a steady job, and you probably could be a damn good musician, it just seems to me you got tied up with the wrong people. When you're feeling better, I'm sure you'll find a decent job, and maybe you can get in a part-time band. I have a couple friends in New York that play in a band part-time. One of them runs a business, and the other's a lawyer. They certainly don't need the money, but they enjoy playing music."

"Yeah, but with me it's not a part-time thing, it's an obsession. I mean I got all screwed up with it."

"What do you mean Johnny?"

"I thought I was going to make it big, you know, records, concerts, I don't know what it is to have a steady job."

"Well how 'bout this, you get counseling for drug and alcohol abuse, get a job at a music store during the day, and form a band. Do you write music?"

"A little bit, here and there—you know."

"Well, if you want to make it big, you're going to have to write your own music, right?"

"Well yeah."

"Well then get to it. I've known a few musicians throughout my life, and I know it can be a pretty mixed up, frustrating business. You have to get serious; you have to control the music, don't let it control you."

"Janet, you're really making my legs feel good. How do you know so much about the music business?"

"I like music, I've read a lot about artists who have made the big time, and for most of them, it was no picnic."

"Well for me it seems like an impossibility."

"It's not impossible Johnny, I think you just have some problems you have to work out, and then you can get busy."

"You make it sound so damn easy."

"I know it's not easy, but I think before you can make a go of it, you'll really have to change your living habits."

Johnny slowly turned on his side. "You know, I don't understand it, I hardly know you and you've given me more vital information and made me feel a lot better than I've felt in a long time. You're certainly different from the other girls I've known. I really got lucky when I met you." Johnny gently pulled her close to him and held her tight. "Ow!"

"What's wrong?"

"It's these damn ribs, they keep hurting."

"Here wait, turn over on your back." Janet pulled the covers over the both of them. Johnny took a deep breath. He was very frustrated.

"Johnny, what's the matter?" she asked.

"Janet I'm so freakin' pissed off all this happened. I mean look at me, I'm a wreck, I can't even make love to you."

"I'll tell you what, when you're better, I'd like you to take me to dinner, and then we can go dancing. Then you can take me home and do what you want to me."

"Now that is worth waiting for. I feel better already."

7

* * * * * * * * * *

THE FOLLOWING THURSDAY AT 9:00 A.M., JOHNNY WAS WAKENED BY A loud knock on the door. The knocking continued as Johnny slowly got out of bed. "OK, OK, I'm coming. What the hell you want to do, break the door down?" Johnny slowly made his way to the door. When he opened it, there stood Danny Rosco.

"Johnny my man, how you doing?"

"Keep it down, will you, do you have to holler?"

"Sorry man, I'm just glad to see you."

"Well come on in."

"Here, I brought you a couple of egg sandwiches, some coffee and donuts too."

"Come on, you can set them on the kitchen table."

The two men took a seat at the table. Danny had some coffee and donuts. Johnny had no problem polishing off the two sandwiches.

"Hey Johnny, how would you like to come work at Sigway Shoes?"

"You mean sell shoes? Put shoes on people's feet? Come on man, you got to be kiddin."

"No man, I'm serious."

"Are you nuts? I'm not going to put shoes on anyone's feet."

"What the hell are you going to do? You can't just hang

around all of your life. I mean there's more to life than Harry's Bar and Frankie Benelli. You've got to get it together Johnny. I mean, we're not kids anymore."

"Danny, why are you busting my chops so early in the morning?"

"What do you mean man? I'm trying to help you."

"Look Danny, there's a lot happenin' right now. I mean I just got out of the hospital a week ago, they want me to get counseling, I'm not playing music, you know how it is man. I mean I know you want to help me, but you're asking me to go sell shoes. What the hell do I know about shoes?"

"You don't have to know anything about shoes, I'll train you, you'll work for me."

"Listen, I'm starting to get around a little better now. Give me a few more days to think about it. Maybe it's not such a bad idea, but I'm not sure."

"Johnny I didn't come here to get you pissed off, I just don't want to see you waste your life away because you didn't make it as a musician."

"You have to rub it in, don't you?"

"Don't forget, I paid my dues too, you know. All those rehearsals, all those stinkin' nightclubs, I had all of the same hopes and dreams that you did. I know how you feel Johnny, I know how you feel." Danny was being very sincere.

"I know you know how I feel," said Johnny, "but we did have a lot of fun, didn't we?"

"Yeah, nobody can say we didn't have our share of women. Boy did we have lots of women."

"Yeah we made it big in that department. How about all the wild parties when we played Wildwood? We never got to bed till at least six in the morning. We were the only guys in Wildwood without a tan." They both began to laugh.

"Yeah we were nuts, weren't we," said Danny. Danny checked his watch. "Johnny, I gotta get down to open the store."

"Aw, that's too bad, I wish we could have talked a little more."

"Listen man, you know where I'm at, and I know where you're at."

"You still living in New York?"

"No, I'm on City Line Avenue. I'll give you a call. And listen, don't forget, let me know about that job. I gotta fill the position by next week, or my district manager is going to be filling my position."

"Thanks man, but as soon as I get better, I think I'm going to go see my cousin Cosmo, he owns a meat house down on Tenth St."

"OK man, have it your way, but keep in touch." Danny opened the door and waved good-bye.

Johnny was feeling much better now and decided to do some cleaning around the apartment. The place was a mess, and he was really getting sick of it. For the next three hours he moved about the apartment slowly, straightening up the bedroom, cleaning the bathroom, and the kitchen. At 12:30, he took a warm shower. He was feeling a bit tired and his ribs were very sore. "Maybe I shouldn't have done all that cleaning," he mumbled to himself, "maybe I'll just lay down and get a few hours sleep." By then Janet should be calling, he thought.

Johnny slept till 4:00. When he checked the clock on the night table, he wondered why Janet hadn't called. Johnny made a call, and ordered a pizza. He sat and watched TV and waited for the pizza to arrive. At 5:00, the pizza was delivered. By 5:30, Johnny had eaten half the pizza and then decided to call Janet. Janet's phone must have rung ten times. Finally, she answered.

"Hello."

"Janet!"

"Johnny."

"Janet, what's wrong? You sound funny."

"Nothing's wrong."

"Why'd it take you so long to answer the phone?"

"Uhh... well I was in the shower."

"Janet, what the hell's going on? You said if you didn't stop over right after work, you would call. You did neither."

"Well to tell you the truth Johnny, I'm just not feeling too well."

"Janet, what the freak's happening? Look if there's a problem, I want to know." For a moment there was silence. Suddenly Johnny was hurting inside. He knew something was up.

"Johnny I'm sorry."

"What do you mean, 'sorry?'"

"Look Barry called."

"Barry! Who the hell's Barry?"

"Barry's the guy I told you about."

"Yeah, but I thought there was nothing heavy between you two."

"Look, I have a long weekend and he wants me to meet him in Boston."

"Boston?! I don't get it. You said when I got better I could take you out to dinner. I had everything planned for this Saturday. I can t believe you're doing this to me. Janet, I'm burning for you. If I don't make love to you I'm going to go nuts."

"Johnny please, take it easy, don't do this to yourself."

"I'm not doing nothing to myself, you're doing it."

"I'm not doing anything to you. I need a weekend away, sometimes I get tired of looking at sick people."

"Oh, I get it, I was just another sick person to you."

"Johnny, please don't talk that way."

"Janet look, couldn't you just tell Barry you can make it another time? I mean, I really need you."

"Johnny, when I get back we'll get together, I promise."

"Janet, why are you really going to Boston?"

"OK you want the truth?"

"Yeah."

"You got it. Barry really cares about me. He likes my career, he doesn't want me just to be a good wife and have his children, he's a good guy. He owns a construction company and he has a solid future, and I have to start thinking about my future. So please don't confuse me, let it be this way."

"Yeah, let it be this way. He'll probably talk you into marrying him."

"Look Johnny, nobody talks me into anything. Look I have to go, I have to start packing. I'm leaving early tomorrow."

"Yeah sure, have a good time Janet." Johnny slammed the phone down. He felt as though he had never been so hurt in all his life. Johnny walked slowly to the bedroom and flopped on his bed. He took a deep breath and said, "Man, what a freaken' loser I am."

Fortunately, that night Johnny got a few calls from some friends and little Joey paid him a visit so Johnny could help him with some new drum techniques. The phone calls and little Joey's visit really helped him keep his mind off Janet.

ON FRIDAY MORNING, JOHNNY LEFT THE APARTMENT FOR THE FIRST TIME since arriving home from the hospital. He was beginning to feel much better and the bruises that were on his face had cleared up. His insides were beginning to heal where he was bleeding internally, although his ribs were still sore. He had an appointment to see Dr. Barnes at ten o'clock. He took his time and drove carefully through the city. He was feeling a bit lazy from sitting around the apartment too long.

When he arrived at the doctor's office, the waiting room was crowded. Oh shit, he thought, I'll probably be here till twelve o'clock. Everyone was looking at Johnny because he was a bit hunched over, very pale, and ten pounds underweight. He took a seat and sighed. To the right of him on the little table was a popular magazine. The front page displayed a picture of a well-known musician, Mark Barnett. It read: "Musician Mark Barnett Institutionalized for Nervous Breakdown—Alcohol and Drugs Linked to the Cause."

Johnny thought to himself, my first day out and I gotta see this, I wonder if they have any sports magazines laying around here. Ah, here's something, let me see how the Sixers are doing. Johnny was patient enough to wait about an hour. Finally, the nurse came out.

"Mr. Covini?"

"Here I am."

"The doctor will see you now. I'm sorry you had to wait so long."

"Oh that's OK, I've only been here an hour," Johnny said sarcastically.

"We do our best here, Mr. Covini."

"I hope Dr. Barnes is checking me over today, and not an assistant." As they walked toward the examining room, Johnny heard a voice.

"Johnny!"

"Doc', how you doin'?"

"I'm fine. How are you? Come on, step into the examining room, let me check those ribs. Did you have any problem driving over?"

"Nah, no problem, except for the usual crazy motorists."

Dr. Barnes just grinned. "Here, take your jacket off and have a seat. Take that shirt off for me."

As Johnny took his shirt off, the doctor could see him making faces because of his ribs still hurting him.

"Still a little sore, huh Johnny?"

"Nah, I'm doing just fine doctor."

"Here let's take a look." Dr. Barnes pressed gently on Johnny's rib. Johnny jumped.

"Doc', take it easy."

"I hardly touched it Johnny, what have you been doing? Have you been doing anything strenuous?"

"Just a little cleaning around the apartment."

"Well listen, for the next couple of weeks please don't do anything, you need to heal up."

"Well how long will I have to keep this wrapping on my ribs?"

"About two more weeks—four tops. The incision is healing very well. Have you had any blurred vision, dizziness, vomiting..."

"No, why do you ask that?"

"Well you took a pretty good shot to the eye, I was very concerned about your vision. Have you contacted Mr. Schatz, the counselor I told you about, and what about the family doctor?"

"Tell you the truth doc', these last couple weeks I didn't feel like talking to any doctors."

"Have you been eating well? You look a bit pale and underweight. Is there anyone helping you?"

"Yeah I got a couple of people from the neighborhood"

"Well it looks to me like you're coming along fine. Let me check your blood pressure."

After checking Johnny's blood pressure, he said, "Your blood pressure's very low, Johnny. I'm going to give you a prescription for some iron tablets and a multiple vitamin, and be sure you take them."

The doctor proceeded to check Johnny's heart and lungs, and everything checked out OK. "OK Johnny you can put your shirt on. I want you to see me in two weeks. Then be sure and pick up your vitamins and get in touch with the counselor. Be sure to get yourself a family doctor."

"OK, Doc', OK. Now when can I get a job and start working?"

"Well I'm glad you're interested in getting work, but you're going to have to wait until you get that wrapping off your ribs. Maybe you could find a job in one of the delis around the neighborhood, you know running a register or something like that temporarily."

"Yeah I guess I'll find something to do. Doc', I got one more problem."

"And what's that?"

"I don't have any medical insurance. I can't pay you right now, not to mention the hospital."

"We will notify you and set up a payment plan, just do the best you can."

Johnny buttoned his shirt and quickly slid on his jacket. "Doc', thanks for all your help. I'll see you in two weeks."

"OK Johnny, take care of yourself. You're still a young man and you still have a lot of time ahead of you; use it wisely."

8

* * * * * * * * * *

On Monday morning, Johnny decided to get up early and go see his cousin Cosmo to ask him for a job at his meat packing company. When he reached the outside of his apartment, he stopped for a moment. He looked around the neighborhood. He thought to himself, I gotta get out of this place, I have to change my life—this place is becoming old news. The time he had spent recuperating gave him a lot of time to think and reevaluate his life. He looked around once more on that sunny April day and then jumped in his car and headed for the meat packing company. He knew it was time to get a regular job with regular hours and a steady paycheck. He needed to change his life drastically. He still hadn't taken Dr. Barnes' advice to call a counselor. It's only Monday, he thought, maybe I'll call some day this week.

He hadn't seen his cousin Cosmo in some time. In fact, the last time was at Cosmo's father's funeral three years before. Cosmo had told him about his successful business, but complained about how hard it was to find good help. He was hoping that Cosmo would be glad to see him and give him a job.

Johnny entered the parking lot, turned off the ignition, and took a deep breath. "Well, here goes nothing," he said. As Johnny walked toward the big building, he saw the big sign "Gianetti's Meats." He stopped for a moment and just stared. He imagined his name up in bright lights. He then looked down and shook his head; that's a joke, he thought to himself, I better learn to stop fantasizing.

As he opened the door to the big building, a big fat man wearing a white coat brushed up against him. Johnny looked at him and there was a big ugly cigar dangling from his mouth. The man stunk from the combination of slaughtered meat and cigar. Johnny tried to get the man's attention to ask him for directions to his cousin's office as he rushed by.

"Excuse me," he said with a note of sarcasm. The fat man stopped and glared at Johnny. He was very mean looking. He had a flat nose and bulgy, wrinkled cheeks. He barely had a neck. He stood about six-foot and very wide. He must have weighed about 280 pounds. "Do you know where I can find my cousin Cosmo?" Johnny asked. Johnny made sure he mentioned his cousin Cosmo in case the man didn't like him for some reason.

"Yeah," the man mumbled. "He's over there, in the last freezer." He pointed toward the back of the building.

"Thanks," Johnny replied. Johnny started to walk in the direction of where the fat man had pointed. He started yelling out loud, "Hey Cosmo, Yo Cosmo—are you in there, man?" He then pulled the partially opened door and yelled again. A man with a very dark complexion and a bushy moustache looked up from the table inside the freezer.

Johnny's cousin was a good-looking character about six foot-two, and must have weighed 190 pounds. He was very strong and a good businessman. He was wearing a big, white coat and a white hard hat. Good looks must have run in Johnny's family. He looked up and smiled. "Johnny Rock'n'Roll, my main cousin," he exclaimed. "What's going on? Are you on TV yet?" He paused. "Wait a minute, what the hell are you doing here at Gianetti's Meats? Don't tell me you came down here just to see me work!" Cosmo walked quickly toward Johnny and went to grab him.

"Wait Cosmo, I got busted ribs."

"What happened, you got in an accident?"

"No, I had a little trouble."

"Well let me shake your hand." When they shook hands, Cosmo patted Johnny on the left cheek. "How's my cousin doin'?" he said.

"Eh Cosmo, it stinks in this place."

"You got that right. You won't find none of that sex, drugs, or rock'n'roll here." Cosmo shut the door to the freezer and walked over to the sink and washed his hands. "So Johnny, what brings you down here?"

As Cosmo dried his hands off he said, "Johnny what's the matter, you look pale. And what happened to your ribs?"

"I told you, I had some trouble."

"Eh you don't want to talk about it? Somebody beat you up? Tell me who it was, you know I know guys who don't smile. If you need somebody taken care of, you let me know. Me and you we been goombas a long time now, right? Let's go to my office and grab some coffee, I've got some Danish too."

"Sounds good to me," said Johnny.

When the two men entered the office, inside was a chair and matching sofa. Under the window was a beat-up-looking desk and another chair. Cosmo's desk was full of paperwork and the office looked like it hadn't been cleaned in some time.

"Hey Johnny, I'm sorry the place don't look too good, but we don't get much time to clean around here." Cosmo poured the two of them some coffee and told Johnny to have a seat. Cosmo took off his hat, took a sip of coffee, grabbed the cigarettes from the desk, and lit one up. He turned to Johnny and shrugged his shoulders. "What's happening with you, Johnny?"

"I need a job, Cosmo," he replied in a low key voice.

"Job? You mean in the meat house?"

"Hey Cosmo I'm serious. You know the music business didn't quite cut it for me." Johnny's eyes dropped to the floor. He was feeling sort of embarrassed. Suddenly there was silence. He looked up at Cosmo and made a half grin.

"Listen Johnny, you want a job, you got it. You come in here when you heal up completely, and I'll put you to work somewhere."

"Thanks Cosmo, I appreciate it."

"I know you do Johnny." Cosmo leaned forward and patted Johnny on the back. Cosmo started asking Johnny questions about some of the guys they both knew, and they avoided the subject of employment. Johnny was glad, because he was feeling uneasy about working at the meat company.

As they continued to talk, Johnny kept inhaling the odor of slaughtered meat. He thought about asking Cosmo if you ever get used to the smell, but he changed his mind.

Someone knocked on the door and told Cosmo they were having a problem with a meat packing machine. "Where the hell's the maintenance men?" Cosmo asked.

"They're working on the grinding machine."

"OK, I'll be right out. Eh Johnny, we got to get that machine running, let me see if I can go fix it. We got a lot of orders and you know with that machine down, I don't make no money. Look, I'll see you in a couple weeks, right?" Both men stood up and shook hands. Cosmo gently gave him a hug and patted him on the back again. He then looked to Johnny. "You take care of yourself, OK?"

"I will Cosmo." The two men left the office and said goodbye. Johnny stopped and shouted, "Hey Cosmo, thanks man."

"Hey Johnny, no problem—you're my cousin."

For the next two weeks, Johnny spent time watching TV, reading, and keeping his apartment in order. He had given little Joey a couple of one-hour drum lessons, and in turn, Joey helped Johnny polish his drum set out in the garage. Johnny would occasionally take a walk around the block and visit some of the neighborhood merchants. Most of the merchants knew him from his childhood. He made sure to stay away from the bars, but he still remained confused and worried. He tried not to even think about cocaine. He neglected to call Mr. Schatz, the counselor, or hook up with a family doctor. Johnny needed counseling really bad and didn't realize it.

On Friday morning, Johnny went to see Dr. Barnes for his second visit, and the wrapping was removed from his ribs. Dr. Barnes told him his ribs seemed to be pretty well healed, and he could go to work now. Later that day Johnny called his cousin Cosmo and told him he could start working on Monday. Cosmo was very glad to hear from him and told him everything was OK and he'd see him Monday morning. He hadn't heard from Janet at all, and thought it would be best not even to try and contact her. This girl might end up getting me all screwed up, he thought. "Forget it," he said.

ON MONDAY MORNING, THE ALARM RANG AT 6:30 AND JOHNNY JUMPED up. He was in a sweat. Must have had a bad dream, he thought to himself. His heart was racing very quickly and it continued even after he took a shower. As he put his clothes on, he could feel his body trembling. He had felt this on and off the previous week. He attributed the shaking to not drinking or doing any drugs. It was a body action that he had no control over, and even though it scared him, he thought anything's better than waking up with a dreadful hangover.

He quickly made himself some tea and toast and relaxed at the kitchen table for a few minutes. He soon calmed down.

The ride to the meat company was quick and he kept changing the radio stations to keep himself from thinking about the smell of meat. When he arrived at Gianetti's Meat Company, Cosmo was standing in the parking lot with a group of truck drivers. He was holding a clipboard in his hand and must have been giving them their schedules. Cosmo saw Johnny pull up and he smiled and then he turned back to the group. After Johnny parked his car and started walking toward the front door, Cosmo walked over and put his arm around him.

"Glad to see you cousin, how are you feeling?" Cosmo asked. "Are you ready to start moving that stinking meat around?"

"I'm ready," he replied reluctantly.

"Cheer up Johnny, listen, when lunchtime comes, the deli next door has the best hoagies in the world." A young guy strolled past them as they were talking. He must have heard the conversation because he looked at them and said, "And Rosanna, she ain't bad either."

"Hey Mike," Cosmo replied, "you have a good wife, don't be talking about Rosanna like that." Cosmo started to laugh, and Mike waved his hands in the air.

"Who's Rosanna?" Johnny asked.

"Rosanna is an Italian delight, but I think with her, they'll probably ship somebody in from the old country when they think she's ready for marriage. Her father won't let nobody talk to her unless it's about hoagies." Johnny laughed. "Let's go inside and see Charlie," said Cosmo, "he handles personnel for me."

Gianetti's Meat Packing Company was a huge brick building that was once a warehouse. The sign at the top of the building was white with bright red lettering. All the woodwork on the windows was gray as well as the entrance. On the right side of the building was a huge parking lot with ten truck terminals for loading and unloading. All Gianetti trucks were red with silver trailers displaying the Gianetti name and logo.

When the two men walked inside the building, Cosmo hollered to Charlie, "Hey Charlie, come here. Charlie, this is my cousin, Johnny Covini."

Charlie was a short thin man about thirty years old. He wore round wire frame glasses and fair complected. You could see his dirty blond hair covering his ears as he sported a white hard hat. He was very intelligent-looking. Charlie and Johnny shook hands.

"Charlie, sign him up in shipping and receiving. He's ready to start today. Make sure he fills out all the necessary paperwork." Cosmo gave Johnny a slap on the shoulder and told him he'd see him in a few minutes.

Charlie directed Johnny to his office and followed after him. As they walked, Charlie asked, "So tell me Johnny, where did you work before?"

"Well uh, I was a musician."

"A musician? What instrument?"

"Drums."

"Drums? Very interesting, I play a little piano you know, in my spare time."

"You mean you play on weekends?"

"Oh no, just a hobby at home, whenever I get bored."

"Oh that's pretty good."

The two men entered the office and Charlie handed Johnny an application and the necessary forms to be filled out. "When you're finished Johnny, just leave everything on my desk, and then go see your cousin Cosmo. If I have any questions about the paperwork, I'll let you know."

"OK, thanks Charlie." Johnny spent about an hour filling out his application and the other forms. He'd never had to do this type of thing before, and had a lot of questions for Charlie.

When Johnny finished, he went to Cosmo's office. When he entered, Cosmo asked, "How'd everything go with the paperwork, OK?"

"Well I left a few blanks, but I'll check back with Charlie."

"Yeah, Charlie will take care of it Johnny. Come on, let's go get you a coat and a hard hat."

When the men went out into the work area, there were people packing meat, people moving skids from one place to another with the forklifts, people loading freezers, and so on. The place seemed to be very busy, and Johnny didn't quite know how to act.

Cosmo took Johnny to the locker room, got him a clean coat

and a hard hat, and issued him a locker. He then told Johnny to go see Tony on the loading dock and that he'd catch up with him for lunch at noon. He also told Johnny he would get him a time card and to be sure to clock out when he went to lunch. Cosmo pointed to the loading dock when the men left the locker room.

Johnny was on his own. There he was in a meat company. How the hell am I going to do this, he thought, I never had a steady job in my life. Oh well, what the hell, he thought, anything's better than hanging around the apartment.

Johnny walked over to the loading dock and asked a worker where he could find Tony. The worker pointed to a guy standing near the end of the dock. It was the same big fat guy with the cigar who had bumped into him two weeks ago. Oh great, he thought, I'm getting off to a good start already. He walked to the end of the dock and tried to get Tony's attention. "Are you Tony?" he asked.

"Yeah I'm Tony. Who are you?" he asked in a raspy voice.

"I'm Johnny Covini." He thought for a second and decided to tell him he was Cosmo's cousin. "My cousin Cosmo the owner told me to see you."

"Oh yeah, Cosmo told me you were coming to work here." He extended his hand toward Johnny. Johnny smiled and shook his hand. The fat man had some strong hand shake, he thought, but he's not a bad guy after all.

"Have you ever worked in shipping and receiving before?" Tony asked.

"Well I never had a real job."

"Oh yeah, well what did you do?"

"I was a drummer."

"Hmmm. Drummer. Come here and I'll show you what you'll be doing." They started to walk toward the work area and Tony turned his head and looked Johnny in the eyes. "What's the problem, no money in music?"

"I don't know, I guess I just never caught the right break. Not everyone makes it to the top."

"I guess I know what you mean, this is where I've been for the past twenty years." They walked for a few more minutes and finally arrived at the end of the loading dock. "This is the place," Tony announced to Johnny.

Johnny looked around and saw pieces of meat lying around on the ground.

"Today there won't be any livestock coming in, and we could use your help cleaning up and rearranging this area. We've been a little short of help the past month. The thing to know about this department is that everything that comes in alive leaves here dead." The fat man laughed out loud.

Johnny made a face and could feel his stomach move. It sounded disgusting to him, but he couldn't show how he was feeling to Tony. "While you're waiting for the orders to come through to go out, you can start by organizing this area and cleaning up anything that was left from Saturday. Frankie Sorrano will be in tomorrow, he's the guy that will show you exactly what to do and what your job is all about. For the next few hours, just clean up and get it all ready. Monday is usually our slowest day. Do you have any questions?"

"No. Count it done." Tony walked away from the area and left Johnny standing there. There was Johnny surrounded by tables and scraps of meat. He was glad Tony left so he could think about just what he had gotten himself into. The smell was horrible. How the hell was he going to withstand the odor, and better yet, be able to touch anything in the place? I must be crazy, he thought. Maybe he should have considered the job Danny offered him at Sigway Shoes. "Feet instead of meat," he laughed.

Johnny looked around for a broom, walked over and picked it up. He took a deep breath and began to sweep all around the tables. He actually was doing pretty well considering this was his first job. He kept himself busy for close to two hours and another guy came back to where he was cleaning up some papers on a desk. He told him he needed his help in shipping something out.

Johnny was apprehensive at first, because he thought he might have to touch the meat, but when he followed the guy over to the area where the trucks were, he only wanted him to load half a dozen cartons onto a truck. Johnny was very relieved.

After he finished loading the truck, he returned back to the other area to continue to clean. Noon time came pretty quickly and suddenly Johnny heard someone shout, "Hey Johnny it's noon time—let's go grab a bite to eat!" It was his cousin Cosmo. "You look hungry."

"I'm starved."

"Let me buy you a hoagie."

"Sounds good to me Cosmo, I'm ready if you are." The men quickly hung their coats and hats and washed up. They walked through the plant and out the front door. Johnny was glad to be seen with his cousin Cosmo, so the other guys would know he was OK.

As they walked toward the hoagie shop next door Johnny asked, "Hey Cosmo, will it get a little busier here tomorrow? I mean the time kind of dragged this morning."

"You'll get used to it Johnny, Monday is definitely not our busiest day. And don't worry, there will be plenty of work for you. Don't knock it when we have a slow day." As they arrived in front of the hoagie shop, Johnny noticed that it was packed inside.

They walked in and several people acknowledged Cosmo. He must be well-known around here, Johnny thought. Cosmo introduced him to some of the guys, and they nodded at him with approval. Cosmo found two spots at the counter and motioned to Johnny to hurry up and sit down before someone else grabbed the seats.

When the men took a seat, Cosmo asked, "What are you in the mood to eat Johnny? I'm buying today."

"I'll have one of those hoagies you've been bragging about." A dark-haired girl wearing a white uniform appeared in front of Johnny and Cosmo. She was standing behind the counter where they were seated.

Johnny was scanning through the menu that was placed in front of him just to see what other types of sandwiches they served. He looked up from the menu and glanced directly into two beautiful big brown eyes. He wanted to speak, but no words came from his lips. They stared at each other in silence for a few seconds. It was so intense that Cosmo broke the silence.

"Hey, can we order our lunch?" He realized that they were staring at each other.

The girl finally looked away from Johnny. Her cheeks had turned bright red against her fair complexion. She felt a bit embarrassed by Cosmo's statement. "Sorry, what can I get you Cosmo?" she asked.

"We'll have two regular hoagies. One for me and one for my cousin Johnny here. Rosanna, this is Johnny, the best drummer in the world." Cosmo waved his finger and pointed to Johnny. Johnny was still staring at Rosanna, he couldn't take his eyes off of her. He felt a wave of heat come over his face as Cosmo told her about him.

"Oh, you're a drummer."

"Well I used to be. Now I'm just a meat man."

Rosanna looked at Johnny's face; she stared at him closely for a second or two. "You're a drummer, not a meat man," she said very sternly.

"Oh yeah? And how do you know what I am?"

"I know a drummer when I see one. I meet a lot of people every day here, and one thing is certain—you're not a meat man."

Johnny laughed and so did Cosmo. "Hey Johnny, Rosanna knows a lot about you. What, do you two know each other or something?"

Behind Rosanna was a large window with a ledge. Several orders were beginning to fill the ledge area. A chubby face appeared in the window. It was Rosanna's father, and he looked angry. "Rosanna—yama yama." He began to shout at this beautiful girl. "We have orders here and you're busy talking, get moving."

Rosanna jumped and turned away from Johnny and Cosmo to pick up a few plates on the ledge. She then walked away. Cosmo leaned over to Johnny and quietly whispered, "That's Rosanna's father, couldn't you tell?"

"Not a real happy guy, huh."

"Johnny it looked to me that you and Rosanna might have something in common."

"Hey Cosmo, a little flirting don't mean anything. You know, she's a pretty girl, what do you expect me to do?"

"Hey, I know flirting. The last time I saw looks like you two were giving each other was when my wife and I met, and look what happened to me. We have three kids, and we're still in love today."

"How is Maria doing anyway?"

"She's good, but I wish she'd lose some weight, she's getting like a real bimbo."

"Cosmo, from what I remember, Maria's a good woman, and you shouldn't talk about her like that. You know what I mean?"

"Yeah, I know she is Johnny, I know she is. I have to show you a picture of the kids."

"How are the kids doing anyway?"

"Real good. They're smart, they get good grades in school."

"Ah, they take after their mother."

"Don't get smart. Look why don't we get the food and head back to my office. We'll eat there and I'll show you pictures of the kids and we can talk for a while."

"Sure, why not. We really haven't had a chance to talk."

Rosanna returned in front of the men. "Your hoagies will be done in a few minutes," she said.

Johnny couldn't help himself; he was staring at Rosanna again.

"Hey Rosanna," said Cosmo, "do me a favor, tell your father to make them hoagies to go. And put two large cokes in there."

Rosanna quickly looked at Johnny as he stared at her. "Oh, you won't be eating here today," she said.

"No, me and my cousin want to talk in private. We haven't seen each other for over three years."

"Oh OK, I'll tell him to make them to go." Rosanna was disappointed. When Rosanna turned to tell her father the sandwiches were to go, Johnny gazed at her long black curly hair. Her body looked perfect. God she's beautiful, he thought. He tried not to let Cosmo see just how taken he was by this girl. He really was disappointed they were leaving. He could have stared at her all day.

Rosanna appeared with the two hoagies and handed them to Cosmo. She looked into Johnny's eyes, but this time only for a second. She couldn't look at him for too long because she was feeling jumpy inside. She had never been quite so mesmerized.

Again, Johnny couldn't speak. The two men and the girl walked toward the register. Cosmo handed her the money. Johnny wanted to say something to her, but he couldn't think of anything appropriate. Rosanna quickly smiled at him before she gave Cosmo his change. Johnny knew this was not just some silly flirtation on either of their parts.

Rosanna handed Cosmo the change and said, "I will see youse tomorrow?" She was looking directly at Johnny. Johnny's heart was racing.

"Yes Rosanna, Johnny will be in tomorrow," said Cosmo.

"See you tomorrow Cosmo."

Cosmo exited first then Rosanna said, "Bye Johnny," just as he was about to leave.

"Bye Rosanna," he said in a low, nervous voice. He barely got the words out. She was so beautiful and making him feel very uneasy.

Rosanna's father had bought the business a few years back. They had previously lived in Brooklyn, and when he found out the business was for sale in South Philadelphia by one of his relatives, he decided to purchase it. He had been looking to go in business for some time, and he was told this was a gold mine.

The place looked a bit old-fashioned. At the counter the stools had red leather seats and were fastened to the floor. Some of the chrome was rusted and the leather torn. The counter was white formica and the floor was tiled red. There were no booths, only tables. They were also white, and the chairs were red vinyl—also a bit rusted and torn. The walls were green and the ceiling white and certainly could have used painting. The cash register was the original from the store's opening in 1960. Outside hung a sign above the two bay windows and the old green door which needed painting. It read: "Angelini's Hoagie Shop."

Johnny and Cosmo walked back to the meat house at a slow pace. Cosmo was going on and on about the family and how no one ever gets together anymore. Johnny tried to pay attention, but he kept thinking about Rosanna. This girl was overwhelming his thoughts.

As they approached the front door of the meat company, several workers were hanging around the lot. Cosmo nodded to them and when he saw that he had their attention, he stopped walking. "Hey guys, it looks like Rosanna met her Italian sweetheart today." Johnny had stopped walking also and listened.

"Cosmo, give me a break will ya!"

"Your break's over in about fifteen minutes," he laughed. "Come on, let's go inside and eat. We'll look at those pictures I was telling you about, and then it's back to work." The guys in the lot just motioned to one another and laughed.

The two men went inside the building and directly to Cosmo's office. As they were eating, Johnny said, "Cosmo, you're right, these hoagies are great—best I ever had!"

Cosmo showed Johnny pictures of his children and his wife. Cosmo also had some pictures of Johnny's mother and father at a picnic with Cosmo's parents. When Johnny looked at one of the photos of Cosmo's daughter Angela, he couldn't believe the close resemblance to his mother. There had always been pictures of his mother as a child around the house when he was growing up. And now, looking at a picture of Angela, the similarity was frightening. Johnny's mother had been dead for five years now, and his father had died five years prior to her death.

He had never been able to establish a relationship with his father. The man was an alcoholic for as long as he could remember. His mother was the sweetest woman anyone could have met. The woman died suddenly of a heart attack on New Year's Eve in 1974.

After she died, he blocked his family out of his mind completely. He was alone. He had no brothers or sisters to share his grief. Johnny was an only child. He had already been doing his share of drugs and alcohol, but when his mother's death came on suddenly, he really became abusive. He had been very close to his mother, and now looking at these pictures after so many years made him feel very lonely. He thought for a minute about his cousin Cosmo who had a wife and three kids. He still had no one.

When the two men finished their lunch, Cosmo told Johnny to go back to the area where he had been working during the morning hours. When he returned to the loading dock, Tony found some other odd jobs for him to do, but assured him that tomorrow would be a busy day. Johnny kept himself very busy the remainder of the afternoon.

At four o'clock, he cleaned his area and quickly hurried to the time clock near the front door of the building. He had forgotten to punch the time clock in the morning. He wrote in his morning time, and then punched out to leave. As he was ready to open the door, he heard Cosmo yelling.

"Eh Johnny, wait up! You wanna go have a beer?"

As Cosmo approached him, Johnny said, "Thanks Cosmo, but it's been a long day for me, and I think I should go home and cool out." Cosmo was being very nice, Johnny thought, really making him feel welcome at his company.

"OK, have it your way." He caught up with him by now, and they went through the door together. Before Cosmo walked across the street to the bar, he gently slapped Johnny on the cheek and began to squeeze it like he was a little boy. "I'll see you tomorrow, right cousin? Don't forget-eight o'clock."

"Eight o'clock it is. I'll see you tomorrow Cosmo." As he started to walk toward the parking lot, he paused for a minute to think about the girl he'd met today at the hoagie shop. He put his hands in his pocket and slowly looked back to the shop aside the meat company. He was surprised he felt as good as he did for having worked a full day.

Suddenly the door of the hoagie shop opened and out came Rosanna. She began to walk toward him. Her face was all smiles and she was carrying a small bag in her hand. He looked her up and down, and then looked toward the sidewalk, kicking his feet on the cement. When he looked back at her, he felt his heart racing. He couldn't believe how infatuated he was with this girl.

As Rosanna got closer to him she began to speak very quickly. "How did your day go?" she started to ramble.

"Eh, I'm living."

"Living isn't good enough Johnny, you have to live, and you should be doing what you like."

"You seem to know an awful lot about me for being a total stranger," he replied. He was starting to get tense for some reason.

"Johnny, I'm sorry, but I think we feel something for each other. I don't feel like a stranger. I saw the way you looked at me today. I couldn't stop staring at you either. I'm not usually this forward, but something happened today that has never happened to me before. Look, I meet a lot of guys every day at the shop. None of them ever made me feel as uneasy as you did today." She sighed and took a deep breath.

Johnny could not believe what he was hearing. He had spent most of the day thinking about her, and now as she stood there in her white uniform and long black curly hair, she was practically telling him she was crazy about him, but he couldn't seem to let down his guard and tell her he felt the same way too. He just kept looking at her face and her beautiful 5'6" frame. Her hair was hanging over her right eye. He had the urge to push it off her face. He wanted to touch her, but he just couldn't. What the hell is going on, he thought, I'm afraid of a girl?

Rosanna was obviously waiting for him to say something. She had just put her feelings on the line and was waiting for his reply. She just kept waiting and did not speak. His eyes were looking down at the ground. Johnny finally decided he better do something. It was becoming a rather uncomfortable situation for both of them. His heart was pounding so loud, he thought for sure she could hear it.

"Rosanna," he gulped, "I think you're really nice." Nice, he thought, she's gorgeous and I'm telling her she's nice! He looked at his watch for lack of something better to do with his eyes. "I think I better get going. I mean this is crazy." Rosanna looked up from the ground and she appeared hurt. "I mean, you're a nice girl, but..."

"But what Johnny?"

"You know, I just met you. What's going on here?"

Rosanna handed him a brown bag. "Here, I thought you might like another hoagie for dinner or whatever. I'm just trying to be nice to you. Sometimes I just talk too much."

Johnny felt stupid that he had just told her she was nice. He just couldn't seem to get it together, this girl was making him crazy. He had never lost his cool with a woman in his entire life. He wanted to run. Again, he looked at his watch. "Listen, I'll see you tomorrow and we'll talk then. Thanks for the hoagie, and you have a nice night." He took a long, deep breath and looked across the street.

"OK," she said and then looked into his eyes. She quickly leaned toward him and kissed him on his left cheek. She turned away quickly and ran back to the hoagie shop.

Johnny continued to watch her until she got in the store. He felt chills running through his body. Man, this can't be love, he thought to himself. "Nah, can't be." Johnny walked to the parking lot and jumped in his car. When he got inside he looked in the mirror and touched his cheek where Rosanna had kissed him, and smiled back into the mirror. He felt soaked with perspiration. Rosanna had kissed him and he was a mess.

Again he went over in his mind the brief conversation that had taken place between them. He put his arms over the top of the steering wheel and said to himself, "This can't be love at first sight. I never did believe in that bologna." He turned on the ignition and drove away.

He started to drive in the direction of his apartment, but he was feeling very shaky. As he drove along, he made a left instead of a right to go to his apartment, and before he knew it, he was parked in front of Harry's Bar. He thought for a few minutes about what the doctor had told him about alcohol. He wanted to go in and see everybody at Harry's, but he knew he would have a drink. He drove off and headed home.

As he drove down the street, he saw a large man about six foot who must have weighed 230 pounds. The guy must have been a body builder. He had absolutely no fat—all muscle. He must have had a 32" waist and a 56" chest. His pectorals were huge, like somebody pumped them up with air. With his 20" biceps, and wide, muscular back, he looked like a guy nobody would mess with. The man was about to enter Johnny's apartment building.

As Johnny pulled in front of the place, the man turned and looked. His black hair was slicked back and he had almond shaped eyes. His nose was pointy and his neck very muscular. He wore a lightweight black jacket with a white sweat-shirt underneath. He sported faded jeans and white sneakers. He needed a shave. He was dark complected and looked really rugged.

Johnny turned off the ignition and looked once again; this time he recognized the man. It was Mookie, a local drug dealer who had supplied Johnny with cocaine. Aw man, what the hell's he want, he thought to himself and let out a burst of air.

As Johnny got out of the car, the man said, "Johnny my man, what's happening? I was in the neighborhood and thought I would pay you a visit. I have a present for you, man."

As Johnny approached, the man extended his hand to him. Johnny shook his hand. "Yeah Mookie, how you doin'?" Johnny said in a low tone. He wasn't happy to see Mookie.

"Johnny, why do you sound so down? Hey man listen, I heard about the beating you took from Benelli and his goons. Man, I don't even know why you messed with them guys, they're some real wackadoos, you know that?"

"Yeah, well that's all over now Mookie. I got myself a normal job now. Look Mookie, I'm tired, I want to get upstairs and get something to eat. You know—first day at work and I'm beat."

"Yeah sure Johnny. Look here's something to ease the tension tonight." Mookie attempted to give Johnny a bag of cocaine. "It's on me."

"Look Mookie, I'm clean—I don't want anything. It's all over for me. Cocaine is a thing of the past."

"I don't believe it. You can't make it without it. You're just a washed-up, burnt-out musician Johnny. You need this stuff just to stay sane. Geez, look at you right now, you look terrible."

"Look Mookie, I don't care what you say, I don't need no more cocaine. And do me a favor, hit the pike, will ya?"

"Hey Johnny, don't get crazy with me. I'll break both your arms. I mean I'll fix them so you never play drums again."

"All right, all right, I'm sorry. But I don't want no more drugs from you. Please stay away from me."

"Sure Johnny, but just in case you get down, here's a little gift from me." He reached over and stuffed a small packet into the top pocket of Johnny's shirt.

Johnny wanted to hand the packet back to Mookie, but when he looked at this 230 pounds of solid muscle that was feared by many people in the neighborhood, he didn't want to refuse it. The last thing he needed was to be roughed up by anyone. He had taken a bad enough beating from Benelli and his thugs. He thanked Mookie and told him if he needed him, he would call. Mookie finally accepted this response and said good-bye.

As Johnny headed up the steps inside the building, his little pal Joey was coming down. "Hi Johnny, you want to go in the garage and bang on the drums a bit?"

"Nah, not today kid, but bang some for me."

The little boy looked disappointed, but he smiled at Johnny anyway. "OK Johnny, see ya later."

As the boy began to run down the steps, Johnny turned and shouted, "Hey Joey, keep practicing!"

Johnny went inside his apartment and headed for the bedroom. He threw off his jacket and flopped on the bed. "Damn I'm tired," he said. "This working for a living is no picnic." Johnny thought of the conversation he just had with Mookie and reached for the bag of coke in his top pocket. He got up off the bed and headed for the bathroom.

He lifted up the toilet seat and looked at the bag of cocaine in his hand. He was confused. He wondered if he should flush it down or put it somewhere. Will I need this or not, he thought. The temptation was strong. Johnny really loved the feeling he got from cocaine.

He walked back into the bedroom. He looked around and decided to hide the bag in the top dresser drawer. The telephone rang. "Hello-" he answered.

"Hey man, how are you? It's Danny."

"Hey Danny, what's going on?"

"How's the drummer doing?"

"The drummer is no more."

"What?!"

"You heard me, it's all over. I've had enough. I got a job at my cousin's meat company."

"But Johnny, that doesn't mean you have to quit playing drums."

"Sorry man, I've played my last drum solo."

"Come on Johnny, stop it. You don't mean it."

"Hey Danny, I'm serious."

"Look Johnny, I just joined a part-time band, and it just so happens—"

"Yeah I know, I know—they need a drummer."

"Look Johnny, give it a shot. We'll have a ball—it's only fun, you know, a weekend thing."

"Look Danny, I'm really glad you called, but I just can't do it anymore."

"Johnny you just can't hang up your sticks just like that. You've been playing too long now."

"Yeah, you said it—too long!"

"Johnny will you at least think it over for a couple days? This guy won't be leaving for another three weeks and I could probably get you an audition this weekend."

"Look Danny, don't try to fast-talk me, I don't want no parts of it anymore."

"Man, you're really serious aren't you?"

"I'm afraid so Danny."

"OK, well listen, if you get a chance, stop by the shoe store this weekend. I'll be there Saturday from 10 to 4."

"Yeah, maybe I'll do that."

"Hey Johnny, let's not lose it, I mean let's keep in touch."

"Hey Danny, my door's open any time, you know that. Just don't ask me to join any bands."

Danny laughed, "OK, Covini, you got it, I get the message. Listen Johnny, you take it easy, OK? I'll give you a call, and I hope everything works out for you."

"Thanks Danny, see ya man."

When Johnny hung up, he stared at the phone for a moment and thought of how he would have liked to jump at the chance to join a band with Danny, but he just couldn't get involved again. He shook his head.

He walked into the kitchen and looked for something to eat. He remembered the hoagie he had gotten from Rosanna. Rosanna, he thought. He smiled. He sat down and quickly devoured the hoagie that served as his dinner. Man I'm beat, he thought to himself. His first day on the job had made him very tired. He wasn't used to normal living habits.

He grabbed a quick shower, then sat in front of the TV and by nine o'clock, he was in bed and asleep.

AT SIX O'CLOCK ON TUESDAY MORNING, JOHNNY WAS AWAKENED BY A loud alarm clock. He felt like something was totally wrong. Six o'clock, he thought, this is crazy. The alarm made him feel like he had bells going off in his head. He reached over and shut it off. He just couldn't seem to get out of bed. He rolled over and went back to sleep. When he woke again, it was almost eight o'clock and he jumped up quickly. "Damn! It's only my second day and I'm late." He threw on some clothes, threw some water on his face, and out the door he ran.

He drove quickly to the meat company, exceeding the speed limit. It was a miracle he didn't get stopped by the police. He parked the car and tore into the building, and forgot to punch his time card. He headed straight for the locker-room for his white coat and hard hat, and then to the loading dock. As he came rushing by, he saw Tony on the phone.

"Hey Covini," the fat man shouted, "you're late. It's only your second day. I was just trying to call you." Tony hung up the phone and he sounded angry.

"Hey Tony, I'm sorry, I gotta get used to this getting up early."

"Frankie's not going to make it in today, and you're gonna have to learn your job pronto. And Covini, don't let it happen again."

"Hey come on man, I'm sorry, it won't happen again." Johnny

was definitely not used to taking orders, especially from some slob like Tony.

"You better not, or you're out the door." He was shouting at Johnny.

Cosmo was walking down the dock and heard the shouting. "Eh-eh, what's going on here? Johnny, how you doin'?"

Tony said, "Cosmo you better straighten your cousin out, it's only his second day here and he's late. We got a lot of work to do here. I hope I don't have to put up with this all the time. We should have started loading this truck half an hour ago."

"So why didn't you load it?" Johnny asked with a cocky tone in his voice.

Cosmo laughed. Tony looked at Johnny and said, "How about if we go outside so I can shut that wise mouth up for you punk."

Johnny wanted to speak, but Cosmo interrupted him. "OK that's enough from both of you. I got enough to worry about. There's a lot of work to do, so let's get to it. I don't want to hear no more. You guys understand? It's finished."

Johnny just stood there and didn't speak. Tony had cooled off real quick. Johnny could see he was upsetting his cousin, and the last thing he wanted to do was ruin the relationship they had reestablished. Cosmo looked real angry, he thought, he'd better smooth things over with him right now.

"I'm sorry Tony," he said.

Tony shrugged his shoulders and looked at Johnny. "Don't worry about it," he mumbled. He picked up his papers from the table near the edge of the wall, and walked away.

Cosmo still looked annoyed. He raised his hands in the air together and waved them in front of his face. His eyebrows were raised high on his forehead and he turned away from Johnny and began to walk toward the end of the dock.

Johnny yelled out, "Hey Cosmo, I'm sorry man."

Cosmo continued walking, but turned back for a second to look back at Johnny. "Go to work Johnny, will ya?" he yelled. He walked a little further and headed for the doorway. Seated at a small wooden table near the door was a young, long-haired boy who handled the scheduling of the trucks that arrived all day long. Cosmo stopped when he reached the table and looked to the young boy. "These guys, this place, some day it's gonna give me a heart attack—I know it."

As Cosmo began to walk away, the young boy just looked and shook his head and said, "Man I'm glad I don't have his troubles."

Johnny watched and waited till Cosmo was out of sight. He really didn't know what to do with himself. He thought for a minute about going home, but figured that Cosmo would never speak to him again if he did. Maybe I should go look for Tony, he thought, not that he wanted to say anything else to him, but he couldn't stand around there doing nothing much longer. He had already caused enough problems by showing up late.

Johnny walked toward the end of the dock and saw Tony talking with one of the drivers. He waited on the side several feet from them, but made sure Tony could see him. Tony finished talking to the driver and approached Johnny. "Eh Tony, do you want me to get started unloading one of these trucks?"

"No, I told you that truck has to get loaded on the other side."

"Look Tony, could you at least come over and show me how you want this loaded?"

"Look Covini, I told you Frankie won't be in today, and I don't have time to do his job, so just go load the truck and do the best you can."

Johnny took a deep breath and walked toward the truck in question.

Tony mumbled to himself, "Man sometimes I wish this place would just blow up." His cigar was practically hanging over his chin.

Johnny began loading the truck the best way he knew how. He couldn't believe how heavy the boxes were, but he wasn't about to complain about anything. He decided to keep his mouth shut and just work. He could feel the anxiety building, he was never exposed to this type of pressure before. He really should have taken Dr. Barnes' advice about getting counseling. His withdrawal from drugs and alcohol was making things worse. He prayed that the time would pass quickly.

Johnny managed to work at a steady pace throughout the morning. He glanced at the clock against the wall, and it was almost noon. He was thrilled. Tony never bothered to tell Johnny that he got a break in the morning. Johnny just worked straight through, and he was glad it was lunchtime. This working all day was certainly going to take some getting used to. Johnny threw one more box in the truck and headed to the washroom to get cleaned up. He threw his hat and coat off and headed for the hoagie shop. He hadn't thought about Rosanna, and now he was on his way to lunch, and the thought of seeing her made him happy.

When he entered the shop, he immediately spotted Cosmo sitting in the far corner with two co-workers. Cosmo waved his arms and motioned to him to come over. Johnny nodded and headed for the table. He was glad Cosmo didn't seem angry any longer.

"Johnny, sit down here, I saved a chair for you. I'm sorry I didn't ask you to lunch today, but I had to get over here a little earlier. Johnny, I want you to meet Pete Seitz and Ray Darden. They work in the slaughterhouse."

"Man, Cosmo, not at lunchtime."

Guys I want you to meet my cousin Johnny." The men shook hands.

Ray, the black man looked to Johnny and said, "What's the matter Johnny, you never seen dead meat before?" The three men laughed.

Johnny just held his stomach. "Hey guys, can we talk about something else? My stomach's starting to do flips."

Pete looked to Ray and said, "Come on man, lighten up."

"OK, OK."

Cosmo put his arm around Johnny's shoulder. "Hey Johnny,

don't worry about what happened with Tony this morning. I know it's going to take a little time to get used to this eight to five stuff. These guys used to work with Tony, and they got used to him, and so can you."

"Yeah man, don't let old Tony get the best of you. He's just an unhappy fat guy," said Ray.

"Not to mention, he stinks of cigars," said Pete.

"Yeah, and I had to put up with him for the last three years," said Cosmo, "I should have gotten rid of him when I took ownership." By now the four men were laughing together and Johnny felt a lot better.

Rosanna was standing at the table next to them and Johnny did not see her. Cosmo turned and said, "Hey Rosanna, hurry up, I'm getting hungry."

Rosanna finished taking the order, and then walked to the guys' table. Johnny gulped.

"Rosanna, you get more beautiful every time I see you," said Cosmo. Ray and Pete smiled. Johnny began to blush. He was beginning to get a bit uncomfortable, but he knew he had to say something to her. He looked up and she was staring at him with her big brown eyes, just like the day before, but today she was smiling. He felt uneasy with her standing next to him. He didn't really want to look at her again. Cosmo was staring at him now, and Johnny couldn't look at him either. For a few seconds there was silence.

Cosmo looked puzzled. "What's with you two? Yesterday there were fireworks going on and today youse can't talk. What's the story?"

"There is no story Cosmo," said Rosanna, "now can I take your orders?"

"You know I know you two are crazy about each other, I just know it."

"Come on Cosmo will ya, cool it," said Johnny, "these guys don't want to hear about my life, right guys?"

"It's pretty hard to cool it when things are this hot." Cosmo laughed.

Johnny looked to Rosanna and said, "Hey Rosanna, I'll have a cheese steak with onions and a large coke. I mean if these guys aren't going to order, the heck with them."

"Yeah me too, I'll have a cheese steak Rosanna," said Cosmo.

"Yeah me too," said Pete.

"Make that four," said Ray.

Rosanna took the order and walked away. "Hey Johnny, when you gonna ask her out?" said Cosmo. "She's a beautiful woman you know, Johnny."

"Eh Cosmo listen, Rosanna and I—we're not good for each other."

"Why not? You just met her yesterday, how do you know?"

"What do you mean how do I know? I just know."

"Hey Johnny, you don't meet girls like this everyday, you should jump at the chance."

"Hey Cosmo, why are you so concerned about my love life?"

"Because you're my cousin, don't you think I want to see my cousin meet a nice girl, get married, I mean come on—what are you, thirty-one now?"

Johnny saw that Rosanna was walking toward the table. Keep it down Cosmo, here she comes with our sodas."

Rosanna placed the sodas in front of the three men. When she placed the fourth soda in front of Johnny, Cosmo placed his hand over hers and said, "Hey Rosanna, my cousin wants to take you out, but he's afraid to ask you."

Johnny couldn't believe what Cosmo had said. Rosanna's face turned bright red. Johnny looked up at Rosanna. He felt so bad for her. Cosmo finally let go of her hand, and had done a good job of embarrassing the both of them. "Hey Rosanna, don't listen to this guy, he's got a big mouth. You know what I mean?"

"Yes I know, I've been serving him for the last three years."

"All right, all right, I'm sorry."

"Yeah, well you oughta be," said Johnny.

"It's OK Johnny," said Rosanna. Rosanna went to take some more orders.

"Hey Cosmo, why'd you have to embarrass her like that?"

"Eh come on Johnny, I'm just having a little fun."

"Yeah well some things you just don't joke around about, you know what I mean?"

"All right Johnny, from now on, no more joking around about Rosanna. Now, when you gonna ask her out?" The four men laughed.

AFTER LUNCH JOHNNY PUNCHED HIS TIME CARD, GRABBED HIS COAT AND hard hat, and headed back to the dock. He was hoping he wouldn't see Tony. Unfortunately, Tony was standing talking with another guy.

"Hey Covini," he shouted, "you made it back in time, I'm surprised."

Suddenly Johnny stopped and looked at Tony. He just stared. Tony's statement really rubbed Johnny the wrong way.

"What are you staring at? You want to say something, say it. What's the matter, the little Italian girl in the hoagie shop give you a hard time? I heard you and her might have something going on."

"You're a real funny guy, aren't you Tony." Johnny's tone was bitter.

"What's the matter, you got a problem with joking around?"

"Maybe."

"You know what, I think you been in that rock'n'roll business too long."

"Oh yeah?"

"Yeah." The two men were beginning to get upset.

"You know what Tony, I'm gonna straighten this out right here and now. I know you don't like me."

"You're right."

"Well how 'bout this, and I'm only going to tell you one

time, from now on, you don't say nothing to me. You got it? Nothing."

"Listen punk, you watch how you talk to me, or I'll put you in a meat grinder."

The man that stood next to Tony said, "Eh Tony, look forget it. Eh look man, why don't you go back to work?"

"Not until I'm finished what I have to say."

"Oh yeah," said Tony, "and what do you have to say?"

"You know what you are Tony? You're a real slob, a first-class slob." Johnny was pissed off and didn't care to deal with Tony any longer.

"All right punk, I m going to rip your tongue out, you said enough for one day."

Johnny noticed a crowbar hanging on a pole. He quickly reached over and grabbed it and yelled, "Come on, rip my tongue out!"

Tony could see that he had pushed the wrong button and that this guy was dangerous. Johnny looked like a raving maniac. He never could stand anybody harassing him. He obviously had a short fuse.

"Look kid, take it easy," said the other man.

"Look, you stay out of this, this is between me and him. I'm going to bust his head wide open."

Tony didn't move. He had dealt with many guys like this through the years, but this guy was crazy, he thought, I could lose my job, plus get my head busted open. "OK that's it. You're done. Get out of here," he yelled. His face was turning bright red. "The last thing we need around here is a tough guy. There's no room for your kind around here."

When Cosmo heard the commotion he came running. "Man don't tell me you two guys are at it again. Johnny what the hell are you doing with the crowbar in your hand, what are you cracking up! Tony what the hell's going on here?"

"Ask him."

Cosmo looked at the other man and asked, "Bill, what happened?"

"This guy here, he said he's going to bust Tony's head wide open."

"Look Cosmo, if I'm going to work here, you keep this bum off my back."

"Hey Johnny, calm down and give me the crowbar." Johnny just stood there and wouldn't hand the crowbar to Cosmo.

"Johnny let me have it." Johnny began to squeeze the crowbar tighter. It seemed as though he was beginning to have a fit. He broke out in a sweat. "Johnny are you OK?" Cosmo asked.

Johnny couldn't speak. He looked at Tony and then to Bill, and then finally he looked at his cousin. He threw the crowbar down and then looked at his cousin again and ran out of the building. He was feeling out of control and he knew he better get out of there quickly.

As the anxiety built and his heart began racing, he could hear Dr. Barnes' voice in his mind, "We found traces of drugs and alcohol in your blood, you better get counseling. You better get counseling, you're not a well man. You're not a well man." Johnny couldn't understand what was coming over him.

Cosmo quickly ran after Johnny. Johnny ran to his car and started the engine. As Cosmo entered the parking lot, he shouted, "Hey Johnny—Johnny! Wait a minute! What's wrong man?" Johnny quickly backed up the car and raced out of the parking lot. Once again Cosmo shouted, "What's the matter with you—what's the matter with you?"

Johnny quickly pulled out onto the street, not looking to see if any cars were coming. Horns were blowing and tires were screeching. Johnny went racing down the street. He was so overcome with anxiety, he didn't even hear Cosmo shouting at him. Cosmo just stood there and shook his head. He was confused, and had no idea what the hell was going on.

Rosanna and some patrons rushed out of the hoagie shop to

see what all the commotion was. She saw Cosmo walking back toward the meat company's entrance. She walked toward him quickly and asked him what had taken place.

"I don't know Rosanna, Johnny had a little argument with one of the workers and ran out of the building in a rage. I don't know what the hell's going on. I don't know, maybe something's bothering him. I just don't know." Cosmo headed for the entrance slowly, shaking his head.

Rosanna just looked up the street sadly and wondered if she would ever see Johnny again.

9

* * * * * * * * * *

"HEY BARTENDER, LET ME HAVE A BEER WILL YA?"

Harry had his back turned to Johnny as he straightened up some bottles. He knew by the sound of that voice it could only be Johnny Covini. As Harry turned, Johnny leaned over the bar and looked Harry in the eyes. "Johnny Boy! How the hell have you been?" Harry quickly extended his hand and greeted Johnny. The two men were happy to see one another.

"I'm OK Harry, I'm doin' real good."

"Tell me Johnny, is it true?"

"Is what true?"

"That you're working down at Gianetti Meats?"

"Man, news really travels fast around this neighborhood, doesn't it."

"Eh Johnny, this is South Philadelphia—your business is everybody's business."

"Yeah, well that job is history."

"Couldn't make it, huh kid. I always said you were different, didn't I? You don't belong in a place like that anyway. I always picture you on TV or in movies—you know, bright lights and excitement." Harry handed Johnny his beer.

Johnny looked up at the clock above the dart board. "Harry will you make sure you let me know when it's two o'clock?" Johnny snickered. "Two o'clock in the morning, that is."

"Hey Johnny, don't go getting yourself all drunked up now."

"I'm not going to get drunk Harry, I just want to have some fun."

"Look Johnny, just don't get in no trouble. I mean I'm still recovering from that incident with Benelli. I mean I thought you died."

"Look Harry, don't worry, there won't be any trouble. Just let me know when it's two o'clock." Johnny spent the remainder of the afternoon sitting at the bar talking with most of the regulars that hung out there everyday, and put away quite a few beers. He rambled on and on about being a drummer. He even told one guy about being offered a job selling shoes.

They all laughed with Johnny and listened to him describe the great feeling of being in front of an audience when he played. They listened to him tell of his dreams and hopes. He had a captive audience. None of these guys had ever done anything worthwhile with their lives. Some even believed that Johnny was close to being a star. Some were factory workers, sanitation men, and some were just unemployed, lost, and lonely.

The day passed by quickly and when it was close to six, Harry looked at Johnny and told him no more booze. Johnny's face just about touched the bar as he slumped over. He looked pretty messed up. "Come on Harry, just one more and that'll be it—I swear."

"Can't do it kid, you're drunk and you're flagged for the day. I probably should have stopped you hours ago."

"OK it's your bar." He slurred his words, and even sprayed some saliva on Harry's face.

"Yo— lean back, you're givin' me a bath." Harry just wiped his face and thought to himself, "Man, Johnny's gotten worse. He's pathetic."

"OK Harry, I'm outta here." Johnny lifted himself off the bar stool and started toward the door. He took three steps and ended up near a table on the side of the room. He grabbed onto the chair beside the table, but didn't have enough leverage to stand up straight. The chair moved and he fell back and landed on the floor.

Harry had been watching the whole time, and rushed out from behind the bar. One of the guys who had been seated at the bar jumped off his stool and came over to help. They both went to grab his arms, and Johnny pushed them away. "I'm OK, I'm OK," he yelled, "I can get up myself! I can play drums drunk or sober, can't I?" He was slurring his words and shouting at that point.

"Johnny we've got to get you home," said Harry. He looked down at Johnny sitting on the floor. He picked up the chair and pushed it underneath the table.

"Don't worry about me, I'll get home." Johnny grabbed onto the chair again and lifted himself up. Harry held onto the chair so he wouldn't fall back on the floor.

"Why don't I call you a cab?" Harry asked.

"I don't need a cab." Johnny sat down and tried to gather his thoughts. "Harry, where's my buddy Lefty? Where is that guy?" He laid his head down on the table and said, "I haven't seen him around here. He's my best friend, you know, he's a good old guy."

Harry was having a hard time understanding him because his face was flat on the table. Johnny got quiet for a second and tried to lift his head up. He managed to get about six inches in the air, and then his face crashed back down, and he passed out.

Harry tried to wake him, but failed. "I better call him a cab," he said to the other guy.

"Yeah, he ain't goin' nowhere Harry," replied the man.

Harry quickly went to the phone and called the cab company. Johnny just slept. A few patrons asked Harry who the guy was.

"He's Johnny Covini," Harry replied.

One guy asked, "Hey isn't that the guy who supposedly died?" Then another chimed in and said, "Yeah, it happened right here, didn't it Harry?"

A third man said, "Yeah, well he still looks dead to me!" The three men laughed.

"Hey fellas give me a break, will ya," said Harry.

When the cab driver arrived, Harry just pointed to Johnny lying on the table. The short black man with the black cabbie's hat looked at Johnny and shook his head. "Aw man, no way," he said, "I'm getting tired of this."

Harry walked from behind the bar to assist the man. Harry had known the driver from previous calls similar to this one.

"Harry man, why don't you just get these drunk people and throw them out in the alley? What am I supposed to do if he gets sick in my cab? The company sure ain't gonna clean it up!"

"Look Ronny—"

"Yeah I know, it goes with the territory."

Harry reached in his pocket for the cab fare. "Here's ten dollars for the fare, and ten for you. Now quit complainin', and let's get him the hell out of here." Together the two men lifted Johnny off the chair. Johnny was mumbling something about music, but he could barely be understood. Harry assisted the driver in getting Johnny to the cab. When they finally got him into the back seat, Johnny's body just went limp and he sprawled across the seat.

"Man Harry, this guy's pretty messed up," said the driver.

"Yeah I know Ronny, Johnny's one messed up guy."

"Where's he goin' to Harry?"

"734 ½ Spruce Street, second floor. And Ronny, make sure he gets upstairs safely."

"No problem Harry. You know anybody needs a cab outta town, tell them who to ask for."

The driver took Johnny to his apartment and did just as Harry asked. As the driver began helping Johnny up the steps, little Joey was coming out of his apartment. He was about to run down the steps and suddenly stopped. He looked puzzled. The driver looked up and smiled at him.

"Hey what's wrong with Johnny?" Joey asked.

"Do you know this guy kid?"

"Yeah, he's my friend."

"Do me a favor will ya, when I get to the top of the steps, reach in his pocket and see if you can get his keys while I hold him up."

When the driver and Johnny reached the top of the steps, little Joey did as he was asked. At that point, Johnny started to come around a little, and then he saw Joey's face.

"Johnny what's wrong? You look sick."

"Yeah I'm sick all right, sick in the head." He could barely speak.

Joey found the keys and managed to open the door for the driver. The driver helped Johnny inside and placed him on the bed. He looked to Joey and said, "Look kid, just leave the keys on the kitchen table. You better go now, just let him sleep it off, he's not feelin' too well."

The little kid looked very confused. He felt sorry for his friend Johnny.

"Come on kid, do like I told you. You can see him tomorrow."

IT WAS SEVEN THE FOLLOWING MORNING, AND JOHNNY OPENED HIS EYES slowly and then rolled over on his side. He reached for some covers to pull over him, and couldn't find them. He then lifted himself up a bit and found himself fully clothed. He turned to the clock and saw what time it was. He lifted himself even more and his head began pounding. The room was spinning. He quickly laid himself back down on his back and rubbed his hand through his hair. "Holy shit," he said to himself, "what the hell's goin' on?"

He knew he had gotten drunk by the way he felt, but he couldn't remember a thing that had happened the night before.

He slowly lifted himself off the bed, and again felt dizzy. He held onto the dresser. He made his way to the bathroom, stripped off his clothes and jumped into the shower.

He let the lukewarm water run on his head for at least five minutes. He could barely move. The water was beginning to make him feel a bit better. After letting water run on him for ten minutes, he slowly washed himself down with soap, and rinsed off.

As Johnny dried off, he heard a knock at the door. He quickly grabbed his jeans and slipped them on. The person at the door was pounding loudly. "OK, OK I'm coming," Johnny yelled.

Johnny finally got to the door. There stood his landlord. "What gives Covini? It's April 25th and no rent. It was due the 15th, or did you forget? I've got bills to pay you know. Let's get it together or I'll have to toss you out on the street. Do you have my money or what?"

Johnny just stared at him and said, "You know, someday you're going to knock on the wrong door."

"The money," said the landlord and stretched out his hand.

"I'll have it for you Friday."

"Friday it is, or you're out. I mean it this time." Johnny slammed the door in his face. What a jerk, he thought.

He walked over to the sink and filled up a pot for some tea. He strolled slowly into the bedroom to put on some clean clothes. He felt miserable. He had a rotten hangover, his rent was due, he lost his job with Benelli, and no one had called him for any music jobs. He had absolutely no money coming in. He remembered he had a little over a thousand dollars in the bank and that would have to hold him over till things started to pick up. Where do I go from here, he thought.

When he opened the top dresser drawer and reached for his socks, he saw the bag of cocaine he had stashed there. He looked at it for a second and pulled it out. He wanted to feel better and figured the drug would pull him out of his hangover. He quickly opened the bag and poured the white powder onto the bureau. With the edge of a matchbook cover he made a straight line. He leaned over and snorted the cocaine. He then finished dressing and walked back to the kitchen.

He could feel the drug taking its effect. He managed to have some tea and toast. Johnny was beginning to feel a lot better. Suddenly, the phone rang. Johnny walked over and picked up the receiver slowly. "Hello," he said.

It was Mookie, his cocaine supplier. "Johnny boy, how was the coke?" he asked.

"You're up pretty early for a guy that don't work, aren't you Mookie?"

"Yeah, well you know, the early bird catches the worm. I gotta be competitive with a lot of dealers out there Johnny. I want to be there when they try to steal my business. I want to crush them."

"Look Mookie, I don't have much time to talk, let alone listen to your nasty attitude."

"Listen I got some good stuff, and you're the first guy I'm callin'. I know you're interested, right?"

"Look I don't know Mookie, I'm kind of short on cash right now."

"Hey Johnny, did I ever question you about money? Your credit's good with me, you know that. Look if you need anything, I'll be at the playground on 9th Street most of the day hangin' out. Come on down, maybe I'll even buy you some lunch. I'll be there from about 11:00 on."

"OK maybe I'll see you later," said Johnny and he hung up. Johnny went back to the kitchen and gulped down his tea. He then rushed to the bedroom, threw some cologne on and gave his hair the once over. He looked in the mirror and said, "Today you'll find a new job." The cocaine made Johnny feel very confident. He brushed his hair one more time and buttoned his collar. He walked to the closet, threw on a lightweight jacket and rushed out the door.

When he got outside, he couldn't remember where he parked his car. He looked up and down the block. Where the hell is my car, he thought. Suddenly, his memory started to come back. The cab driver, he thought, my freakin' car's at Harry's, I was too drunk to drive home. Harry called me a cab. Johnny began walking back to Harry's.

Johnny quickly made it to Harry's Bar and saw his car. He jumped in the car and headed for center city. He was on his way to find a new job. Traffic was heavy and it took him a while to get to center city. Johnny's patience was starting to run out, and the cocaine was wearing off.

Finally, he found himself driving along 8th Street. As he drove slowly down the street, he saw a sign that read: "The Music Emporium." Surprisingly, there was also a sign in the window advertising for help. The sign read: "Salesman/teacher wanted." Suddenly Johnny became excited. He hurried down the street to find a parking spot.

Luckily, there was one at the end of the block. He parked quickly, turned off the engine and looked in his rearview mirror. He took a deep breath, he then reached into his glove compartment where he had a small bottle of mouth freshener. He gave a quick spray and put it back. "Well, I'm as ready as I'll ever be," he said to himself.

He quickly jumped out of the car and began taking large steps as he walked speedily towards the music store. Man what a job, he thought, this is perfect—I can sell drums and teach drums. Johnny slowly entered the doorway of the store and took one more deep breath as he closed the door. It was early in the morning and the store had just opened.

Johnny stopped for a moment and looked all around him. There must have been 20 drum sets all along the wall in various sizes and colors. There were guitars covering the whole back wall. Their colors alone would want to make anyone want to buy. Guitar amplifiers and synthesizers covered the center of the store. Along the back of the sales counter were hundreds of sets of guitar strings, microphone cords, microphone displays, and various other accessories. Hundreds of drumsticks were piled neatly in a bin that rested on the sales counter.

Johnny was amazed, just the smell made him feel happy. I gotta get this job, he thought, this is perfect. He slowly walked toward the sales counter. A salesman walked from the back of the store. Johnny waited patiently as the man approached him. "Can I help you with something today?"

"Uh, yeah... I saw the sign in the window. I want to apply for the position."

"Just walk to the back of the store and ask for George." The salesman pointed to a little office in the far corner of the store. "He'll give you an application and interview you."

"OK thanks a lot," said Johnny. Johnny headed for the back of the store, still very excited. He was happy that his headache had gone away and he felt much better. The door to the office was open. Johnny stuck his head in and there sat a chubby man with long black curly hair and wire-rimmed glasses.

"Excuse me, are you George?" he said.

"Yeah I m George, how can I help you?"

"I'm here to apply for the job that's advertised in the window."

George extended his hand to Johnny, and introduced himself. "I'm George Baker, the store's manager."

"Johnny Covini." The men shook hands and George offered Johnny a seat.

"Look Johnny, I'm going to get right to the point, I don't want to waste your time, and as you can see by all the paperwork in front of me, I need all the time I can get. I have three questions for you. Number one: can you read music? Number two: can you play drums? And number three: have you ever had a sales position before?"

"I'm a drummer, and I know how to fix drums, and I can definitely, teach."

"But can you read music?"

"Well, no."

"Can you sell?"

"Yes, I can sell."

"I mean, have you ever had a sales job in a store?"

"No, but what's that have to do with it?" Johnny asked.

"Look Mr. Covini, I need experienced help here."

"Look, I can sell, and I can learn to read, I know I can." The confidence Johnny had come in with was being chopped down quickly.

"Look Mr. Covini, I have a lot of work to do. I'm very sorry, but I just don't think this would work out. You have to know how to read music, and you absolutely must have sales experience from the get-go. I'm sorry, really."

"Yeah, sure you are," Johnny answered angrily. Johnny jumped off the chair quickly and walked out of the room. He brushed shoulders with the salesman who had initially approached him, and didn't say a word to him.

George the manager just shook his head and said to himself, "When the hell am I going to get some decent help in this store?"

Johnny rushed out of the store and slammed the door behind him. The salesman said to his co-worker, "What the hell's that guy's problem?"

Johnny walked back to his car, flopped down into the driver's seat and slammed the door. By this time, he was pretty frustrated and really pissed off. He didn't know where to drive to, but he started up the engine and took off. He was full of anxiety and anger. He drove through the streets without a destination.

He wanted that job real bad, and he was turned down because he couldn't read music. Johnny was a good drummer, but he could never sit down and learn the art of reading music. To him, it was totally confining. He always had a natural ability and was self-taught.

He continued driving around and never even thought of turning on the radio. It was quiet, millions of thoughts were jumping around in his head. He wondered about his cousin Cosmo and thought that one day soon he would call him and apologize for walking out the way he did. He thought about Rosanna. She was beautiful, he thought to himself; the first girl that left him speechless. He remembered how he couldn't even speak to her, she made him so nervous, but now he would have to forget about her, there were more important things at hand and he couldn't be worrying about Rosanna.

Not paying attention to where he was driving, he turned into a small side street and realized he was almost into the heart of South Philly by now. He looked at his watch and remembered Mookie said after eleven, so he decided to go and find Mookie. He figured that maybe some cocaine would help him figure out what to do with his life. He headed in the direction of the playground on 9th Street. When he made the turn onto 9th, he saw Mookie at the end of the block standing aside his Lincoln Towncar. The car was jet black with a black convertible-type top. The spoke wheels with white wall tires were cleaned to the hilt. The car looked as though it had just been waxed. The interior was pure white leather, equipped with a telephone, and custom stereo system.

Johnny noticed a parking spot and quickly parked the car. He slowly got out of the car and was reluctant to approach Mookie. Johnny was always afraid that Mookie was under surveillance. He knew that sooner or later the narcs would bust him. He began walking toward Mookie.

When Johnny reached Mookie they shook hands. Mookie had always told Johnny to shake hands with him when they would meet, it looked less conspicuous. "Johnny, how's the music?" Mookie asked.

"The music's history man, listen I need some money, I'm broke. And I need some coke too."

"Hey Johnny, no problem. Just so long as you know I gotta charge you three dollars on every five."

"Three dollars! Man, that's a disgrace."

"That's life in the fast lane. You take it or leave it. Didn't your mother ever tell you to save money for a rainy day?"

"Yeah well, I only got a grand in the bank, I want to try to keep it there. I got this psychological problem, if I don't have any money in the bank, it's a crime."

"Hey Johnny, you got psychological problems, go see a shrink. I'm a businessman—you want money or not?"

"Yeah I want money."

"OK, how much you need?"

"200."

Mookie reached into his pocket and pulled out a wad of money. There were two separate wads, one was all twenties, and the other all hundreds, and they were thick. Mookie peeled off two hundred dollar bills and handed them to Johnny. "OK Johnny, now that we got that straightened out, I know you want some of this good coke that I just got."

Johnny took a deep breath. "Yeah, I want some coke too."

"Wait a minute, I'll get you the stuff from my car." Mookie turned slowly and walked cautiously to his car. As he sported his black sunglasses, he looked all around before he opened the car door. Johnny just leaned up against the wire fence that surrounded the playground. He folded his arms on his chest and was looking around nervously.

As Mookie opened the car door, he noticed directly across the street a car with its hood open and two men were looking into the engine. Suddenly Mookie stopped and stared. The men looked up at Mookie at the same time. He knew something was going down. He had been in these situations before and he smelled a rat.

Johnny turned toward Mookie and saw him and the two men. He knew something was happening, but wasn't quite sure. Johnny took a deep breath and began biting his upper lip. He didn't know whether to split or hang around. There was no way he wanted to get involved in any drug bust.

Mookie slowly reached in his car and underneath his seat for his gun, a .357 Magnum. No way is anyone going to bust me, he thought, I m not going to jail again—I had enough of that place. He reached over to the glove compartment and got a couple packets of cocaine for Johnny. He just wasn't sure if these guys were narcs or ordinary people fixing a car. He stuffed the gun in his pants and closed his jacket, and slowly got out of the car. As he closed the car door, he saw Johnny looking at the two men.

It seemed as though the two men were trying to fix a problem under the hood, but Mookie wasn't taking any chances. When he thought the two men weren't paying attention any longer, he stretched his hand slowly across toward Johnny, trying to keep it out of sight with his back toward the men.

As Mookie touched Johnny's hand with the cocaine, a voice shouted from across the street, "Freeze!"

The men had guns pointing directly at Mookie. Johnny panicked and grabbed the coke from Mookie. He looked toward his car and started to run, he had never been in a situation like this and he felt as if his heart was coming out of his chest.

Mookie reached in his jacket and quickly pulled out his gun. He turned swiftly, raised his gun and aimed with two hands. He fired and one of the guys grabbed his shoulder and fell against the car. Mookie had hit him.

By now, Johnny had reached his car and opened the door quickly. He was in such a state of fear, he couldn't get his key into the ignition quick enough. His body was trembling, he couldn't think clearly.

The two men managed to get on the other side of their car for cover. Mookie took cover in back of a car two spaces behind his. He knew he had to get to his car quickly and get out of there.

People who had been eating outside at the steak shop on the corner quickly dropped to the ground and took cover. Traffic halted and people began to panic. No one was firing a shot, and things quieted down.

The narcotic agent said to his wounded partner, "You OK?"

"I'm OK, I can still fire a gun. Let's get this bum." He then shouted across the street, "Mookie, throw down the gun! There's no way you're going to get out of here."

Johnny just sat in his car with the engine running. Suddenly he froze and didn't know what to do. Mookie decided to make a run for it. Suddenly he jumped up and began firing his gun rapidly. As he moved sideways toward his car, the two narcotic agents knew this was their chance. They aimed quickly and fired.

They both hit Mookie directly in the chest. The white t-shirt under his black jacket suddenly became red. His chest was ripped open from the devastating bullets. The force drove him into the fence. Mookie dropped to the ground and died instantly.

Johnny decided to drive off. He knew if he stayed there, he might get himself killed. He couldn't believe his eyes. He had never seen anyone killed like that. The screaming from all the women in the area was eerie as death filled the air. As Johnny quickly pulled out of the parking space and sped down 9th Street, the wounded narcotic agent said, "I'll call and tell them to track him down."

Johnny sped down the Street. He continued down 9th Street and when he got to Washington Ave., he saw a police car to the right. He panicked; his entire body was soaking wet. Now what, he thought, I better keep going and try to get away. He couldn't think clearly. He slammed his foot down on the gas pedal again. From the left side, a car tried to pull out in front of him. Johnny put his hand on the horn and held it there. He smashed the right front side of the bumper, and it fell off the car. He kept going.

As he continued, he hit another car on the right-hand side. Johnny felt drips of perspiration land on his upper lip. He reached up and wiped his brow with his sleeve. His head was soaked. As he sped down 9th Street, he heard sirens coming from the rear. He continually sounded the horn as he ran red lights. He glanced in the rearview mirror, but saw nothing behind him.

Several blocks behind him were two policemen in a car speeding up 9th Street after him. They knew they had to apprehend him before he did any real damage or killed someone.

As Johnny sped farther and farther up the street, he considered turning off onto one of the side streets, but each time he got to one, he changed his mind, because he was driving too quickly. He noticed a sign that read, "Ben Franklin Bridge," and decided he would head for Jersey.

As he headed toward Vine Street, a truck pulled out from a street on the right. He slammed his hand on the horn and shouted out the window at the truck driver, "Get out of the way, you screwball! Out of the way!" He grabbed onto the steering wheel and veered to the left of the truck. The front of the car went up on the sidewalk and he brushed alongside of a wall. He continued to steer the car and bounced off the sidewalk and back on the street, landing in front of the truck.

For a brief moment he lost control of the car and hit the back fender of a parked car. He gained his composure and held onto the wheel and straightened out the car. Thoughts of Mookie's bloody chest were running through his mind. He then looked into his rearview mirror and saw the police car that had been chasing him ram into the front of the truck's cab and turn sideways. He smiled and felt a slight sigh of relief: Vine Street was only four blocks away.

As he approached Vine Street, he saw police cars blocking his way. The two cars made a v-shape, and others were parked along Vine St. halting traffic. As he glanced to the right and the left to possibly turn off, he saw police cars at the end of the block. He went through the last intersection before Vine, and slowed the car down. As he coasted slowly toward the police, he thought about jumping out of the car and running. Where the hell would he run, he thought.

He slammed his foot on the brake and threw the car in park. He opened the door and began to get out of the car. He placed one foot on the ground and then looked up at the police cars ahead of him. He took a long, deep breath, pulled his leg back inside the car and slammed the door shut. He was angry, scared, and mixed-up. He knew there was only one thing to do: try to make it to Jersey.

Johnny was not thinking rationally, there was no way he would make it. He took another deep breath, put the car in drive, and floored the gas pedal. His car went soaring up the street as his tires screeched loudly. Johnny looked at his speedometer, and it read 60 m.p.h..

As the policemen stood behind their cars, one said to another, "I don't believe it, this guy's actually going to try to get through." The sergeant shouted, "Quickly, move those cars out of the way! This guy's a nut."

Johnny was too close, and the men wouldn't risk it. "He's too close Sarge," the men shouted, "we'll never make it!"

"OK, everybody out of the way! You other men get in your cars and get ready to follow him, he may head toward the bridge." There were some people standing on the corner one block before 9th and Vine as the odometer on Johnny's car hit 80 m.p.h.. They were actually waving their hands in the air and encouraging him. He heard someone yell out, "Go for it man, go for it!" Johnny grinned. Johnny was finally getting some attention, unfortunately not for being on the stage, though. As the speedometer reached 90 m.p.h., he slammed into the front ends of the two police cars, breaking apart the blockade.

He banged his head on the steering wheel, and his neck snapped back up. He looked in front of him and couldn't believe he was on Vine Street. The car was out of control, but he managed to hold onto the steering wheel and turn to the right.

He hit the gas hard and headed toward the Ben Franklin Bridge. The police followed. When he passed 7th Street, he saw a police car turn onto Vine. The car was alongside of him and one of the officers was yelling to him through a loudspeaker, "Stop the car, you'll never make it! You're going to kill yourself and others as well. Stop the car immediately!" he shouted.

Johnny was weaving in and out of traffic. He continued driving toward the bridge, and running red lights. He sped past the other cars and saw the beginning of the bridge. There were plenty of police cars following him and several police cars lined up at the bridge. They had only left one lane open for bridge traffic.

Johnny looked straight ahead and instead of going to the bridge, he made a sharp U-turn to the other side of Vine Street and headed in the opposite direction. The police car behind him slammed into the side of his car, forcing him to veer to the right and hit the truck that was driving alongside of him. The truck was dragging him slowly down the street. Finally the truck came to a stop.

A police car pulled in front of both Johnny's car and the truck. Johnny managed to maneuver his car away from the truck and quickly backed up, and sped off once again around the police car. The officer behind the wheel said, "I can't wait to get this son of a bitch. By now there were four police cars directly behind Johnny.

Johnny looked in the rearview mirror and was suddenly confronted with a flashback of Mookie's bloody chest. As Johnny was lost in that thought, a tractor trailer was turning onto Vine Street from Broad. When Johnny came out of his thoughts, it was too late.

Frightened to death, he slammed the brake pedal and began skidding. The car turned sideways and the driver's side smashed into the rear tires and side of the trailer. The driver had seen Johnny coming and stopped the truck immediately. The left side of Johnny's head smashed into the driver's side window. Johnny was knocked unconscious, and his body fell sideways onto the passenger's seat.

10

* * * * * * * * * *

THE LIGHTS ABOVE HIS HEAD WERE EXTREMELY BRIGHT AND HE TRIED TO shield the glare by raising his arm over his face. Johnny realized he couldn't look straight up or the lights would blind him. He looked to the left and saw a tall man in a gray suit standing with a man that looked like a doctor. It didn't take him long to figure out he was in another hospital and that he didn't make it across the bridge to Jersey.

When Detective Lou Kelvani saw he was moving, he got closer to the bed. "Mr. Covini, can you hear me?" he said.

Johnny nodded.

"I have a warrant for your arrest. You have the right to remain silent."

Johnny turned his head in disgust. What the hell am I able to say anyway, he thought.

"Anything you say can and will be held against you in a court of law. You also have the right to an attorney." The doctor who had been standing with the detective walked closer to the bed. He lifted Johnny's eyelids and shined a light into them. He told the detective to leave him alone and that he needed some rest, and then left the room.

Detective Kelvani moved away from the bed. By now, his partner Detective Townsed entered the room. "Hey Lou, what do you want to do with this guy?"

"We'll put two officers outside, he shouldn't be in here too long. They tell me he's got a slight concussion and possibly a fractured shoulder. They just want to keep him in here a couple days for observation."

Officer Townsed looked down at the front of the bed and noticed Johnny's name. "Hey is this the same guy that got beat up down at that Harry's Bar?"

"Yeah, they tell me he was dead, and the way he hit that truck, it's a wonder he's not dead again." Detective Kelvani looked to the nurse who was checking Johnny's blood pressure and said, "Hey nurse, you think this guy's going to be able to move tomorrow? I mean we gotta bring him in."

"Give him a day or two. We have to make sure he's not bleeding internally and be sure he has no major head injuries. Right now we have him sedated."

"OK, we're going to have to leave two officers outside, and we'll be back tomorrow. This guy was involved in a major drug bust. We don't know if he was just a user or a dealer."

"Well you'll just have to wait until he heals up."

Officer Townsed whispered, "They oughta let the bastard die. I'm sick of these freakin' drug dealers."

"Hey Townsed, don't get so pissed off. They got Mookie, and that ain't bad."

"Where they holding him?"

"Well right now, at the morgue."

"Mookie dead?! I don't believe it."

"Yeah, he tried to shoot it out..."

"Yeah, well he was a screwball anyway." The officers finally left and Johnny spent the rest of the afternoon and evening resting quietly.

ON THURSDAY MORNING JOHNNY WAS WAKENED EARLY FOR A BLOOD

pressure check and the usual procedures. He managed to eat his breakfast and was feeling pretty good physically. He had a slight headache and a sore shoulder, but other than that it felt like he could get out of bed and go home.

After breakfast, Johnny began thinking about his next move. He knew his car must have been demolished. He had no job and only one thousand dollars in the bank—That was his life savings. And he was forgetting one thing... he was placed under arrest.

The doctor entered the room with the two officers who were on duty. "Mr. Covini, how you feeling? I'm Dr. Lang. This is Officer Swan and Officer McGrady."

"Hey doc, what are the cops doing here?"

"You're evidently a little groggy, and you don't remember anything."

"I remember fine. I was being chased by the cops and I smashed my car up."

Officer Swan interrupted. "You don't remember a man being shot? An Anthony Boleiro?"

"Anthony Boleiro, who's that?"

"On the streets he's known as Mookie."

"Mookie?! Yeah, Mookie! Now I remember. I can see the blood coming out of his chest." Johnny suddenly gathered his thoughts and knew he had better act dumb. He didn't want to be involved in any drug bust. "Yeah I remember, I was eating a steak, and suddenly I heard gunshots. I got so scared, I threw my steak down and got in my car and took off. Next thing I know I was being chased. At first I thought it was these guys who had beaten me up before. You know, I thought they were coming after me again."

Officer McCrady chimed in, "Look Covini, we know all about you and Benelli, and it wasn't him that was chasing you, it was the police. The narcotic agents saw Mookie giving you drugs, and you know it was the police who were chasing you. Don't play dumb!"

"Look man, I know Mookie from the neighborhood, but I don't mess with drugs. How is Mookie anyway?"

"Mookie's history Covini," said Officer Swan.

"You mean he's dead?" Swan just nodded his head at Johnny.

Johnny couldn't deal with the pressure and just gave in. "OK, OK, I take cocaine. I'm an addict. Mookie was my supplier, but I never sold drugs to anybody, believe me."

"That's not our department Covini, we just have to take you downtown when you get better."

Dr. Lang interrupted. "We're going to do some tests on you today Johnny. I want to x-ray your head and shoulder. I want to make sure you don't have any serious head injuries." He then turned to the officers and said, "If all goes well, and the tests show negative, you can take him in first thing tomorrow morning. I'll call Detective Kelvani."

"OK, we'll be outside doc'," said Officer Swan.

ON FRIDAY MORNING JOHNNY WAS ESCORTED OUT OF THE HOSPITAL AND into a police car. All Johnny's tests had shown negative, and he left the hospital with a clean bill of health.

When they arrived at the precinct Johnny was led to a desk in the rear corner. They went through the necessary procedures of booking him and finally someone told him he was allowed to make one telephone call. He was handed a phone and left alone for a while.

Johnny looked around the old precinct. The walls were dull and needed paint; the floor was filthy. The desks looked like they were a hundred years old. You could hardly breathe for the smoke from all the lit cigarettes. Johnny didn't know who the hell to call. Who can get me out of this mess, he thought. He thought for a second, and like a bell going off in his head, he remembered his Uncle Al.

As Johnny sat there and thought, he looked to the floor. Suddenly he saw someone walking toward him. He looked up and saw a tall dark haired man looking down at him. It was Detective Kelvani and he looked angry. "Hey Covini, I don't have all day. Make the phone call and get it over with."

"Just a couple more minutes, I'm trying to remember the phone number. Can I call information first?"

"One phone call Covini. Now get on it."

Johnny finally remembered his uncle's number. He thought hard and could remember his mother always telling him to call his Uncle Al, and the number came back to him. He could remember as a little boy how his mother would say, "555-5257." Gee, I hope it's the same number, he thought, I haven't called him in years."

Born Alphonse Mundella, Johnny's uncle started as a bookie in South Philadelphia many years ago, and through the years, developed one of the biggest numbers operations in Philadelphia. He also knew a lot of people, including some top officials in politics.

Uncle Al was Johnny's mother's brother. His mother always told him if anything should ever happen to her, Al would be there for him. Uncle Al was a short, medium built, very Italian-looking man probably close to 60 years old by now. Johnny remembered his pitch-black hair always worn slicked back. Uncle Al had come here from the old country with very little, and at the time, taking bets seemed like a fast way to make money. Johnny hadn't seen him for probably close to five years.

Johnny dialled the number and hoped it hadn't changed. What if he moved by now, he thought. The phone kept ringing. Please answer, Johnny thought. Finally someone picked up the receiver.

"Hello," a man's voice said.

"Uncle Al?" Johnny sighed, "How you doin?"

"Who's this?"

"Uncle Al, it's me, Johnny."

"Hey Jewon, how's my nephew? How come you don't come

to see me anymore?"

"Listen Uncle Al, I've got trouble. I'm at the 16th precinct."

"You mean you're in jail! You've been arrested? But what happened Johnny?"

"Look Uncle Al, I can't go into it right now. I gotta get somebody down here to bail me out. I don't have any money, my car's been demolished, I don't have a job—Uncle Al, I don't know what I'm going to do. I m sorry I haven't called you in so long."

Al felt sorry for Johnny as he listened to him practically cry. "Uncle Al, I didn't mean to stay away so long, I guess I've been all mixed up. Please, I need your help. A man was killed. I bought drugs from him." Johnny kept babbling on.

"Johnny calm down, everything's going to be OK. I should have tried to look you up. I'm sorry I forgot you too, Johnny. Look, I'm going to send my lawyer down there. Hopefully he is not in court. His name is Tony Fario. He'll be there as soon as I get him on the phone, don't worry. I will be in touch with you soon as possible. Your Aunt Carmella and I are leaving for Italy this afternoon. We will be there for about a month. Tony will take care of everything, and don't worry about money, and we'll get you another car. I'll call you from Italy, and when I get back, your Aunt Carmella and I will see you. Maybe you can come and live with us."

"Thanks Uncle Al, I'll never forget this."

"I'll see you Johnny, and don't worry about anything." Al hung up the phone.

As Johnny placed the receiver down, Detective Kelvani walked toward him. He told Johnny to stand up and accompany him. Johnny followed him to another room. The man closed the door behind him and told Johnny to sit down. Also sitting at the table was a red-haired, light-complected rugged-looking man. It was Detective Townsed.

Kelvani began pacing his 6'2" frame around the room. "Look Covini, I got a lot of questions and I want some valid answers."

Johnny took a deep breath.

"Look relax Covini," said Detective Townsed, "just cooperate and we'll make this easy as possible."

"We found a packet of cocaine in your car, and we also know you were tied in with Mookie." Officer Kelvani paused for a moment. "Incidentally, did you know he was killed by one of our narcotic agents?"

"Yeah, I found out in the hospital," Johnny said with a note of sarcasm.

Kelvani continued. "What I need to find out from you is just how tied in you were with this guy." Kelvani stopped and folded his arms against his chest. "Look Covini, you're in really big trouble, and anything you tell me might help you out."

"Listen," Johnny said, "I'm a cocaine addict, I admit that. Mookie was my supplier, but I haven't sold any cocaine to anyone ever. Listen, I don't want to say any more until my lawyer gets here."

Detective Townsed got angry. He grabbed Johnny by the shirt and picked him up off the chair. "You listen to me Mr. Covini, maybe you don't know it, or maybe you just don't care, but we have a drug problem in this city, and we have reason to believe that Mookie was tied in with New York people. Now, I want some answers, Covini, you got it?" Townsed threw him back in the chair. "You want to wait till your lawyer gets here." Townsed was frustrated and breathing heavily, "That's all I ever hear from you creeps."

"All right, take it easy Townsed," said Kelvani. "We need your cooperation Covini, you might know something that could help us in some way. We may be able to help you in return. Maybe we can get you off easy. You got problems: you got caught with drugs and you resisted arrest."

"What more can I tell you? I'm not a pusher, I'm an addict. I hardly knew Mookie. He used to bug me every day to buy drugs, he even threatened me on a few occasions."

Kelvani leaned on the table and looked Johnny in the eyes. "Covini we need more than that, you're holding back." Kelvani was getting hostile.

At that point the door opened and in walked an officer. He walked over to Kelvani and told him Tony Fario was outside.

"Tony Fario!" Kelvani looked to Johnny. "Who the hell do you know? Get up off that chair you slime." Kelvani grabbed Johnny by the shirt and pulled him close to him till their noses almost touched. "I'm going to get you Covini. Everywhere you look, you're going to see my face. You're not going to be able to sleep at night. You're going to have nightmares about me."

Tony Fario appeared at the door. "OK Kelvani, let him go before I get you for brutality."

"Fario, so you're representing slime now."

Tony just ignored Kelvani's remark. Tony Fario was a smart, confident lawyer. He was medium-built and stood about 5'9". With his slicked black hair, black pin-striped suit, and good looks, he stood there with a very expensive-looking briefcase. "Come on Johnny," he said, "I'm bailing you out." He walked up to Johnny and shook his hand. "I'm Tony Fario."

"Man, am I glad to see you!"

"Don't say another word till we get out of here."

Kelvani looked to Townsed and said, "And I thought this guy was smart!"

Fario looked to Kelvani and said, "You know Kelvani, I'm just waiting for the right time and place."

"And what are you going to do?"

Tony looked to Johnny. "Let's get out of here Johnny, it stinks in here." Tony posted bail for Johnny and together the men walked to his car. As they walked Tony asked, "What did you tell them in there?"

"All I told them was I was a cocaine addict and that I purchased cocaine from Mookie."

"Who's Mookie?"

"He was just some dealer around the neighborhood."

"What do you mean he *was?*"

"He was killed."

"By who?"

"The narcotics agents."

"Why were you arrested?"

"They saw me purchasing cocaine from Mookie. They told him to freeze, but he ran to his car, pulled out a gun, and started shooting."

"And what did you do in the meantime?"

"I ran to my car and took off." At that point the two reached Tony's car, a large black Mercedes.

"Here's my car, we'll talk some more on the way."

When Johnny climbed into the front seat he rubbed the tan leather seats before Tony got in. Pretty nice, he thought, I wish I was driving something like this myself. As they drove away, Tony began asking more questions.

"So what happened when you drove away Johnny?"

"Well, I was speeding down 9th and the next thing I know, cops are following me."

"So what'd you do then?"

"I tried to outrun them and I ended up crashing into a truck."

"Did you get hurt?"

"Had a slight concussion, they had to bandage up my shoulder—slight fracture. Listen Tony, can I go to jail for this?"

"Can you go to jail? You were caught buying drugs, you're linked with a drug dealer. Did you destroy any city property while the cops were chasing you?"

"A little."

"Did they find any drugs on you?"

"They found a bag of cocaine in my car."

Tony rubbed his forehead and rearranged his tie. "Look Johnny, all I can tell you is don't get in any trouble before your trial comes up. I'm going to take you home, and I'll be in contact with you. Are you working?"

"No."

"Start looking for a job. If you don't have a job when you go
in that courtroom, it's going to look pretty bad. And whatever you
do, don't come in the courtroom drunk or drugged, because if you
do, they won't show any mercy. And listen, don't tell anybody
anything, especially those two cops that were giving you a hard
time. They may come by your place and try to get information. If
they start bugging you, just give me a call."

When they arrived at Johnny's apartment, Tony handed him
a card with his address on it and instructed him to be there at 9:00
sharp Monday morning. He then gave Johnny $200 and told him
not to worry about money.

AT 9:00 ON THE BUTTON MONDAY MORNING, JOHNNY ARRIVED IN CEN-
ter city after taking the subway. He wondered where his car was
and thought that he should discuss it with Tony.

When he entered the law firm the receptionist told him to
have a seat and that Mr. Fario would be in shortly. Tony arrived
moments later and motioned to Johnny to follow him into his office.

Everything in the office appeared just as Johnny expected:
rich-looking. Tony told Johnny to have a seat as he opened his
briefcase to get some paperwork out.

"Hey Tony, I was wondering about my car."

"Johnny, just pay attention, your Uncle Al knows a lot of
people in this town. He made some calls before leaving for Italy,
and he managed to pull some strings to get you a quick hearing. If
we're lucky, we could be in court by the beginning of next week.
Now, I need you to tell me what you've been doing for the past
few months. What types of jobs you've had? Are you a heavy
drinker? And, I assume, you take drugs. Tell me, how have you
been earning a living?" Tony took a seat behind his big desk and

took a tablet out of the drawer.

"Well, I had been playing drums in different bands on weekends. I also repaired drums and sold them," Johnny hesitated. "I was also taking bets—You know, numbers, horses."

"Who were you taking bets for?"

"Frankie Benelli."

"Frankie Benelli! That guy's a scumbag. How'd you ever get hooked up with scum like that?"

"Eh Tony, I needed money and a friend of mine turned me on to him."

"Well what about the music?"

"Tony, you don't make no money playing in barrooms. I spend more than I make on drugs and alcohol."

Tony shook his head in disgust. "How come you're not playing now? And I assume you're not taking bets anymore."

"Nah, me and Benelli had a run-in."

"Well that's no big loss. What are you doing now?"

"Right now I'm not doing anything. I had a job at my cousin's meat house, but I had a little problem with a coworker. Besides, that place stunk."

"What about drumming? Why don't you go back to it?"

"Well I'll tell you Tony, I decided I'm not playing music anymore."

"Look Johnny you gotta do something. And like I told you, you should have a job before you go into that courtroom, but most of all, stay off the drugs and booze, and make sure you have a good attitude at your hearing. Look Johnny, here's the story: this guy Mookie was small time in the neighborhood, but he had connections with some big time people. Your Uncle Al has been a buddy of mine for a long time and anyone he sends me, especially a relative, I'm going to go out on a limb for. Your uncle has always been good to me. You have to follow my instructions, and only my instructions. I'm going to have my secretary type up a list of all probable questions you'll be asked by the other attorney, and the answers you're going to give. Don't think about getting creative and saying anything that I didn't tell you to say, or you'll screw yourself right into jail. On the morning of the hearing I'll meet you an hour before to go over everything again, so that everything will be fresh in your mind. I'm going to keep you out of jail if you play your cards right. Any questions?"

"Yeah, where's my car?"

"Your car. Forget about your car for now. Let's concentrate on the hearing and we'll deal with that afterwards."

Johnny took a deep breath and looked disgusted. "Hey Tony, you sure you're going to get me out of this? I mean, I never been in jail before."

Tony stood up and came around from behind the desk. He put his arm around Johnny and shook his shoulders a bit. "Listen, I'll take care of everything for you. My secretary will mail you the questions and answers today so you'll have a few days to go over them. Read everything carefully, and I'll call you in a few days to give you all the information about where to be and when. Give your address and phone number to my secretary when you leave."

Johnny stood slowly. "Hey Tony, thanks." The two men shook hands. Tony escorted Johnny through the door and pointed to where his secretary was sitting. Johnny walked over to her and gave her the information she needed.

When Johnny left, he headed directly to the subway. He was anxious to get back to his apartment. He was feeling pretty scared and made up his mind to stay in his apartment as much as possible until the hearing. He knew that the last thing he needed was to get into any kind of trouble or get drunk. He stopped at the corner store for some groceries before heading up to his apartment.

Johnny spent the week rearranging and cleaning his apartment. He even did some painting. He really didn't feel like looking for a job. He didn't want to talk to anyone. Johnny's fear had overcome him. He was definitely afraid that he would have to go to jail. He even took ten minutes every night before bed to pray.

All through the week he had nightmares of Mookie being shot, and crashing into the truck. It seemed as though Johnny's past was continually flashing through his mind. Johnny had stumbled across some old pictures he had stacked away in the closet. Excited that he still had them, he spent a couple afternoons remembering his old buddies and memories. There were several pictures of Penny in bathing suits down at the shore. She looked so terrific, he thought.

When the mail arrived on Saturday, along with the envelope from Tony's secretary there was a postcard from Penny. She said she was working in a real classy nightclub, nothing like the ones back in Philadelphia. At the bottom of the card she said to please write back. He thought that maybe he would write her a letter on Sunday. First he needed to go over all the papers Tony had sent him regarding the upcoming hearing.

He read all six pages carefully over the weekend. Some of the questions were personal about whether he ever used or sold drugs. Some of them were about traffic violations, and some about alcohol abuse. Obviously, there were several questions about Anthony Boleiro, a.k.a. Mookie. Johnny laughed when he read the name. He never thought about Mookie ever having any name but Mookie. Funny, he never ever thought about him being anything but Mookie, the guy who sold him drugs.

On Sunday Johnny reviewed the questions and answers once again and decided to write a brief letter to Penny. He told her about the pictures he had found, and how great she looked. He didn't mention anything about the fight, nor the hospital, and definitely not about Mookie. Penny hated drugs and she never liked Mookie. Johnny told her he was doing fine and working at his cousin's meat house. A little white lie would keep her happy and she wouldn't write back and harass him if she thought he was doing the right thing with his life.

ON MONDAY MORNING AROUND 9:30 THE PHONE RANG, AND IT WAS TONY Fario. "Johnny, did you receive my package in the mail?"

"Yes, and I read it over quite a few times."

"OK, the hearing is set for Wednesday, 10 A.M. Do you know where the courthouse is located?"

"Yes, I've been there with a friend."

"OK, be there at 9:00 sharp so we can go over everything again. It's courtroom B. By the way, wear a jacket and tie. You do have a jacket and tie, don't you?"

"I don't know, I have to look around the place."

"Look, go down to Anderson's Mens Store and ask for a guy named Jack Harmon in the shoe department. Get yourself some new shoes, and then he'll direct you to the suit department. He'll also get you a shirt and tie. And don't get anything flashy! I'll give him a call. He'll be expecting you and charge it to my account."

"OK, I'll get down there this afternoon."

"Any more questions before I hang up?"

"Yeah, any news on my car?"

"Again with the car, I'll check into it and let you know on Wednesday. Now don't forget, 9:00 sharp Wednesday morning."

"Thanks Tony, I'll be there."

Johnny did just as Tony requested. He went to Anderson's department store and got the clothes he needed for his hearing. He stayed in all day Tuesday and relaxed. He had a very restless night. Tuesday night Johnny hardly slept a wink.

WEDNESDAY MORNING CAME TOO SOON. JOHNNY SHOWERED, DRESSED, and out the door he went. He was too nervous to eat. He arrived at the courthouse at 8:45 and headed directly for courtroom "B". Johnny couldn't wait for the hearing to be over. The anxiety was killing him. He found a bench and sat down. Several minutes passed and Johnny was becoming uneasy. Everyone walking by seemed to be in a hurry. Finally he saw Tony coming down the hallway. As usual, Tony was dressed to perfection.

"Johnny, have you been waiting long?"

"About ten minutes."

Tony took a seat next to Johnny. "Johnny, I got some good news.."

"What do you mean Tony?"

"I'll be able to get you off. No prison."

Johnny took a deep breath. "I feel like I've been born again."

"There's only one thing Johnny."

"Oh no, I spoke too soon."

"You're going to have to spend time in rehabilitation."

"You mean I'll have to go to them A.A. meetings?"

"No Johnny, I'm talking rehabilitation center."

"Aw, wait a minute Tony—why do I have to go to a rehabilitation center? I don't need that."

Tony leaned over closer to Johnny's face. "Listen to me Covini, don't act like you're an angel. If you were hooked up with this bum Mookie, you're not just smoking pot once in a while. You're a cocaine man, I'm not stupid. And you better take this deal if you want to stay out of jail. Don't make me angry, and more importantly, don't make your uncle angry. This deal wasn't easy to put together. It cost your uncle plenty. One more thing, your car is down at Joe's near the airport. You might as well forget it, you bent the frame up pretty bad, the car is totaled. Besides, you won't need it. Figure on being up there six months to a year."

"Tony, why couldn't I just get probation?"

"Look Johnny, Mookie was hated by every cop in Philly. I'm telling you, if it wasn't for your Uncle Al, you would've gotten at least 3 to 5 years. You better count your blessings."

Johnny sat there looking at Tony in amazement. A rehabilitation center, he thought, tears came to his eyes as he took a long, deep breath. He couldn't speak. He just continued to sit there in silence. He wondered what kind of place they would send him to. Johnny started getting hyper and moving around the bench. Tony saw that he was getting very anxious and tried to calm him down.

"Listen Johnny, you'll probably get sent to Jeffersonville. Depending upon how quickly you clean up your act is how quickly you'll get out. The judge will make the decision about how long you'll have to stay initially. It's really not a bad place, very pretty as a matter of fact. Look, of course there'll be some restrictions, but anything beats the hell out of prison. God knows what could happen to you there."

"Where the hell is Jeffersonville anyway?"

"It's about 25 miles west of Center City. I've seen the place a couple times and it's really a nice place."

"I remember playing this nightclub in Pottstown, PA along time ago. Anywhere near there?"

"About twenty miles east."

For a moment Johnny reminisced about the good ol' days of wine, women and music, when life was carefree and he had no troubles.

Tony looked down at his watch and saw that it was 9:20. "We'd better go inside, this judge likes to begin on time." Johnny and Tony stood up. "Look Johnny," Tony said, "just plead guilty and nothing else. If you don't, you blow it. Everything is arranged, don't worry about the questions and answers that I sent you, this won't take long. Are you clear on everything?"

"Sure. Just send me to a rehabilitation center." Johnny snickered and Tony did not acknowledge his actions.

"Let's go." Tony held open the courtroom door, and Johnny walked inside. The courtroom was empty except for a man who was sitting at a desk up front. Tony walked in front of him and waved to the man. Tony and Johnny sat down. They waited quietly and within five minutes, the judge entered the room and approached the bench. The three men in the courtroom stood up as the judge approached.

The judge was an elderly man about 70. The man stood about six foot and had a full head of gray hair. He looked very stern and before he took a seat, he looked Johnny right in the eyes. Johnny's insides began to shake. He thought to himself, Oh God, don't let him send me to jail—he looks like he wants to crucify me. The bailiff told them to be seated.

The Judge asked Tony Fario to approach the bench. As he approached, Johnny's forehead broke out in a sweat. While the judge and Tony conversed quietly, Johnny strained to hear them, but couldn't understand a word. He felt helpless and scared to death. What if the judge told him he'd have to go to jail for five years? Who would stop these people from taking him away? Despite all that Tony had told him, Johnny's imagination was running rampant.

Finally Tony returned and took a seat. The judge asked Johnny to rise. Johnny looked to Tony and he nodded in approval. Johnny stood up slowly as his whole body began to shake and perspire. He prayed to himself that things would go as Tony said.

The judge spoke. "Young man," he peered down at his papers and hesitated, "your name is Johnny Covini, right?"

"Yes sir," Johnny replied in a low voice.

"Speak up man."

"Yes sir," Johnny replied a little louder.

"I have decided not to waste the tax payers' money on you. I have come to a conclusion and will forego the normal question and answer period to proceed right to your sentence."

Johnny's heart began to pound when he heard the word sentence. He thought for sure he was going to jail.

"Due to the severity of your wild police chase and your involvement with drugs, I have decided to recommend you enter the Welsley Drug and Alcohol Rehabilitation Center in Jeffersonville, PA. You obviously need to clean up your life and get rid of your dependency on drugs and alcohol. I recommend you remain there for a minimum of one year, unless the center feels you should be released at an earlier date, at which time they will notify me, and I will make a final decision."

"Incidentally, if you get smart and try to leave the place on your own, you will be picked up and then sent directly to Graterford Prison for three to five years. I suggest you think positively and obey all the rules at Welsley. Personally, I think you're getting off too easily, but I hope you prove me wrong. Do you have any questions?"

"Yes sir, when do I have to leave to go there?"

"I will give you the remainder of the week to get yourself organized. On Monday morning, you will be escorted to the Welsley Center. Any other questions Mr. Covini?"

"No sir. No more questions."

"This hearing is adjourned."

Tony asked Johnny to be seated. "Johnny your Uncle Al is good to everybody and he cares about you. He'll come to see you soon. Don't disappoint him. Get off the booze and drugs, don't kill yourself."

"Tony, tell my Uncle Al thank you." The two men stood up. "And Tony, thank you too." The two men shook hands.

11

* * * * * * * * * *

As the blue Ford van entered the grounds, on that sunny day, Monday, May 13th, Johnny just sat in the back seat in a daze. He couldn't believe this had happened to him. After 31 years of life, this was all he had to show for it. He thought things would be so different. How he wished his life would have been more successful. A beautiful home in the country, a wife, some children, a career as a professional musician—that's really all he ever wanted. He couldn't help but continually wonder why things had turned out this way.

Suddenly he was startled. A voice from the front of the wan yelled, "OK Covini, let's go." Johnny thought to himself, maybe when I get out of the van I can run, they'll never catch me. Where the hell would I run to, he thought?

When Johnny got out of the van he took a good look around. The Welsley Center was really a nice place. The smell of the fresh-cut grass made Johnny feel a little better. The building looked new. It was plastered in a beautiful off-white color. The shingles on the roof were bright red. Everything looked so clean and in order. Some of the patients who were walking on the grounds looked and smiled. Johnny could definitely sense a feeling of friendship. Maybe this place isn't so bad after all, he thought. Maybe I can make it through this.

The two officers walked Johnny up the steps and through the beautiful glass doors. When they entered the lobby, the three men took a seat. In front of the men stood a big brown desk. The rugs were red with black checks. The walls were painted beige, and beautiful pictures hung everywhere. Johnny thought to himself, this place looks more like a resort than a rehab center. The two officers sat quietly and didn't say a word.

Suddenly a woman about 30 years old entered the lobby. "Good morning, welcome to the Welsley Center." The three men stood up.

One officer spoke. "I'm Officer Craig Beacon, this is Officer Mark Hausman."

Before Officer Beacon could introduce Johnny, the woman said, "And this must be Mr. Covini." She looked Johnny up and down and then smiled at him as she looked into his eyes. "I'm Mildred Stone." She extended her hand to Johnny and said, "It's very nice to meet you Mr. Covini, I hope you enjoy your stay here at the Welsley Center." Mildred seemed to have been overcome by Johnny's presence.

"Yeah, nice meeting you too, Mildred," Johnny responded in a sarcastic voice.

Mildred was not very pleased by Johnny's poor attitude. She wanted to tell him a word or two, but was trained in these matters, and held her composure. She just took a deep breath and smiled. Mildred looked to the two officers and said, "Officer Beacon, Officer Hausman, if one of you would be good enough to sign this admissions form, I'll take Mr. Covini to the admissions office."

Officer Hausman signed the form and he and Officer Beacon said good-bye.

"OK Mr. Covini, just follow me."

Johnny picked his duffle bag off the floor and followed Mildred. On the way to the admissions office there was silence. Johnny began staring at Mildred's derrière and shapely legs. This place is getting better and better, he thought to himself.

The two entered the office and Mildred told Johnny to have a seat. She then took a seat behind her desk. Mildred took out some information which had already been sent up to the center. "I'm going to need you to fill out a couple forms for me, and then we can get you organized. Tell me, how long have you had a chemical dependency?"

"A chemical dependency? What's a chemical dependency?"

"Please Mr. Covini, let's make this as easy as possible. I know you've been through quite a bit in the last few days, but please try to cooperate."

"Eh look, um... what's your name again?"

"Mildred Stone."

"Oh yeah, Mildred, I'm serious."

"What I'm trying to ask you is how long you've been taking drugs."

"Hey look Mildred, I'm not a dope addict. I like to snort cocaine once in a while, and you know, just like everybody else, I like to have a few drinks now and then." Suddenly there was silence and eye contact only.

Mildred felt embarrassed for a moment and looked away. She had been working at the Welsley Center for over ten years, and had met all sorts of characters. But this one was different, she thought, to her Johnny seemed a bit mysterious, someone who had been in his own world. She also saw an angry man full of guilt and fear. Mildred had first come to the Welsley Center to be cured of a barbiturate dependency. Her parents had told her either to get help or live somewhere else. After she was cured, she went into the field of drug rehabilitation and the center offered her a job.

Her interest in drug rehabilitation became so important, she even enrolled in a local college, attended classes at night, and eventually received a degree. Her job at the center was directing admissions, and counseling new patients.

As Mildred wrote some information on her note pad, Johnny filled out the necessary forms. Suddenly, he looked up and began staring at Mildred. He thought to himself, man this woman is good looking.

Mildred was light complected. Her hair was reddish-blond and very curly. She had these shiny big blue eyes. Johnny just kept staring at her shiny hair that sat so well on her shoulders. Her face seemed to be perfectly shaped. Mildred looked up as she felt him staring at her. Suddenly the two seemed to have gotten a bit aroused. They smiled at one another and then continued the paperwork.

As the two continued to write, an extremely tall man approached the admissions office. It was Jerry Simon, the center's head of counseling. "Hi Mildred."

"Hi Jerry, how are you this morning? Jerry, I'd like you to meet someone new at the center." Johnny looked up at the tall man. "Jerry, this is Johnny Covini. He'll begin rehabilitation today."

Jerry quickly extended his hand. Johnny slowly reciprocated, and never bothered to get up off the chair. "I'm Jerry Simon, head of counseling here at the Welsley Center. It's good to meet you."

"Yeah it's good to meet you too, Jerry." Once again he spoke sarcastically.

Mildred and Jerry just looked at one another knowingly. "Look Johnny, why don't you get squared away here, and I'll be back in 15 minutes to show you around the facility. We can go over your schedule at that time, and some of the programs we have to offer you. See you in a bit." Johnny just shook his head.

Johnny finished filling out the forms and handed them to Mildred. Mildred then stood up. Johnny went back to his seat as Mildred looked over the forms. Mildred walked slowly from behind her desk and leaned up against the front of it. As she looked the forms over, Johnny began staring at her again. Mildred was wearing a white long sleeve blouse and a black skirt. She also wore black lace nylons with black heels. It so happened she was to attend a board meeting that day and wanted to look her best. She stood about 5'8" in her heels and had a perfect body to go with her good looks.

When Mildred looked up and was about to speak, she caught Johnny staring at her legs. She let out a slight cough. Johnny's face suddenly got red.

"These forms seem to be in good order. Looks like we can get things under way as soon as Jerry gets back. So tell me Mr. Covini, or better still, how about if I just call you Johnny?"

"Sure, you can call me Johnny."

"Jerry told me you're a drummer."

"I was a drummer."

"You mean you don't play drums anymore?"

"You got it."

"Why did you stop playing? "

"Too many problems, too many ups and downs. I was getting tired of all that. It's like a big rat race."

"Maybe you went about it the wrong way."

"How do you know about music? You either hear it or you don't."

"Maybe you mean you either have it or you don't."

"Now what the hell's that supposed to mean?"

"Do you have it?"

"You know Mildred—or whatever your name is—do me a favor, lay off will ya? Besides, you're asking too many questions." Johnny's anger was definitely aroused. Mildred certainly hit a sore spot.

"I'm sorry Johnny, I was only trying to make conversation."

"Yeah, well don't make conversation, just leave me alone, will ya?"

At that point Jerry entered the room. "Is there a problem in here, Mildred?"

"No Jerry, no problem. Johnny was just telling me some crazy story about the music business."

Jerry picked up Johnny's bag. "You didn't bring very much, did you Johnny?"

"Yeah, well I don't have much."

"Come with me, I'll show you around." Johnny stood up and looked at Mildred. By now she was sitting on the edge of the desk.

"I'll see you later Johnny," she said. Johnny just turned and followed Jerry. Mildred smiled and shook her head. Even though the conversation with Johnny became heated, she hadn't felt that comfortable speaking with someone in quite some time. Johnny's presence at the center was quickly beginning to arouse Mildred's interest. She actually felt something for this crazy, mixed up musician. She couldn't figure out if it was just his good looks or his rebellious attitude, whatever the case, to her it was something new and different and she certainly needed a change of atmosphere.

Johnny continued walking down the long hallway. Jerry stood about 6'4" and weighed about 220 lbs. He was well conditioned and always made it a point to work out at the center's gym at least three times a week. He basically was an average-looking guy with short black hair. He was definitely a gentleman and knew how to handle people. Johnny found it easy talking to Jerry.

"I understand you're a drummer Johnny, and a pretty damn good one too."

Johnny just rolled his eyes. Again with this, 'I heard you were a drummer,' he thought to himself. "You know Jerry, I just got here and how does everyone know I was a drummer?"

"I got a call from Tony Fario. After you told him you were a musician, he heard some good things about you. He's been a friend of mine for quite some time, you know, he told me a little bit about you. He believes you've got a lot of potential."

"Yeah well if I have potential and I'm such a good drummer, how the hell did I get myself in this mess?"

"Hey Johnny, even the professionals have their ups and downs, you know. We've had quite a few musicians in here. Some rich, some poor. But just the same, they were in here for the same reason—to get cured."

"Yeah well I don't have to worry about music no more, it's all over. It's just one less worry I have."

"You know Johnny, you may find out it's more of a worry not being in music. You better think about it. Running from drugs and alcohol is good; running away from music may not be such a good idea."

Suddenly Johnny stopped, then Jerry stopped a few feet in front of him and looked back. "Why are you stopping Johnny?"

Johnny took a deep breath. "Look Jerry, all I want to do is do my time here and go back to Philly. I'll get a job in a factory and try to be happy. So please, don't keep bugging me about music, I want to forget I ever played drums."

"OK Johnny, you made yourself clear. From now on, no more about music. Come on, I'll show you your room."

Johnny couldn't believe how clean the Welsley Center was. The walls were beige and the big white tiles on the floor shined like glass. The acoustic ceiling was immaculate. The place smelled so fresh and new. "Tell me Jerry, how long has this place been here?" Johnny asked.

"This building has been here just a little over a year. The old building is just down the road. The Welsley Center has been in existence for over 25 years."

"You people sure keep the place clean."

"Yeah, well we want our residents to feel comfortable as possible." Finally the two men reached Johnny's room. "Here's your room, let's go inside."

When they entered, Johnny couldn't believe it. Gray carpeting wall to wall, the walls in the room were the same as in the hall—beige, and the ceiling acoustic. Everything looked new—the bed, the bureau. "Man, I can't believe this Jerry. I'm actually going to live here?"

"Yes, this is your living quarters."

"Man, how do I rate?"

"You don't rate Johnny, everybody gets the same treatment

here. Of course, you'll only spend a little time here in your room. We will keep you active with different programs and counseling therapy. As you can see, you have a phone and a television. Of course, you'll pay for your own telephone bills, but your television's free." Jerry checked his watch. "Oh Johnny, I just remembered something, I have a board meeting in fifteen minutes. I want to make a couple calls first. Why don't you unpack some of your clothes, get situated, and I'll be back in about an hour or so. Then we can get some lunch. I'll get Mildred to join us."

"OK, sounds good to me." Before Jerry left the room Johnny said, "Hey Jerry, thanks."

As Johnny began unpacking his duffle bag, he felt a bit warm and decided to take off his shirt. Suddenly he heard a knock at the door. He slowly walked to the door and opened it. There stood Mildred. For a few seconds she stared at his upper body.

"Oh I m sorry, I didn't know you were getting changed."

Johnny was glad to see her. "It's OK." For a moment there was silence. "Well what is it you wanted?" Johnny asked.

"I wanted to see how you were coming along."

"I'm coming along fine."

"Do you always treat everybody this way when they come to visit you?"

"What do you mean?"

"I mean do you just let them stand at the door and don't ask them in?"

"Come on in Mildred."

"Thank you." Mildred couldn't help being forward, but she couldn't let Johnny know she was infatuated.

Johnny walked over to the bed and continued to unpack. Mildred took a seat on the edge of the bed opposite him. "So how do you like your room?"

"I like it. I like it a lot, as a matter of fact, I'm surprised. I thought I was going to go to some ugly-looking place out in the middle of nowhere."

"No, I think you're going to find it very good here. We have a good staff. We know how to keep people busy."

"What exactly does go on here?"

"You'll be going to therapy every day. You'll be attending group therapy."

"What's group therapy?"

"Well you get together with 10 or 12 other people, you know, kind of like a support group."

"You mean I'll have to sit with other people and talk about myself?"

"Yeah, kind of something like that."

"So I sit in front of 10 people and tell them my life story?"

"Look Johnny, it's not that bad. A support group is good for you. You'll be able to express yourself. It will make you feel better. It will make your rehabilitation much easier." Suddenly Mildred remembered, "Oh my God! The board meeting! I have to go Johnny."

"Will I see you later?"

"I'll see you in about an hour or so."

When Mildred left, Johnny flopped on the side of the bed. He was really happy to know Mildred was around, then he thought, he couldn't leave this place for at least a year, how was he going to do it? Would he be able to adapt to the change? Away from his neighborhood, no freedom, and what about drugs and alcohol— Would he be able to quit? Fear began to grip him. Anxiety and depression were quickly crowding him. He felt sacred and alone. It was like a whole new world. It was like someone had just left him off like an abandoned child.

Johnny finished unpacking and got situated. He then decided to lay down until Jerry returned. Johnny dozed off and fell asleep. He became engulfed in a horrible dream about Mookie. He saw Mookie walking around the streets of Philadelphia asking for Johnny Covini. Mookie's chest and face were covered with blood. Suddenly Johnny woke out of the dream, shaking and sweating all over. The feeling of fear that he encountered was enough to give anybody a heart attack. His pulse must have been 200 beats a minute. He could barely catch his breath. He sat up on the edge of the bed and began taking deep breaths.

After a few minutes he began to calm down. He placed his face between his two hands and rubbed his forehead. He stood up for a second and looked in the mirror. He looked old and tired, he thought. His hair was too long and he looked pale. He sat back down on the bed and broke out crying.

Jerry had received an important phone call and wasn't able to go up to Johnny's room right after the board meeting. He asked Mildred if she would go and ask Johnny to join them in the cafeteria for lunch.

As she approached his room, she heard noise coming from inside. She picked up her hand and was about to knock on the door when she realized the noise she heard was crying. She hesitated and listened. She turned and started walking down the hallway. She thought it best to leave Johnny in his room to have a cry alone. After all, she had been in his position once too.

Twenty minutes later she returned to Johnny's room and knocked at the door.

"Come on in," he yelled. When she entered, Johnny was lying on the bed watching TV.

"Johnny, Jerry asked me to come up and see if you cared to have lunch with us."

"No, I think I want to skip lunch."

"But aren't you hungry?"

"Nah, I don't feel so good."

Mildred shut the door quietly behind her and walked to the edge of the bed. "What's wrong Johnny?"

"There's nothing wrong, I just feel a little sick. Probably tired, maybe I'm coming down with something."

Mildred knew Johnny was just scared and confused. "Is there anything you would like to talk about Johnny?"

Johnny didn't speak, but he looked up at her intently. He slowly raised himself off the bed, looked Mildred in the eyes, and put his arms around her. Mildred then put her arms around Johnny. Johnny held her tight and said, "I'm sorry, I just need somebody close to me."

"I know you do. Hold me as long as you wish." Mildred seemed to have needed Johnny as much as he needed her. "How would you like to have dinner with me tonight?" Mildred asked.

Johnny took a deep breath and felt relieved as his head rested on Mildred's shoulder. "I'd like that. Gee, I don't know what's wrong with me Mildred. I feel like I'm losing it. I feel so damn angry inside, it's killing me. I really didn't mean to be rude to you when I first arrived here, it's just that I've been through some bad times."

Mildred pulled her arms from around Johnny and sat him on the edge of the bed. "Don't worry Johnny, you're in a place where we can help you. You will be able to deal with your anger and your fears a lot better when you leave here. We have a good staff here and they'll work with you 100% if you let them." Mildred sat down beside him.

Johnny smiled at her. "You know—Mildred," he laughed.

"Why are you laughing? Are you making fun of my name? You are, aren't you!"

"I'm sorry, it's just that you're too pretty to have a name like Mildred."

"Well at least I got a compliment out of that."

"How long have you been with the center?"

"Just about ten years."

"Well, what made you get into this kind of work?"

"Well I didn't really just get into it, I was a patient here at one time."

"You? A drug addict?"

"A chemical dependency."

"Oh yeah, that's right."

"Say it."

"A chemical dependency. You want to talk about it?"

"Well it's really very simple, actually when I was a bit younger, I used to follow all the local rock bands around."

"You, a groupie?"

"Yes, I admit it, I was a groupie."

"You mean you used to wear them blue jeans and high heel boots?"

"Well, used to wear the jeans, but not the boots." They laughed. "Well anyway, believe it or not, I got involved with a musician, I mean I really fell for him. The only problem was, he was on a big ego trip. He was really good-looking and a good talker. Every girl in town was after him, only I was too naive to see all this happening. I mean, I put up with a lot. His band worked five nights a week, and I was there at least two of them every week for one year. I really believed he was going to quit that rock'n'roll business and find a real job and someday, he would marry me. I mean, everybody liked him—my mother, my father, my friends— he was just a great guy. But I just didn't realize how much he loved music."

Johnny listened intently, he knew how much the music business could control one's life...

"Hope I'm not boring you with all this, you're the patient."

"No, on the contrary, go on!"

"Well anyway, he couldn't resist all the other girls out there, and told me we had to end the relationship. To make a long story short, it hurt me pretty badly."

"You really fell for him, huh?"

"It felt like I fell to my death, and that's when I started taking prescription drugs. Or, as the street addicts would call it, pharmaceuticals."

"Oooo, pharmaceuticals, that's a biggie."

Mildred just grinned. "And on top of all that, I began drinking heavily. That's when my parents gave me an ultimatum: either get help or get out of the house."

"How long were you on the booze and drugs?"

"It lasted 4 years, Johnny."

Johnny sighed and shook his head. "I'm really sorry Mildred."

"Oh, that's OK, I'm clean now. Now my job is to get you clean."

Johnny seemed to be amazed by Mildred's story. "So you were rehabilitated, and now you're rehabilitating others."

"That's it. I know what it is to be strung out, and I want to help others who are strung out."

"You know Mildred, I've only known you a couple of hours, and I feel like I've known you for a couple of years. Tell me, this guy, you know, the one who let you down, what instrument did he play?"

"He was a drummer."

LATER THAT EVENING, JOHNNY AND MILDRED SAT AT A QUIET TABLE BY A window in the center's cafeteria having dinner. The room was bright and the carpeting looked new—it was a pretty shade of brown, and just like the rest of the building, it was spotless. Mildred had informed Johnny where the food stations were located, and also informed him of the meal schedules and procedures.

They finished dinner quickly and spoke only of the center. Johnny didn't want the conversation to turn to him personally. He noticed that Mildred was staring at him several times when she thought he wasn't looking. He had a feeling about this lady; he knew she liked him.

As they were finishing their coffee, Jerry Simon, who was sitting with some of the center's staff, stood up from a table on the other side of the room, and walked over. "Good evening, Mildred. Johnny, how are you?"

"OK, Jerry, OK."

"I hope I m not disturbing anything." Jerry looked at Mildred curiously. He wondered why it was only the two of them at the table.

"No, please have a seat," said Mildred.

Jerry took a seat and explained a little more about the center. He told Johnny that he and Mildred would give him a tour of the building and the grounds, and asked them to meet him in the hallway in five minutes. As they stood up to leave and wait for Jerry, Johnny and Mildred looked intently at one another and smiled. Emotions began to rise. Mildred's face looked flushed; he had managed to embarrass her this time.

They waited in the hallway for Jerry, and he soon appeared. The three of them proceeded to tour the building and grounds; each time they entered a room, Jerry gave Johnny a detailed explanation of what went on, and handed him a pamphlet. Johnny almost felt like he was at a resort. There was a gym for exercise and weight training, a quarter-mile running track behind the rear of the building, a room for playing pocket billiards and ping pong, a swimming pool, and several comfortable-looking rooms where they held group lectures and discussions. The discussion rooms had big chairs and sofas in them, like big living rooms.

Johnny was completely amazed; he had already met two good friends and his new home was beautiful. The only problem was, he was beginning to feel a bit shaky. His nerves were beginning to signal him for alcohol. His mind was telling him cocaine. Johnny knew he had a big fight ahead of him. He had tried on occasions to quit on his own, but he just couldn't do it: this would be his biggest fear.

When they had finished touring the Welsley Center, Jerry asked Johnny and Mildred to accompany him to his office. The three of them walked back together, and when they arrived at the office, Mildred indicated she was going home. She looked at Johnny and told him she would see him in the morning, and then she left.

Jerry wanted to give Johnny some schedules of therapy sessions and activities. He also explained to him that these sessions and activities were mandatory in the morning hours, and in the afternoon he could pick and choose some other activities. The only other mandatory requirement was every Tuesday and Friday he would have to meet with an assigned counselor on a one-to-one basis for one hour.

Johnny had remained fairly quiet during the tour and Jerry's explanation of the schedules. He seemed to have been concentrating more on Mildred.

"So Johnny, what do you think so far?" Jerry asked. "You must have some questions. You've been very quiet since we started going over everything."

"Well the place seems to be not so bad, Jerry, and I really appreciate the attention you and Mildred have given me today."

Once again, Jerry looked curious. He wondered what type of attention Mildred had given him, but he thought it better not to say anything at that point.

Johnny continued, "My only problem, Jerry, is I feel pretty shaky. I haven't done any cocaine or had any booze in quite a while and I feel miserable. I mean, I feel confused. I feel scared and weak, you know, like I'm lost or something."

"You may not be able to get too much sleep the first few nights you're here, but as time goes on, you will become more comfortable and relaxed. I'm going to be straight with you Johnny, this rehabilitation may take some time. Like anything else, you will have your good days and bad days. Alcohol and drug addiction are very serious matters. It's one thing to quit; it's another thing to overcome its loss. It's like losing a good friend or family member, or better still, it's like losing a girlfriend who you really loved. Quitting drugs and alcohol can cause a devastating emotional crisis in one's life, that is why one needs counseling and therapy, and most of all, support from other people. Don't hold back Johnny, if you have something on your mind, share it with others. Pour your heart out. If you feel like crying, cry. Here at the Welsley Center we've learned the horrifying effects of withdrawal.

That is why we support our patients to the fullest. You're going to make it Johnny, just follow our program and we'll have you better in no time.

Now one more thing, I know you don't want to talk about music, but I have to tell you this just in case you change your mind: I have a pretty good friend who is a drummer. He also spent time in this place. Now he's a part-time counselor. He can help you get on your feet again, musically. In addition to being a counselor and a drummer, he's into physical fitness and he's one hell of a martial arts expert."

"I don't know, Jerry, it sounds like too much at one time," Johnny replied. "I just don't know."

"OK, you just relax. After you've been here a week or two, we'll talk about this again."

"Why all this emphasis on music, Jerry?"

"Look Johnny, how long have you been playing drums?"

"Gee I don't know, maybe 25 years, I mean I started when I was a kid."

"If you quit after 25 years, it could take a big toll on your life. I mean, I just don't think you should quit, even if you do it as a hobby. Listen, I'll see you at breakfast tomorrow morning, then I'll introduce you to your counselor, you know, the one for individual sessions. Also, in case you didn't know, you must attend my group therapy class every morning."

Johnny was glad Jerry spoke to him again about music. He was really hoping he would have talked a little longer on the subject. The two men stood up and shook hands.

"Welcome to the Welsley Center," said Jerry.

When Johnny got back to his room, he just laid down on the bed and watched some TV. He was feeling a bit restless, but just the same, he didn't feel like doing anything else. By now it was 9:00 P.M.

Finally, Johnny dozed off. Suddenly the phone rang and startled him. He grabbed it quickly. "Hello? He wondered who had his phone number already.

"Hi Johnny.

"Who is this?"

"It's me, Mildred."

"Mildred, how you doin'? You startled me, I must have dozed off."

"I'm sorry Johnny, I didn't mean to disturb you. I was just sitting here watching TV and wondering how you are."

Johnny sat up on the bed. "Mildred—"

"Yes Johnny."

"I need you here. I want to be near you. Is there any way you can come back tonight?"

"I'll be there in twenty minutes." Mildred was hoping Johnny would lead to asking her to come and see him. They hung up the phone at the same time.

Johnny sat on the edge of the bed. Feeling fidgety and excited, he leaned forward and opened the drawer of the night table next to the bed. Inside was a Bible. He slammed the drawer. A Bible, just what I need now, he thought.

The twenty minutes flew by and soon there was a knock on the door. He barely heard it and jumped up. When he opened the door, Mildred rushed in. "I don't want anyone to see me, obviously," she began babbling.

"Hey calm down, will ya? It's OK," Johnny closed the door quietly. He felt much happier now that Mildred was there.

"I really shouldn't be here, Johnny."

"Yeah, well just the same, I can't tell you how glad I am that you are."

"Yeah, me too." Mildred was dressed very casually: faded jeans, a lightweight black jacket, and pink bedroom slippers. She did manage to apply a little make up, a light coat of lipstick, and fixed her hair. Mildred attempted to unzip her jacket.

"No wait, let me do it." Very gently, Johnny slowly began to unzip her jacket. Underneath she wore a pink tank top. As Johnny slowly pulled the jacket over her shoulders and off her arms, it fell quietly to the floor.

They looked into each other's eyes with great intensity. Slowly, Johnny moved his eyes to Mildred's breasts. His emotions were set on fire. He hadn't been with a woman in quite some time, and he was hungry. He was feeling nervous and excited at the same time. He took Mildred by the hand and slowly escorted her to the bed. Mildred showed no resistance whatsoever. She knew she would be Johnny's for the night.

12

* * * * * * * * * *

THE FIRST MORNING SOUND TO JOHNNY'S EARS WAS NOT THAT OF Mildred, instead it was a knocking on his door. He opened his eyes, and for a brief second, he couldn't move. He looked at Mildred sleeping next to him. She wasn't moving, apparently she didn't hear the knock. Again, there was a tap on his door. He wasn't sure what to do.

"Who's there?" he yelled.

"It's Jerry," a voice replied. "I thought you, Mildred, and I could have breakfast. Are you up and dressed yet?"

Mildred heard Johnny talking and rolled toward him. She barely opened her eyes and in a groggy voice she whispered. "What time is it Johnny?"

Johnny leaned over toward Mildred and smiled. "It's 8:15. Did you say you weren't allowed to be here? Jerry's outside and I think he wants me to open the door and let him in."

"What?!" she exclaimed as she sat up quickly. "Oh my God, I'll lose m job if he finds me in here!" Johnny and Mildred jumped off the bed and began running around the room in a panic. Mildred was looking for her belongings as Johnny located his jeans and put them on. He then ran to the closet for a t-shirt.

"Mildred, go into the bathroom and shut the door," he said. "Take your things, I'll handle Jerry." Mildred was stark naked.

With her clothes in hand she ran quickly to the bathroom without making a sound.

Johnny walked over and opened the door to let Jerry in. As Jerry entered the room, Johnny noticed his eyes moving quickly from one spot to another. He was checking everything. In all the confusion, Johnny hadn't noticed that the room was pretty messy. Jerry's eyes fixed on the bathroom door, and as Johnny looked to see what he was staring at, his heart dropped. There at the doorway of the bathroom was one of Mildred's pink slippers. The expression on Jerry's face changed. He looked away from the door and directly into Johnny's eyes.

"Johnny, can I ask you a question? I know you don't wear pink slippers, do you?"

Johnny took a deep breath and then scratched his head. He snickered but didn't say a word.

"Listen, I don't know what went on here, but someone told me this morning that they swore they saw Mildred come back to the building last night." Jerry hesitated for a moment and then spoke again, this time in a loud voice. "Let's see, they said it was around 10:00 or so." Jerry walked toward the bathroom door and picked up Mildred's pink slipper. "You know Johnny, this looks just about the right size for Mildred's foot. Now, the way I see it, she jumped out of bed, grabbed her clothes, and ran right in this bathroom. As a matter of fact, I have to use the bathroom, if it's all the same to you, Johnny." Jerry placed his hand on the doorknob.

"Jerry wait," Johnny said.

Jerry just shook his head. He then shouted, "I'm going to forget this happened, Mildred. If it happens once more, you're out of here. I hope I make myself clear."

Mildred didn't say a word. Jerry started walking toward the door to leave. Suddenly he stopped and looked to Johnny. "Johnny, don't let this happen again. If the higher-ups should find out stuff like this is going on, they won't hesitate to get rid of you." Jerry exited the room, slamming the door behind him.

Mildred had been listening to every word, and when she heard the door shut, she came out of the bathroom. She was fully dressed by now. She was breathing heavily and a bit shaken up. "I don't know how I'm going to face him, Johnny," she said.

"Yeah I know, we're lucky Jerry's going to forget this."

"Listen, I better get going. I have to run home and get cleaned up. I didn't really plan to stay the night, you know." She leaned over and placed a kiss on Johnny's cheek.

"Hey wait a minute," he said, "come here." Johnny grabbed her in his arms and kissed her lips. Mildred pulled away.

"Johnny please, not now. I've got to get out of here, or I will lose my job."

"Eh, OK, OK," said Johnny. "I'll see you later." Johnny walked Mildred to the door and she left the room. He closed the door and just stood there. He rubbed his hands through his hair and then laughed out loud. He thought for a second about the night, and again he laughed. "Mildred, who ever thought I'd make love to a Mildred," he said.

Johnny hurried and straightened up the room. He took a fast shower, dressed quickly and ran out of the room. Down the steps and into the dining room he went. He looked around the room and saw Jerry sitting at a corner table alone. He then went to the food line and grabbed some bacon, eggs, and coffee. He walked reluctantly to Jerry's table.

Jerry was eating slowly with a disappointed look on his face. "Mind if I join you?" Johnny asked.

Jerry looked up. For a moment he didn't speak. "Sit down Johnny, have some breakfast."

"Thanks."

As Johnny sprinkled some salt and pepper on his eggs, Jerry spoke. "So tell me, besides all the activity of the night, did you sleep all right?" he asked with a hint of sarcasm.

"I slept OK. Why do you ask?" Johnny replied.

"Usually a person's first night here can be pretty rough, but then again you did have lots of help to make you relax, right?"

Johnny was starting to get annoyed. Johnny reached for his glass to get a sip of juice. Jerry noticed his hand was shaking. "Come on Jerry, get off it, will ya? Listen, I'm sorry. Look I haven't been with a woman for quite a while, you know with everything that's been happening in the past couple weeks, I needed someone, and it just so happens that Mildred was there. You know, me and her have an attraction for one another. Look Jerry, it just happened." Johnny was beginning to get upset.

Jerry knew he better calm him down. "All right Johnny, take it easy." Jerry decided to change the subject. So what do you think of this place?" he asked.

"It's better than going to jail, however, I'd rather be in Philly."

"Don't worry, you'll be just fine. Finish eating, we have to get to your first session. Oh, and don't let me forget to introduce you to Ed Clemmings."

"Who's Ed Clemmings?"

"He's your private counselor, you know, the guy you'll see every Tuesday and Friday." Johnny gulped down the rest of his breakfast, and when he finished the remainder of his coffee, the two men walked from the dining room, down the hallway, and entered one of the large rooms. Jerry motioned him to take a seat in the circle of chairs. Johnny responded and found a seat near the window. Jerry sat down beside him.

"Listen Johnny, I want you to feel right at home at your first session. These people are in the same boat as you, and eventually, you will become friends with them. You are all here to receive help and support from one another. I will be leading this session today, and altogether there will be twelve people. They should be arriving any second. Maybe for your first time you might just want to listen. But if you want to participate, feel free to do so."

"Look Jerry, I'll do what I can, but I can't promise you anything."

"It's OK, you don't have to promise, just listen." They sat

there and waited for the rest of the group to arrive. One by one, the other people started to fill the room. They each took a seat in the circle and smiled at Johnny. He felt like they were humoring him, but he smiled back anyway.

Johnny's heart began to pound. He was getting pretty nervous. He was worried he would have to give some big long speech and didn't know what he would say.

"Good morning everyone!" shouted Jerry. "Before we get started today, I'd like to introduce you to Johnny Covini."

In unison they said, "Hello Johnny." It reminded Johnny of a movie he once saw of people in a nut house all talking at once. He was starting to feel very uneasy, but he tried to remain calm.

"OK," Jerry said, "I'd like to get started today by having Marsha Thompson tell us a little bit about herself. Marsha just arrived last week, so let's be very supportive. When our session's over, I'd like to introduce Johnny Covini to all of you personally. OK, Marsha, if you would, I'd like you to begin by telling us some background as to why you came to the Welsley Center for help."

Marsha was seated on the opposite side of the room, directly across from Johnny. Her complexion was pale, almost white. She was very slender with black dyed hair parted on one side and almost covering one eye. She was wearing a black t-shirt and black jeans. She looked just like a junkie on the streets. She began to address the group.

"My name is Marsha Tompson. I'm addicted to barbiturates and alcohol. I'm 18 years old and I've been an addict since I was 13. I starting taking pills so I could fit in with my friends. I've taken valium, librium and qualudes. When I was around 15, I started drinking. At that time my father was also a heavy drinker. He would come home after work and he'd already have a few drinks in him, then he would have two or three more drinks before dinner. My mother didn't get home until after eight or nine. She ran a boutique. My father actually started to offer me drinks so he wouldn't have to drink alone. I felt sorry for him and I went along with it. He seemed like such a lonely guy. He really treated me good. He always gave me money to spend and would buy me a gift at least once a week. I would sit with him and talk maybe two or three hours until my mother got home. My mother would work 12 hours a day, and when she'd get home, she'd be too tired to even talk. My father and I were very close. Before I knew it, I was drinking a half a bottle of gin almost every night. After my mother came home, I would go out and keep drinking with my friends. I think she was just too tired to see what was happening. Her and my father would generally argue at least three or four times a week. Anyway, between the booze and the pills, I was a total wreck. My life got so bad I hardly went to school. I would roam around the neighborhood all night. My father would drink himself to sleep, and my mother was generally in bed by 10:00 every night. She never kept house, and it was a total mess. I did as much as I could. I even used to cook breakfast and dinner for my father." Marsha paused for a moment. Her lip quivered and tears began rolling down her cheek. Everyone stayed quiet and waited for her to continue. She wiped her eyes on her sleeve and went on.

"One day I came home after school and I went to get a drink. For some reason, there was a lock on the door of the bar. There was absolutely no alcohol out. I didn't know why it was locked, maybe my mother was finally catching on to what was happening. I even heard her accuse my father of incest in a heated argument. I looked all over for the key, but couldn't find it anywhere. I tried to pry the door open because I was becoming desperate for a drink. I panicked. I went upstairs and looked in the bathroom cabinet for a razor blade."

At that point, Marsha's eyes were filled with tears. She sniffled a couple times and sighed. The girl sitting next to Marsha handed here some tissues. Everyone listened intently. Marsha continued.

"I couldn't take it anymore. Slowly I undid the package of

razor blades. I closed the cabinet and walked from the bathroom to my bedroom. As I sat down on the bed, I thought of the mess that I had got myself into with the pills and booze and how my father was an alcoholic, and how him and my mother were constantly arguing. All my friends were addicts and boozers, I mean I just couldn't take it anymore, I felt so alone and had no one to talk to about my problems. I thought there was absolutely no hope. With my right hand, I took the razor blade and stuck it slowly into my left wrist. As the razor went deeper, I continued to cut across my wrist."

At that point, some of the other girls in the session had tears in their eyes. One young guy uttered a quiet "Damn." Johnny thought to himself, man this is really gross, this girl's a real nut case. Johnny had really never learned to understand other people's troubles. He never really knew what love was about. He was an angry man by nature and was always very judgmental. He probably hated his own life, but didn't realize it.

"I began crying and shouting out loud, 'I love you Mom, I love you Dad, please forgive me—I'm sorry!' The blood began pouring out of my wrist pretty fast. I took the razor and started to cut my other wrist. Suddenly something stopped me. It was like I heard a voice or something. I was hysterical and started to realize I didn't want to die. That quick I dropped the razor, leaped off the bed and ran down the steps out of the house. I ran across the lawn to my neighbor's house. Fortunately, Mr. Hanlin was home. He was sitting on the porch and saw me running with blood pouring out of my wrist. He ran and got towels and wrapped them tightly around my wrist. Quickly, he put me in the car and rushed me to the hospital—

Well anyway, as you can see, I survived." Everyone clapped for Marsha. "When I came home from the hospital, I realized for the first time in a long time that I wanted to live, and that I needed professional help. I thank the good Lord I'm here today at the Welsley Center." Marsha stopped speaking.

Everyone waited for a moment and finally an older man stood up and began to clap his hands. Soon everyone in the group stood up and began applauding Marsha for her courage to tell her story. Even Jerry applauded and smiled.

Johnny just thought Marsha was a gross, disgusting person like some of the girls he used to take to bed for a night and then throw aside. Johnny was a womanizer, and had absolutely no respect whatsoever. The only woman he really cared about was Penny, and he even treated her badly. Johnny was totally disgusted by Marsha's story and walked out of the room.

Jerry asked everyone to take their seats and told them he would be right back. Everyone looked on curiously. Jerry walked out of the room and looked down the hallway. No one was there. He then ran down the hall, heading towards Johnny's room. He hoped Johnny was there. He knocked on the door and waited. No one answered. He started to walk back to the group when he saw one of the other counselors coming the opposite way.

The counselor was a tall black man, about six-foot. The man sported a red tank top and blue jeans with white sneakers. To first look at him, you'd think he was a mean guy. He was a good-looking character, but always had a serious look about him. He had big, muscular arms and a well-defined chest. He must have had a 30" waist. His hair was short and clean cut. He looked rugged, well-conditioned, and very healthy. His name was Billy Curry, the drummer and martial arts expert Jerry had told Johnny about. Jerry and Billy had become good friends.

"Hey Jerry, what's happening?"

"Billy, maybe you can help me."

"Hey man, take it easy, why you breathing so heavy?"

"I'm looking for this new guy, he just got up and ran out of the group therapy session. He's Italian-looking, six foot, weighs about 175. He's got a light complexion for an Italian guy, you know."

"A white guy."

"Come on Billy, no jokes now."

Billy laughed. "All right, all right. He's in the billiard room. I just came from there a minute ago."

"Where are you going right now?" Jerry asked.

"Well I was on my way to grab a sandwich."

"Look, give me a couple minutes. I want you to meet this guy. You didn't speak to him, did you?"

"No. Why do you want me to meet him?"

"I think you two have something in common and it might be good for you to talk with him. Come on, let's go."

As the two men were about to enter the billiard room, they spotted Johnny standing over the pool table, knocking a few balls around. His back was toward the door and he was alone in the room. Jerry and Billy stoped at the doorway and watched Johnny for a moment. It was obvious that Johnny didn't know he and Billy were there watching him. Billy whispered to Jerry, "Hey man, this guy plays pretty good. Who is he anyway?"

"Come on, I'll introduce you to him." Jerry thought it best not to make a big deal of Johnny walking out of the session, he would have plenty of time to adjust to this place, he thought. Jerry spoke up. "Johnny, I have someone here I'd like you to meet."

Johnny looked up from the table and then turned to the cue ball and made the shot. "Oh yeah, and who's that?"

Billy looked to Jerry and then thought to himself, oh boy, sounds like another bad attitude. Johnny continued shooting the balls.

"Johnny, I want you to meet Billy Curry, you know, the drummer friend I told you about."

Suddenly Johnny stopped and looked up eagerly. His face was full of surprise. He looked directly into the eyes of the man Jerry was introducing. That name sounds familiar, he thought, but from where? He couldn't place him at first. "Hey, didn't you drum for a band named the Rockets?"

Billy smiled. He liked being recognized. "Sure. I worked

with the Rockets for quite a few years. Did you know the group?"

"Oh yeah, I remember the Rockets, you guys had about three albums out, didn't you?"

"Yeah, million sellers too."

"Man, you were hot on them drums!"

Jerry chimed in, "And he's even hotter now, Johnny, you should see him play."

"Whatever happened to the Rockets? Where have you been?"

"I've been doing a lot of session work, you know, doing some recording for some of the big time artists. Of course, I do a lot of counseling here at the Welsley Center also."

"Why counseling work?"

"Well, you know, I've been out there. I've been through it—drugs, alcohol, women. You know the music business can get pretty crazy. Thanks to Jerry here and some other good people at the Center, I got myself clean. And now I'm helping other musicians clean up their acts."

"Anybody in the recording business?" Johnny asked.

"Remember Joey Gilmore of Nightwing?"

"Yeah sure man, he was great, that guy could play a guitar."

"Well he's in therapy here, and doing quite a bit of session work. He doesn't feel quite steady enough yet to play on stage again, but he'll be out there soon. I'm thinking of recruiting him for a band I've been thinking about starting. Do you remember Mike Riggs of Moonshot?"

"Don't tell me he's here too."

"He's here man, and plays drums like somebody out of this world."

Jerry interrupted, "Uh, excuse me guys, it seems like you two have a lot to talk about, so I'll head back to my session and leave you two here. Johnny, why don't you meet me here for lunch around noon." Jerry looked to Billy and nodded as he left the room. Johnny also nodded to Jerry.

Johnny grabbed the cue stick and held it in the air. "Hey, you want to shoot a game?"

Billy glanced at his watch. "Well I've got about an hour before my next session, sure, why not."

"You can break," said Johnny. Johnny racked the balls.

Billy leaned over and took the first shot. "Hey man, what kind of work are you in anyway?"

"You wouldn't believe it."

Billy laughed, "You're a drummer."

"Well I play, well, I did play."

"You mean you want to quit, right?"

"Well Billy, to tell you the truth, I did quit, so I really don't know what kind of work I'm into. I guess it's just all over for me with music."

"It's never all over, Johnny." Billy walked around the table to reach the eight-ball. He reached over and took the shot. He missed. "I never could sink that ball," he yelled.

"Well it may not be over for you, Billy, but for me it is. I think when I go back to Philly, I'll get a regular job and just live."

"Live! That's it? What about living? You know, energy— excitement. The music Johnny, the music. What about the music?"

"Music?" Johnny laughed. "Music played a joke on me, Billy. It gave me a big fantasy, a big dream, then it laughed in my face. I've been in more bands than I can even remember. I've played for drunks and punks in every stinkin' bar I can think of. Half the time, they probably didn't know I was there."

Billy stopped Johnny from rambling on. "Let me tell you something Johnny, dreams and fantasies do come true, but only by hard labor and dedication, nothing else. It's you that holds the power of your dreams."

"Oh yeah, and where do you get power?"

"From God, man."

Johnny put his stick down and leaned against the table. "From God? God? Billy, man, where you coming from?"

Billy set his stick down and leaned against the table. "I'm

coming from the heart, Johnny."

"Look Billy, I've asked him many times to make me a success. You know what I got? Problems, nothing but problems."

"Look Johnny, God will only work for you if you work for him." Johnny looked at Billy. For a moment he paused, he was starting to get confused with this whole God thing.

"What God are you talking about?" he asked.

"The God of love."

"Listen Billy, I think this is getting a little too deep for me."

"It may be deep for you, but I think if you try to understand a little bit more, your life would change and you wouldn't be so down on music. You see man, music is waiting for you to take it. But you have to have some direction, some faith. You have to believe you're going to do something before it happens."

"I don't know Billy. Lately everything seems to be so damn hard for me. Believe this, believe that, struggle, work hard… All I ever wanted to do was play music and be happy. What I don't understand is why all the damn bullshit. I mean, I'm starting to wonder what the hell's going on. You know Billy, I'm 31 years old and look at me—I don't have nothin'." Johnny was beginning to get upset.

"Look Johnny, I know where you're coming from, but you can work this out, and if you really work hard and really believe, you can reach your goals and fulfill your dreams."

"Nah, it's no use Billy. I don't feel it no more. The passion's gone. I think the best thing to do is go back to Philly and live."

"Johnny, did you ever hear of the eagle saga?"

"No, what's the eagle saga?"

"Have a seat, Johnny." Billy followed and took a seat beside him. "Once there was this boy who worked on a farm. One day, he was out in the yard, and he noticed this nest up in the tree. Naturally, being a young boy, he was very curious. He noticed the mother bird. The large bird flew to the nest and brought the young birds some food. A few days had passed and by that time the boy, overwhelmed with curiosity, decided to climb the tree and take a look when the mother bird wasn't around. When he reached the nest he decided to take one of the young birds; it was an eagle. He climbed back down the tree very carefully with the bird in his hand and then went to the barn and placed it with some baby chicks. Now the boy wasn't aware that he had taken an eagle, he just thought it was some regular ordinary bird. As time passed, the bird began to grow larger than the other chicks. It was so beautiful, so full of life. Ready to fly around the world. The others were just content being fed and staying in the barn. They were just happy being where they were. "Now one day, the boy went in to feed the birds, and the eagle was gone. He looked all over the place for that bird, but he was nowhere to be found. He cried for days, you see he didn't realize the bird was different, not wanting to be part of the little family of chicks, not wanting to live in the barn and just be fed. The eagle wanted the freedom to do as he pleased and so he did.

You see, Johnny, people like you and me, we don't belong in straight jobs. We belong in music. Don't quit, man, don't quit. If you need me, I'm here three days a week. I'm willing to help you if you're willing to work." Billy stood up and looked down at his watch. "Hey, I've gotta run, I'll see you later on in the week."

Johnny was speechless, he just shook his head at Billy. The story Billy had told really inspired him. He sat there in a daze for a while and finally when he heard some movement coming from the hallway, he was alerted.

He left the recreation room and headed back to the therapy session. Later he and Jerry headed for the cafeteria for lunch. Johnny got some food and told Jerry he wanted to go back to his room and eat and just relax for a bit. He felt the need to be alone for a little while.

Mildred was in the cafeteria having lunch as she sat at a table alone. Jerry spotted her and decided to join her. "Where did Johnny go?" she asked.

"He said he wanted to go back to his room and relax a bit, he had a pretty tough morning."

"What do you mean?" she asked.

"Well you know, it was his first therapy session and he walked out, but he did come back. After he spoke to Billy Curry, that is."

"Oh, so he met the great Billy Curry," she said sarcastically. Mildred was not fond of Billy. Nobody really knew why, but there had been a rumor that she made a pass at him and he told her no deal.

"Yeah, he met Billy and I think it was the best thing for him. Billy will be a big help to him."

"I think I better go talk to him," said Mildred.

As Mildred got up, Jerry stopped her. "Mildred," he said, "just talk. I've got enough to worry about as it is."

"I'll be right back, I swear."

Jerry began thinking about all the things he let Mildred get away with at the Center. He remembered when she first arrived there ten years ago. She was so screwed up, so insecure. He had only been working there a short time himself and she latched onto him very quickly. He was proud that she had made so much progress and he was the one that recommended the Center hire her after she was cured. She reminded him of his kid sister who had died of a drug overdose in her early 20's. His sister's death prompted him to pursue a career in drug rehabilitation and counseling therapy. He had never married and devoted his life to rehabilitating people from all walks of life. He worked very hard with Mildred so that she wouldn't turn out like his kid sister. She had been his first real success story at the beginning of his career.

In some ways Mildred took advantage of Jerry's good nature. Whenever she pulled some of her old stunts, she knew he wouldn't turn her over to the superintendent. She knew how fond of her he really was.

Jerry cleaned off his hands from lunch and started to feel annoyed. He knew Mildred was getting emotionally involved with Johnny. She had done something like this once before. A young guy had been at the Center for a few weeks and he caught Mildred leaving the Center one night with the guy. He followed them back to her house, and he knew they had spent the night together.

Mildred's husband traveled a lot on business trips and she was often alone. Jerry felt sorry for her, but that didn't give her the right to sleep with other men, especially patients. Anyone else would have reported her, but he just couldn't do it to Mildred. He felt some sort of responsibility toward her and he tried to deal with her actions as best he could. This time he would have to put a stop to it if she was planning on continuing this affair with Johnny. Geez, he thought, they only met yesterday and already she went to bed with him. He would have to have a long talk with her. He wanted to talk at lunch, but it wasn't a good place to be serious.

Mildred knocked on Johnny's door. She assumed he had returned there with his lunch. "Who's there?" a muffled voice replied.

"It's me Johnny, Mildred. Can I come in?"

"Hey look Mildred, I'm a little tired. I'm going to take a nap after I eat."

"I only need a couple of minutes of your time," she replied in a low, desperate voice.

"OK, come on in, it's open." Johnny was a little annoyed. Mildred opened the door quickly and closed it behind her as she entered the room. Johnny just sat on the bed watching TV with a sandwich in his hand and his mouth stuffed.

"Why didn't you come and sit with us at lunch, Johnny?"

"Look Mildred, I'm tired," he grumbled with a mouthful of food. "I just didn't feel like sitting and talking. Can you understand that?" His tone was harsh.

Mildred was sure not to say the wrong thing. Johnny seemed edgy. She felt like she was being ignored. "Jerry told me you walked out of therapy this morning. Johnny, aren't you going to ask me to sit down?"

"OK you can sit down, but just for a few minutes. Look

Mildred I haven't had any drugs or alcohol for quite a while and I'm really feeling miserable, so please don't ask too many questions."

"OK, OK," she replied, "I only wanted to see you." Suddenly there was a knock on the door.

"Aw man, what the hell's going on here?" Johnny griped.

"Oh don't tell me it's Jerry again," said Mildred.

"Who is it?" Johnny shouted.

"It's Rosanna," a meek voice replied.

Rosanna, he thought for a second, who the hell was Rosanna, he wondered. "Rosanna—the hoagie shop!" He sat up straight and climbed off the bed to greet her. Johnny opened the door. "Rosanna?" For a moment he was stunned.

"Hi Johnny," she said, "How are you?"

"Well quite frankly, I'm surprised, I mean I just didn't expect to see you again."

Rosanna looked saddened. "Maybe I shouldn't have come up here, I feel like such a fool."

Johnny's heart was racing, just like the first time he saw her at the hoagie shop. He looked her straight in the eyes. She was beautiful. "Listen, come on in. How did you know I was here?"

Rosanna entered the room. "I saw your cousin Cosmo like I always do. He told me you had some problems and you were going to be here for a while." Rosanna noticed Mildred sitting on the bed right away. "Johnny listen, if I'm interrupting something I can always come back another time, or maybe I shouldn't even be here."

"No, it's OK, I want you to meet Mildred."

"Mildred, this is Rosanna, someone I know from South Philadelphia."

"Hi Rosanna," Mildred replied, "it's good to meet you." Mildred got off the bed and extended her hand to Rosanna. "Look Johnny I have some paperwork to do, I'll talk to you later." Being a professional, Mildred was very nice to Rosanna, but inside she was burning with jealousy. She could sense the joy in both Johnny and Rosanna when they saw each other at the door. Mildred left the room immediately.

Rosanna handed Johnny a package. "Here Johnny, I made this especially for you."

"I know it's a hoagie, this thing smells great." Johnny placed the sandwich down and told Rosanna to have a seat on the edge of the bed. "So tell me, how did my cousin Cosmo know I was here?"

"Well I think he knows this lawyer—his name's Tony something—and he must have told him." She was acting vague on purpose, she didn't want Johnny to know that the whole neighborhood knew what had happened and where he was.

Johnny scratched his head and sat beside her on the bed. "Geez, news travels fast, doesn't it?"

"Johnny, who was that woman?"

"Aw she just works here."

"Oh. I'm sorry for not calling before coming to see you, but I didn't know if you would even see me. You never came back, and I didn't really know what happened to you."

"Actually, I'm really glad you came," said Johnny. He wanted to reach out and pull her close to him, but something stopped him. He was scared of this woman. Johnny grabbed the hoagie from the table. As he began to open the bag he said, "You couldn't have come with this hoagie at a better time. I mean I've only been here a couple days and I'm already tired of tuna fish and egg salad sandwiches. Thanks, Rosanna."

"I didn't know if you like peppers on your sandwiches, so I brought some on the side."

"Are you kiddin'? These things wouldn't be hoagies without peppers." Johnny smothered the sandwich with the hot peppers. As he took his first bite, he looked up at the beautiful face that had come to see him. She laughed as she watched him eat silently. Why did he ever think he could get away from this girl? Better yet, why would he want to get away from her. He couldn't believe she was there at the Welsley Center; she obviously cared about him. "So tell me Rosanna, what brings you up here anyway? I mean I'm really glad to see you, believe me. You know—I know you're really a good girl. I mean, I feel like—somebody special. You know, I've never known a girl like you before. I mean—what I'm trying to say is…"

At that point Rosanna's face lit up. "It's OK," she said, "I know what you mean. You've only been used to the women in nightclubs, right?"

"Yeah, that's right." Johnny took another bite of the hoagie. "How'd you know what I was trying to say?" he mumbled with his mouth full. "You know, I'm really sorry about the argument we had, I had no right to speak to you that way. Rosanna, you scare me, do you know that?"

"Johnny, I've been thinking about you all the time. I asked Cosmo where you were, you know, why you stopped working there. Yesterday he told me he just heard you'd been sent to this place. I was going to wait 'till the weekend to come up, but I couldn't stand not knowing if you were OK. When I got here early this morning, they told me you were in therapy, so I went out and did a little shopping. Tell me, what exactly is this place about and why are you here? I'd like to hear it from you, not the streets." She stopped when she realized what she'd said.

Johnny placed the hoagie on the night table. "What do you mean? What's this about the streets? Wait a minute—does everyone from the neighborhood know what happened? Is that how you found out?" He stood up and began to pace the floor.

"No," Rosanna said, "I told you, I found out from Cosmo." She didn't want him to think he was the talk of the neighborhood, even though it was true.

He calmed down and returned to the edge of the bed.

"Look Rosanna, here's the story, I've been known to do some drugs and alcohol. I got involved with some wrong people and I got in trouble with the law. Anyway, between my uncle and this lawyer, Tony Fario, they worked out a deal for me to come here instead of going to jail. I mean I didn't do anything real bad, besides, there's lots of people here who want to help me. I mean I gotta get off drugs and booze, Rosanna."

Rosanna just wasn't sure what was the truth, but she decided not to press the issue. "I have an idea," she said. "Can we go for a walk? It's very pretty here, and it really is a beautiful day. Are you allowed?" she asked.

"I don't know, but let's go anyway. Sounds like a great idea to me."

JOHNNY REACHED OUT AND TOOK ROSANNA'S HAND AS THEY WALKED along the path down toward the pond. It was a beautiful sunny day in May and for a while, everything seemed perfect for Johnny. He seemed to have felt so calm with Rosanna there. They stayed away from the subject of rehabilitation and drugs and spoke about their backgrounds, family, and about how they grew up. A few times Johnny leaned over and lightly kissed the hand he was holding. He felt so terrific, higher than he had ever been from any drug. Rosanna was innocent and naive, yet she seemed to possess a quality he was crazy about. She had such a calming effect on him, it was frightening. They were so wrapped up in each other and the conversation that they failed to notice Mildred staring out the window at them as they continued to walk along the path that surrounded the main building.

Jerry had come into Mildred's office to find out where Johnny had disappeared to. Mildred reluctantly pointed out the window and showed him. Jerry told Mildred to stay cool and just let Johnny alone for a while. Mildred disagreed with Jerry, but Jerry put his foot down and explained to her that Johnny was not the type to be pressured, especially after only a couple days there. Jerry decided to give Johnny another hour, after which if he hadn't come in, he would go out and speak with him.

Rosanna saw a bench and pulled Johnny over to sit down.

She was feeling everything Johnny was—maybe more. She had led such a sheltered existence and Johnny was the most exciting person she had ever allowed herself to become involved with.

"Rosanna, how did you get away from work to come here?" Johnny asked.

"I told my father a lie. I think he believed me. That man is so overly protective, I swear sometimes I'd like to run away. I mean he worries so much, I think he forgets that I'm 25. And if he's not worrying about me, he's worrying about that business of his."

Johnny just smiled and shook his head. He was glad Rosanna was able to tell him her troubles. He felt so useful for once in his life.

"It's true Johnny, I mean the only time he's content is when he's having spaghetti and wine."

"I remember when my mother used to make spaghetti," said Johnny, "every Thursday and Sunday for sure, and sometimes even on Tuesday."

Rosanna laughed. "Was she a good cook?"

"My mother was a good everything. She would do anything for anyone. In fact, sometimes I think she was too good."

"And your father?" Rosanna asked.

"My father was a good man, but he drank himself to death. When he wasn't drunk, he was working. I really didn't see too much of him, nor did I get to know him very well."

"Johnny, are you going to continue playing the drums?" Rosanna changed the subject when she noticed Johnny beginning to tense as he spoke of his father.

"I don't think so, I really believe I've had enough. I mean I'm really fed up with the whole damn thing." For a moment there was silence. Rosanna was thinking of something to say to make him feel better. She put her hand on his shoulder and pulled him toward her.

"Johnny I believe I care about you more than any woman could ever care about you."

Johnny took a deep breath and stared into space.

"Johnny, please look at me."

He turned his head slowly to her.

"I want you to do something for me," she said.

"What is it?"

"Promise me you won't quit."

"You mean music?"

"Yes, music."

"I don't know Rosanna. I just don't seem to feel it anymore. I mean I feel down, I feel scared. I mean you know, it just don't feel like it used to. It's like I don't feel like picking up drumsticks anymore. I feel like I've lost all my energy. I don't know," he sighed. "It's all mixed up. I'm all mixed up."

Rosanna grabbed Johnny's arms and held him still. "Johnny, listen to me. You can be a success, you've just had some letdowns. Everybody has them, but now you have a second chance. You have people here that want to help you, but you're going to have to want to help yourself. Don't let this thing grab a hold of you. You're on the verge of a major change in your life. Just stay with it. And Johnny," Rosanna looked in his eyes, "I want you to remember one thing, I will always stick by you—no matter what happens. You can do it, I know you can do it."

Johnny just stared at her for a moment. He then took his arms, wrapped them around Rosanna, and pulled her close to him. As they rested their heads on one another's shoulders, Johnny was glad Rosanna couldn't see his eyes filling up with tears. "Rosanna, you're a helluva woman, one helluva woman."

Rosanna stayed wrapped in Johnny's embrace for a few minutes. She managed to get a look at her watch and broke away. "Johnny I better leave, it's getting late. My father will never believe my story if I'm gone too long. I'm sorry, I've got to go."

They both stood up and walked back down the path to her car. As they reached the parking lot, Johnny pulled her near him again and placed his hands on her face. He kissed her lips and held onto her for dear life. He didn't want her to leave. He felt great and scared at the same time. She was his miracle.

"Johnny, I must leave." Rosanna walked quickly to her car. As she entered, Johnny shouted, "Rosanna please come back and see me again."

"I will."

"No, I mean all of the time."

Rosanna smiled, "I will be back real soon, I promise."

Rosanna proceeded down the driveway.

Johnny watched her car pull out and turn on to the highway. Even after he lost sight of her car, he just stood there for a few moments thinking about Rosanna's innocence. She was the most incredible girl he had ever met. What did she see in him, he wondered. He turned around and started walking back toward the building. His thoughts were of the future. The conversation between Rosanna and himself had left him feeling enthusiastic about a future, something he didn't concern himself with very often. He had always lived from day to day. That day he felt he had a future, a future with a beautiful girl and possibly with music. What a feeling, he thought.

He began to run up the driveway. When he reached the building he ran up the steps and decided to go speak with Billy again. He would be the one person there who could help him with his music. He prayed Billy was available at the moment. As he turned down the hallway, Jerry was walking toward him. He stopped when their paths met and Jerry looked at him peculiarly. "Yo, where's the fire?" he said.

"Listen Jerry, I really need to find Billy. There's something I need to talk with him about. Do you know where he is right now?" Johnny was trying to catch his breath.

"Sure I just left him," Jerry replied. "He's in my office at the end of this hallway " Jerry pointed to the end of the hallway on the right-hand side. "What's so important?" he asked, "Do you want to share it with me?"

"I'd like to, but Billy really knows what I'm talking about. Sorry, gotta find him now."

As Johnny began running down the hallway, Jerry shouted, "Hey Johnny, don't forget, you're going to have to get together with your personal counselor Ed Clemmings!" Jerry just shook his head and grinned. I think this guy's going to make it, he said to himself.

Johnny found Jerry's office at the end of the hallway, but when he peered in, he saw no one inside. He went to the next door that was closed. Maybe he's in here, he said to himself. He knocked real hard on the door.

Billy was seated at a desk on the other side of the closed door when he heard the pounding. He couldn't imagine who was beating on the door like that, so he got up from the desk and walked over and opened the door.

Johnny barged in nearly knocking him over. Johnny stopped short in his rush and turned around to look at Billy's face. "Billy, I'm ready."

Billy smiled at Johnny and then he laughed, saying, "Covini you're crazy." He could feel the excitement in the room coming from Johnny. Billy had seen this kind of excitement before in other patients he had worked with.

Having been at the Center for almost two years, he really enjoyed reaching out and getting close to a patient. Billy loved his job at the Center and patients like Johnny were right up his alley. He hadn't expected Johnny to come around quite so quickly, but nevertheless, he was pleased with his enthusiasm.

"Calm down Johnny, calm down! We can't start this minute, but I'll speak to Jerry, and next week we can get started. I'll see if I can work out an arrangement so you can have extra time to work with me. I know that playing drums will be a good form of therapy for you, but you must realize something, you have to attend all the group sessions, and you have to have private counseling, and most important, you have to be serious about never doing drugs or alcohol again."

Billy's face was so intense by now that Johnny became a little frightened. "Johnny, I want you to know this is not a place to play drums and party. If you're not willing to give 100%, I'm not going to get involved and waste my time. Do I make myself clear?"

Johnny's mood had calmed down a bit. He knew Billy was right. He had to make a serious commitment, or he might as well spend his time here and then return to the routine he had been involved with in his old neighborhood. This time he had to make a total commitment. "I heard everything that you've said, and I'm sure I'm ready."

"OK, I'll see you next Monday morning, 8:00 sharp." Billy reached out and grabbed Johnny's hand, slapped him on the back and smiled. He was going to enjoy watching the rebirth of Johnny Covini.

13

* * * * * * * * * *

BILLY SAT AT HIS DESK FINISHING UP SOME PAPERWORK THAT TUESDAY afternoon. The phone rang. It was Jerry.

"Jerry, I'm glad you called. I want to talk to you about Johnny Covini. He was just here, and very excited for some reason. All of a sudden he wants to work with me. I told him you and I would go over the schedule and maybe you could give him some extra time with me. All of a sudden he's really anxious about music. I really believe it's the thing he loves the most and I would like to work with him a little closer than I do with some of the other patients here. I just have this feeling about this guy. Can we work out some extra time in his schedule?"

"I'm really glad to hear this," Jerry replied, "that's exactly why I wanted you two to meet right away. I saw him in the hallway a little while ago. He had just been visited by a very pretty girl, maybe that's why he's all excited. He really shouldn't be having visitors during the week, but I decided to let it go for this time."

"A girl, huh?" said Billy, "Maybe she's the reason his attitude changed so quickly."

"Yeah, I did see him earlier, rushing through the hallway soon after he was with the woman. I could barely get a word in. Well, anyway, I'm glad you guys are going to start working together. I hope it works out for him. Touch base with me tomorrow and we'll work out a schedule. Do you know where Johnny is right now?"

"As a matter of fact I don't know. I don't know where he headed when he left me."

"OK, I'll find him, he's probably back in his room. 0h—and Billy, thanks." Jerry hung up and proceeded directly to Johnny's room, hoping to find him there. He knocked on the door as he turned the handle at the same time. He found Johnny propped up on the bed, just sitting there staring into space. "Johnny are you all right?"

"Hey Jerry, how you doin'? I'm fine."

"Hey Johnny, I spoke with Billy and he told me you're excited about working with him."

"I'm going to give it my best, Jerry, I promise."

"OK, Johnny that's good, but you have to understand there are rules and regulations here you have to abide by. It's not a prison here, but you have to participate in various programs we have set up for you. I know you were outside with a visitor earlier and I didn't stop you because you just arrived here. Now I have to tell you, you can only get visitors on weekends, and you have to follow the schedule that is being designed for you. Billy and I will work out a schedule and starting next Monday, you'll be on a regular routine. Billy and you will have plenty of time for music and so on."

"Jerry, I'm sorry about the visitor. She really didn't know about the visiting schedule. But I want you to know I will follow the rules and regulations, I mean I really want to get rehabilitated, I really want to change, Jerry. I'm ready to start new things."

"I'm really glad about your change of attitude, Johnny, I want you to meet me in about a half an hour in my office. I want to introduce you to Ed Clemmings, your personal counselor, and later this evening we're showing a movie I really think you'll enjoy. See you around 5:30 for dinner OK?"

Johnny raised himself off the bed and extended his hand toward Jerry. "Thanks Jerry, I mean I really appreciate everything everyone's doing for me."

Later that afternoon Johnny was introduced to Ed Clemmings, his personal counselor, whom he would see twice a week.

JOHNNY WAS ONE OF THE FIRST TO ENTER THE DINING AREA A LITTLE after five. He got in line as the food was being brought out and set up. He made small talk with the kitchen help, and when everything was ready, he helped himself to meatloaf, potatoes, and salad. As he turned to leave the line, he noticed Mildred at the doorway, heading toward the line. He tried to avoid eye contact with her, but she saw him immediately. He turned away from her and found the table where Jerry usually sat and placed his tray down.

Mildred wanted to get over to the table where Johnny was sitting, so she avoided the hot food, helped herself to a sandwich, and left the line. She was all prepared to confront Johnny, but as she walked over to the table, he rushed past her quickly and headed for the beverage area. She sat down and waited anxiously.

Johnny returned, but right behind him was Jerry and the center's superintendent, Mr. Abercrombie. Once everyone was seated Jerry nodded at Mildred and looked to Johnny. " Mr. Abercrombie, this is Johnny Covini, he just arrived here."

"Hello." Mr. Abercrombie lifted his hand and shook Johnny's. The man had quite a strong grip. He was 6'3" and slender. He was sporting a brown suit, white shirt, and a tan necktie. He wore wire-rimmed glasses and had hair only on the sides. The top of his head was totally bald. He had a very pointy nose, big blue eyes, and a very broad smile. Despite the man's aging face, he still seemed to be in good shape and quite handsome—at age 60.

"Johnny, Mr. Abercrombie's the superintendent here," said Jerry.

"Oh," Johnny replied somewhat surprised.

"And Mildred, how have you been?" asked Mr. Abercrombie.

"Fine thank you, sir, it's nice to see you—how was your vacation?"

"Very relaxing."

Mildred was staring at Johnny and not even listening to Mr. Abercrombie's reply. Mr. Abercrombie noticed she was not paying attention, but instead, giving the man sitting with them dirty looks. He wondered what was going on.

Jerry felt the tension and began to speak directly to the gentleman about some of the issues that had transpired while he was away on vacation. They seemed pretty wrapped in their conversation, so Mildred leaned over to speak to Johnny. "Who was that girl who came to see you today?" she whispered.

"She's a friend from the old neighborhood."

"Oh, by the looks of it, she seemed to be more than a friend. I saw the way you two walked along the pond today."

"Hey Mildred look, I told you—she's a friend. Besides, what's the big deal here? Who are you anyway—my mother?"

Mildred's voice grew louder as she answered Johnny. "You know you can't have women coming and going from here."

"Hey look Mildred, lay off, will ya'?" Johnny's voice was also rising.

Jerry and John Abercrombie stopped speaking and looked over at Johnny and Mildred. Jerry was tensing again. And then the two men resumed their conversation.

"Are you going to the movie later?" Mildred asked Johnny.

"Yes, I am going to the movie."

"I want to see you after the movie."

"I can't tonight, I'm a little jittery. I think I'll just rest up tonight after the movie, so I'll be in a good frame of mind for therapy tomorrow."

"Oh come on Johnny—why don't you just say it? You took that bitch back to your room, and she wore you out today so you wouldn't have the energy to make love to me tonight." Her voice was starting to get loud again.

Johnny jumped up from his seat. He stood straight up and looked at Mildred. Suddenly everyone in the room got quiet. "Listen, you watch what you say about her, you hear?"

Mildred's expression changed. "Oh, the hell with you, Johnny Covini!" By now John Abercrombie and Jerry had turned their attention to Mildred and Johnny.

Jerry wanted to step in and quiet them down, but before he could get a word in, Mr. Abercrombie spoke up. "Mrs. Stone, I don't know what this is all about, but it certainly is not the time nor the place to have a personal argument. Have you forgotten you're a professional? Why don't you meet me back at my office in a few minutes. I think we should talk."

Mildred was humiliated. She stood up, grabbed her handbag from the floor and quickly left the dining room, not taking the time to say another word to anyone.

John Abercrombie looked at Jerry and then at Johnny, but not a word was said. He then took a deep breath and said, " This is deplorable." He left the table and followed after Mildred.

Johnny couldn't believe what he'd just heard. He looked puzzled as he leaned over toward Jerry. "Jerry, did I hear him say 'Mrs. Stone?'"

"You heard right, Johnny."

"You mean this chick is married?"

"You're not the first, Johnny, believe me you're not the first." Jerry took a deep breath and ran his hand through his hair. He then slouched back in the chair.

Johnny just sat and stared. He could not get a grip on the information he had just learned about the woman who came to his room the night before. Never had he even thought she might be married. She didn't even wear her ring. He just assumed she was single. "Jerry, why would she come to my room late at night if she were married? Where's her husband anyway? What—is she having problems or something?"

"He's on the road most of the time, Johnny, he's a salesman.

I mean big time. He's doin about a hundred and fifty grand a year. I mean Mildred's never in want of anything, she's just lonely."

"Listen Jerry, I think I'll go back to my room and clean up before the movie. See ya about seven?" Jerry was barely listening. "Jerry, did you hear me?"

"Oh yeah, the movie—sure, see you tonight Johnny."

Jerry was thoroughly disgusted with the whole scene that just transpired. Mr. Abercrombie counted on him to keep things running smoothly. The last thing he wanted was the staff arguing with patients. Now here it was his first day back from vacation, and there was a scene at dinner. Just great he thought.

Johnny gathered his dishes and left the table. He didn't bother to say good-bye to Jerry, he figured he wouldn't hear him anyway. After he placed his dirty dishes on the rack near the kitchen entrance, he looked back over at Jerry one more time. The poor guy was sitting in his chair, staring into space. Johnny felt bad for him, but he decided to leave and return to his room.

As he walked down the hall toward his room, Johnny heard the telephone ringing. He began to run and rushed into the room. He was able to grab the phone in time. He thought it might be Rosanna. "Hello," he said, excited and out of breath.

"Johnny, is that you?"

"Uncle Al—is that you!?"

"It's me, Johnny, how are you?"

"I'm fine, how's my favorite uncle doing?"

"Never mind me, how's my nephew doing?"

"I'm OK, I'm really OK. I think this place is going to help me a lot. I really appreciate what you did for me. Where are you calling from?"

"I'm calling from Rome."

"Oh yeah, that's right. How's your vacation going?"

"It's going fine, Johnny. I wish you could be here with us. I haven't told Aunt Carmella about what happened yet, I don't want to spoil her vacation by worrying her. When we get back, we will come and see you. I want you to get better Johnny. You're a good kid."

Johnny laughed, "Well, I'm not a kid anymore, Uncle Al."

"Yes, I know Johnny, I keep forgetting that you've grown up. You were always like a son to me. I promised your mother I'd take care of you, and for years we didn't even speak. I wish we could have stayed in touch."

"Look Uncle Al, don't feel bad—you're a good man. I'm the one with the hard head. I'm the one that's been roaming around. I'm the one who always got mixed up in crazy things, and it's not your fault that I screwed up the way I did. But I'm on the right track now, and this time I'm going to make it. I think this place will be able to help me. And I have you to thank for it, Uncle Al. I won't forget what you did for me."

"Johnny, maybe we could be close again, like when you were a boy. Do you remember the time we went to the carnival with the whole family and you and I snuck off and ate all those hot dogs and I let you drink beer with me? Remember your mother looked at your eyes and she knew what we had been doing. Boy did she give me hell! Do you remember?"

Johnny laughed, "Yeah, I sure do remember, Uncle Al, and there's something I never told you... when you went to the bathroom at the carnival, I threw up behind one of the tents."

"I thought you looked a little pale that day when I came out." For a few seconds there was silence.

"Uncle Al, I would like it if we got close again. I think it would be real good for both of us. I'm really sorry for the trouble I caused you, I mean you really saved my ass. I'd probably be in jail if it wasn't for your help."

"Johnny don't worry about anything, just get better. From now on, when you need help, you just call me. Listen, when we get back, I'll come and see you."

"That's great Uncle Al, I'm looking forward to it! I haven't seen you in quite some time."

"Johnny, I have to go, your aunt's waiting for me."

"All right, I'll see you when you get back, Uncle Al—and thanks."

"Good-bye Johnny."

"Good-bye Uncle Al."

14

✯ ✯ ✯ ✯ ✯ ✯ ✯ ✯ ✯ ✯

"The power comes from God, the God of love. The power comes from God, the God of love."

Someone was yelling words that made absolutely no sense to Johnny as he woke out of a restless sleep. Johnny sat up in his bed and looked around. He hesitated. He realized he was the one uttering the words. He touched his chest; he was soaked with perspiration. He must have been talking in his sleep.

He looked around the room and tried to calm down. He had fallen asleep with the night light on. He couldn't hear a sound except for the racing of his heart. He felt scared. He kept hearing Billy's voice in his head repeating those same words... "the power comes from God, the God of love." He couldn't seem to stop the voice. It kept saying the same thing over and over.

His body was trembling. He looked to the clock on the night table. It was a little after 5:00 AM. He decided to lay down and try to fall back to sleep. He rolled over on his side and faced the window. He curled his body into the fetal position and grabbed the blanket. He was shaking.

It seemed like a long time had passed and he hoped it was time to get up. Disgusted, he reached over to the night stand and opened the drawer. He thought there was some literature he could read to help him relax. He fumbled around with his hands and pulled out a book. It was a Bible. Oh wonderful, he thought, just what I need—more spiritual guidance! Oh what the heck, maybe it'll help me sleep.

He sat up on the bed with the Bible and started flipping the pages randomly, not looking for anything in particular. For some reason, he stopped flipping the pages in the 40th chapter of the Book of Isaiah. He looked down at the open page and began to read from the 31st verse: "But they that wait upon the Lord shall renew their strength. They shall mount up with wings as eagles. They shall run and not be weary. They shall walk and not faint." He took a deep breath and read it again.

Suddenly he realized his body was no longer trembling. He rubbed his chest and it was dry. He felt light-headed, but very calm. He closed the Bible and looked around the room. What was going on, he thought. It was like some unknown force had directed him to read this particular verse. When did he ever read a Bible—better yet, out loud?

He leaned back against the pillow, clenching the Bible in his hands. It was like he had been touched by God or something. He felt alive and so peaceful. Maybe there is something to this Bible stuff, he thought—maybe Billy was right. Could this be the God Billy was talking about—the God of the Bible?

It's sort of like a rebirth, he thought. Johnny remembered watching TV late one night and this preacher put his hand on the head of a lady who had arthritis and was cured instantly. He had remembered saying to himself, "What a bunch of crap." But now he wasn't being so judgmental. He actually felt like someone or something had touched him, a feeling that you can't find in this world.

He thought about Billy and all the things he had spoken about. He figured he must have been sent by some spiritual force to this center to meet Billy. He felt really cleansed and didn't feel confused. This was supposed to be happening to him for some reason... he could feel it. It was like he was given a chance to start over. Yeah, that was it, he decided: he was being given a chance to begin a new life. After all, Rosanna had come to see him out of nowhere, and all this other stuff was happening to him. He closed his eyes and fell asleep with the Bible in his hands.

THE KNOCKING ON THE DOOR STARTLED HIM. HE YELLED TO THE KNOCKER in a groggy voice, "Who is it?"

A hand appeared around the door as it opened slowly. It was Jerry. "Good morning, there's an optional therapy session on Saturdays and I think it would be real good if you came. It starts at 9:45. I didn't see you at breakfast this morning Johnny. Just wanted to let you know it's 9:00 AM., and I hope to see you at the session."

"Sorry Jerry, I had a bad night. I woke up five o'clock this morning and I was really tired. I'll be there shortly, let me get cleaned up."

"OK, I'll see you at therapy."

Johnny hopped out of bed with enthusiasm. He felt pretty good, considering he had slept late. He took a quick shower, got dressed, and headed to the dining room for some coffee. He wasn't feeling very hungry, so he just took some juice and coffee and found a seat. He had about fifteen minutes before therapy. He just sat alone and gathered his thoughts. The dining area was empty. He couldn't believe it was Saturday already and he was there almost a week. On Monday he would begin training with Billy.

When he finished his coffee he walked to the room where the therapy session was being held. There were chairs set up, and only three people were there. He smiled at them. Jerry was sitting behind a desk, speaking with a girl. He waited until they were finished and then walked over to Jerry.

"Hey Johnny, I'm glad you made it, just take a seat. We hold these informal meetings on Saturday for the people who go home on Sunday. They like to share their positive experiences with the new patients. It's good to hear about what they've learned from being at the Welsley Center before they leave to go back in the real world. You'll enjoy this, I'm sure."

Johnny nodded and took a seat. He was feeling excited and full of energy. He wanted the session to begin, but people were still arriving. He recognized some of the people from the session on Tuesday, especially the girl who had told of her suicide attempt. He sat quietly until all the seats were filled. Jerry walked over and took a seat directly across from him. Everyone quieted down when Jerry cleared his throat.

"Good morning, I don't know if all of you have met Johnny Covini yet. He's one of our newest members." Jerry pointed to Johnny. Johnny smiled, but said nothing. "Mary and Phillip are both leaving tomorrow. Which of you would like to speak first this morning and share with us what the Center has taught you?"

A thin girl, probably in her early twenties grinned. "I will start, if it's OK with everyone. I've been here for six months—"

"Excuse me Mary," said Johnny, "I know you want to talk but I've only been here a few days and I really have to get some things off my chest. I'm sorry, it can't wait another minute. Do you mind?"

Jerry's mouth dropped. He couldn't believe what he was hearing from Johnny. He had seen patients make rapid changes before, but this guy was beating all the records. It was like two different people. "Mary, do you mind if Johnny speaks first? It's obvious he has something on his mind he'd like to share with all of us."

"Sure, go right ahead," said Mary, "I know how he feels."

Johnny took a deep breath and as he let it flow out from his mouth slowly he stretched his legs out in front of him and assumed a comfortable position. He was very anxious to begin his story. He was feeling so enthusiastic about the future even though he had only been there for a few days. Meeting Billy and having Rosanna were just what his life needed to bring him back to reality. He felt a strong need to talk about his past and how he had gotten to this low point in his life.

Because he knew he had a possible future, he wanted to talk about the past and just close the book. He looked around at the various people sitting in the circle; each of them had their own story to tell, he thought to himself. Some of them looked real together and some of them looked pretty screwed up.

He took another deep breath and began. "My name is Johnny Angelo Covini, and I want to tell everyone here first of all, that I always wanted to be a success. I mean sometimes the desire gets so strong, I can taste it. I don't know why, but sometimes the very thought of success haunts me. Ever since I was a kid, I wanted to be on top. And maybe, just maybe, by telling you people my story, it could help me overcome my fears and problems that have been holding me back from the success I'm trying to reach.

It was about seven or eight years ago, I was part of this rock'n'roll band, you know, just playing the nightclub circuit. I'll tell you, I felt like I was on top of the world. We were good and always getting better. We were even talking about working on our own material, you know, the whole bit—recording contracts, concert tours—we had big dreams. Big dreams. I was having such a good time performing and partying, that I didn't realize how much I was drinking and how many pills I was taking. Anyway, it all caught up with me, and it got so bad that my performance was beginning to decline—both on and off stage.

Well, one day the group gave me a choice—either get off the booze and chemicals, or you're out,' they said. Well it turned out they fired me shortly after that threat. I continued to play drums here and there, mostly small-time places and dumpy bars. I kept doing drugs and continued drinking heavily. It seemed like it went on forever. I would clean up my act for maybe a few days at a time, but I always went back. Eventually I started doing cocaine, then I got even more screwed up. My friends tried to tell me how bad I was getting, but the more they told me, the more I said I could handle it. I told them I was fine. You see, I've always been the kind of person that if you told me not to do something, I definitely had to do it... seems to be my nature. I'm independent, and hate to be told what to do. And I always thought I knew my limits. You see, it's because of cocaine that I got arrested and sent here. But you know what? I'm glad I'm here because I probably wouldn't have been around much longer." Johnny's voice cracked as he tried to go on with his story. Tears started to roll down the side of his cheek. Everyone had been listening closely to his story, and when they saw him start to cry, the expression on their faces changed to sympathy.

No one had known it, but by the door stood Johnny's personal counselor Ed Clemmings, a medium built man about 5'9". He had a rugged looking face and tortoise shell-rimmed glasses. His hair was dark brown and just over his ears. He just stood there with his arms folded, wearing blue jeans, penny loafers, and a white short sleeve shirt with an open collar. His wide brown belt displayed a large gold buckle. He had a serious look on his face. Johnny's story gave him some good background information which would be very beneficial to both of them in his counseling. He was glad that he had quietly stepped into the room.

Jerry stood up and walked over and placed his arm around Johnny's shoulder to comfort him. One by one, each member of the group stood up and walked over to Johnny, either shaking his hand or patting him on the back, as they expressed some words of comfort and assurance, including Ed Clemmings.

After everyone took their seats again, Johnny thanked the group for listening to him and understanding. He gained his composure and was feeling very relieved. Jerry turned his attention to Mary and suggested that she begin to speak. He knew Johnny wanted the group's focus to be on someone else.

Mary started to tell how she had first arrived at the Welsley

Center. Her family had committed her there when she was close to twenty years old. She had been at the center for one year.

As she spoke about what she had accomplished during the past year, Johnny tried to listen, but he just couldn't pay close enough attention. He began spacing out and pictured Rosanna and himself walking along a beach, hand in hand. Her dark hair was flying in front of her face from the wind, and he kept pulling it away so he could look at her big brown eyes. He could hear Mary's voice in the background, but he didn't hear the words she was speaking. He continued to drift in and out of his fantasy. The next time he tried to pay attention to Mary's story, he noticed Phillip was speaking instead.

Phillip was a good-looking man, probably in his late 40's. Once again, Johnny was trying to pay attention to Phillip's parting words. Phillip was going back to his wife and family for a second chance. Johnny liked the term second chance. That's what he felt was happening to his life, a second chance.

He drifted off into his own thoughts again, but suddenly Mary was leaning over and wishing him all the luck in the world. He looked up at her and around the room and realized the meeting was over. He was the only one there still seated. He smiled at Mary and thanked her, and wished her the best. Finally, he stood up and walked over to where Jerry was standing. He waited patiently until all the people were out of the room and only the two of them remained.

Jerry nodded at him in approval. "I'm really glad to see you're comfortable enough to express your feelings, Johnny. You've accomplished a whole lot in just a few days, you should be proud of yourself."

"Thanks Jerry, but it wasn't me that did it."

"I don't understand Johnny."

"Well, let's just put it this way, Jerry, somebody up there likes me." Johnny looked upward.

"Well, whatever works for you. Since it's Saturday and there's not much happening, why don't we go over to the physical fitness room and check out the equipment? I try to put in extra time there on weekends. That's probably where you and Billy will be on Monday. Maybe you can get a head start."

"OK. Jerry, I'll check it out with you."

The two men walked to the physical fitness room together. When they arrived, there were several people working out on the machines, and one guy with enormous shoulders was working on the free weights. His biceps were incredibly huge as he curled what appeared to be a 150 lb. barbell.

Johnny looked around the room and couldn't believe how many different pieces of equipment the room contained. "Jerry, man—where do I begin? This place has everything imaginable."

"Oh, this isn't everything, Johnny."

Johnny frowned. "What else could there be?"

"Wait until you see the pool and the running track."

"Well you can forget about the running track, lately I seem to have enough trouble just walking. As a matter of fact, forget all this stuff, I'm in no shape for this."

Jerry laughed. "Don't worry, Billy will make a new man out of you in no time."

"Wait a minute!" Johnny said. "You mean Billy's going to make me use this stuff?"

"Oh yeah, plus swimming and running—all of it."

"But I thought Billy was going to help me with my music, not my body."

"Yeah, that too."

"Maybe I just ought to hang around with you, Jerry, it seems much safer and a lot easier." Johnny snickered.

"No Johnny, stick with Billy. He can definitely help you to be the best at what you do. Speaking of Billy, he's rehearsing here today." Jerry looked at his watch. "Why don't we go over to the music room and see if he's there yet. He'll be glad if we stop by and see him."

"I don't know. I got some phone calls to make and..."

Jerry could feel Johnny tensing up, maybe he was pushing him too hard too soon. It seemed whenever he got around to the discussion of music, Johnny clammed up. "Listen, we'll just watch, you don't have to get involved."

"OK, but just for a little while." Johnny really wanted to go, but he felt afraid to show too much enthusiasm for some reason. "You know what Jerry, right now I'll go anywhere just to get away from this physical fitness stuff."

Jerry laughed at Johnny's statement. As they walked toward the music room, the men could hear the sound of a guitar into an accelerating lead. Chills began to run through Johnny's body as he slowed his pace and fell slightly behind Jerry.

Jerry entered the room quietly and Johnny followed him a few seconds later. The smell of instruments was refreshing to Johnny, it brought back many memories.

There stood a tall man with shoulder length blond hair and a black Telecaster guitar hanging from a gold guitar strap ripping through an incredible guitar solo. However, the first thing Johnny's eyes focused on was Billy behind the big red drumset. On the two big bass drums were black drum heads in front displaying the name "Billy Curry." Billy was surrounded by red drums and shiny gold cymbals.

On Billy's right was a medium built man with long black hair over his shoulders pounding out the bass rhythms on his fiery red Fender jazz bass.

When the guitar player finished his solo, Billy took the lead with a very tasteful and unique drum solo. Johnny leaned against the door frame and admired the technique Billy was using. Jerry just took a seat on a bench nearby. Both of the men seemed to have been fascinated. Billy's hands seemed to manipulate the sticks in a fashion Johnny had only witnessed once before at a concert at the Philadelphia Spectrum a few years back. He had heard some of Billy's music on a few albums, bet he never realized the guy had such talent. Johnny was amazed. I'd give anything to play like this guy, he thought.

Billy's solo ended and the rest of the group joined in as they played hard and fast with lots of power and punch. The instrumental continued for a few minutes and then they came to a polished ending. Johnny let out a sigh. "Man, you guys are unbelievably good. Billy, you've gotten better with age."

Billy got off the drumstool, breathing heavily. Sweat was pouring down his face. "Eh Johnny, I'm glad to see you. Jerry, what's happening?"

"It looks like you're happening today, Billy."

"Oh Covini, watch them comments about my age—these guys think I'm as young as they are." Everyone laughed. "Come on over here, I want to introduce you to my bandmates."

Johnny walked over to the drums and looked down at the name. "These Tama Drums, they really sound good, Billy."

"Nothin' but the best, Johnny." Billy introduced Johnny to the band. Johnny smiled and the guys nodded back at him. "Well, what do you say, Johnny?"

"What?"

"You want to sit in?"

Without any hesitation Johnny's whole being perked up. "How could I resist?" Johnny sat down on the stool behind the big red drumset. Billy handed him the drumsticks and took a few steps away from the area where the instruments were. Johnny laid the sticks down on the tom-tom drum, and began to exercise his hands and fingers to loosen up. He hadn't played in quite a while and was feeling shaky and stiff. He picked up the sticks. "Well here goes nothing," he said jokingly.

Jerry folded his arms and relaxed in the corner of the bench. He was excited knowing he would see Johnny play for the first time. Billy grabbed his towel and took a seat next to Jerry. When he began wiping his face, suddenly he heard this loud syncopated rock'n'roll beat. The other guys waited to see what direction Johnny was going in and once they picked up the beat, they joined in simultaneously.

Johnny continued to play, but he was feeling insecure. Even though he had only watched these guys play for a few minutes, he knew they were good musicians and he felt he wouldn't be able to keep up with them.

Billy picked up on Johnny's nervousness quickly. He tried to look at the other musicians without Johnny noticing. They each winked at him and he knew what they were thinking. He was sure they wouldn't want this to go on for too long. Johnny was obviously very nervous and not playing up to par. Billy could tell that Johnny had potential, but was very rusty.

Johnny attempted to do a fill, but his right stick rammed into the side of the mounted tom-tom and threw the beat off for everyone. He could feel his forehead and hands start to sweat. He was starting to get really nervous. Attempting to regain the beat, the stick fell out of his right hand. Billy quickly ran over, picked up the stick and handed it back to Johnny. Again Johnny tried to get back into the beat, and again he dropped the stick. He felt like such a fool. His face began to redden with embarrassment. As Jerry looked on, he felt bad for Johnny, knowing how embarrassed he was.

Johnny stopped playing. He quickly grabbed the stick off the floor, and then laid both sticks on the drum. The other musicians stopped playing slowly as they looked at Johnny with pity. For a moment, Johnny didn't move. No one spoke.

Suddenly Johnny sighed. He then shook his head in disgust. He was so embarrassed, he didn't know what to say.

"Johnny, how's it feel to sit behind the drums again?" said Billy.

Johnny took a deep breath. "It don't feel too good, Billy." Johnny looked to the other musicians. "Sorry fellas, I really screwed that one up."

"Eh, no problem. Everybody drops a drumstick once in a

while."

"Yeah, well I think I just dropped my last drumstick."

"Eh, come on Johnny," said Jerry. "How long's it been since you played?"

"It hasn't been that long, Jerry. I just can't figure it out. I'm a nervous wreck without drugs and alcohol."

"I must be crazy to think I can get anywhere in this business." Johnny got up and walked out. Everyone looked on feeling somewhat sorry for Johnny.

He headed back to his room.

"I'll be right back," said Billy. He followed Johnny to his room. He didn't knock, but rushed in. Billy was angry. "Man, why did you walk out like that?"

"Look Billy..."

"No! You look. I don't have time for quitters. You make a mistake, you roll with it. Some of the best drummers in the world screw up and come back better than ever. Man, you can't just walk away every time a little problem occurs!"

"OK," Johnny replied, "We'll try again on Monday."

"No Johnny. Don't try again Monday—do it today."

Johnny gazed out the window. "I'll see you tomorrow Billy."

"Yeah! See you tomorrow." Billy rushed out, slamming the door behind him.

Johnny felt bad shutting Billy out, but he wanted to be alone.

The phone rang. He picked it up. Johnny yelled, "Hello."

"Hi Johnny, it's Rosanna. What's wrong?"

"What do you mean what's wrong?"

"Why are you shouting?"

"I'm not shouting!"

"Johnny, would you please calm down and talk to me?"

"Sorry Rosanna, I'm just a little screwed up today. I miss you Rosanna, I really miss you."

"I miss you too Johnny, and I'd like to know if I can come up to see you tomorrow."

"You don't have to ask, Rosanna. You're welcome here any time. How's the hoagie shop?"

"It's the same—smells of onions all the time."

Johnny laughed. "How's my crazy cousin doin'?" he asked.

"Oh, he's fine," she replied. "He wants to come up and see you also. Johnny, I have to go. It's almost lunch time and my father's calling. It's starting to get very busy here."

Rosanna hung up quickly without another word. Soon after, Johnny fell asleep for two hours.

THERE WAS A LOUD KNOCK ON THE DOOR. STARTLED, JOHNNY SAT UP ON the bed. "Hold on, I'm coming." Johnny stumbled to the door and opened it.

"My man Johnny! What's happening?" Danny Rosco and Stevie Roselli shouted together.

"What the hell are you guys doin' up here?" Johnny was surprised.

"You don't think we'd forget an old friend like you, do you?" said Danny Rosco.

"Stevie, you're the last person I'd expect to see here!"

"Well, you gonna let us in?" demanded Danny Rosco.

"Yeah," Johnny moved out of the doorway, "Come on in and have a seat!" He looked to Stevie. "Someone told me you got a job with a local band that got a recording contract. I thought you'd be touring by now."

"Nah. They decided to get their old guitar player back."

"Oh. Tough break."

Danny Rosco interrupted, "What's happening up here? We hear you're going to be hanging out with Billy Curry. What do you think about this guy, eh Stevie—hanging out with the big boys!"

"He's just going to work with me a little while," replied Johnny. "You know, therapy... stuff like that."

"Johnny, come on, this guy can help you get your head screwed on right, man!" stated Stevie. "He can make you a clean musician again."

"Yeah, he can make you a good drummer again too." Danny Rosco added.

"So what if he does? I just don't want to be a clean musician, I want to be a successful clean musician. You know what I mean—the Bigs, man. I'm tired of all the nightclubs. Same old one-night stands with them crazy women. Arguing with club owners, they're either telling you you're playing too loud, your breaks are too long, you're not playing the right kind of music—not to mention lugging that equipment around all the time. I don't miss all that craziness anymore. I want someone else to lug my equipment around. I want to play the Spectrum, Madison Square Garden, JFK."

"That's why we're here," explained Stevie, "we want something back for all the time we've put in this crazy business."

"Stevie—what are you getting at?"

"We want to start a band with you Johnny." Danny Rosco spoke up.

"And do what?" Johnny asked.

"Come on man, we got what it takes. We can make it Johnny. All we need is some organization. Some team work. Some people we can work with. The three of us worked together before, we never had any problems."

"He's right, Johnny," said Stevie. "And you remember Jerry Carvelli?"

"Jerry Carvelli! The singer? I thought he quit."

"He did, but he wants a shot at the Bigs too, and he's what we need as a singer and a front man."

"What about keyboards?" Johnny asked.

"Who else? Your pison—Mike Danella."

"Mike? But he's a jazz man."

"Johnny, he can play what we want," Danny Rosco forced, "Trust me, he's one of the best."

Johnny stared out the window. He was confused. Chills were running down his spine. He didn't know whether he was happy or sad. He felt like a kid again starting his first band. Was this a chance at a new beginning—what he had always dreamed of?

Danny broke the silence. "What do you say, Johnny—you in or what?"

"Danny, you always were a good talker."

"Then it's a deal?"

Johnny turned to his friends. "It's a deal." Excitement shot through the room as the three men shook hands.

In an instant the mood was broken. "Hey wait," Johnny realized, "I can't leave here. How am I gonna rehearse with you guys?"

"Who said you have to leave?" laughed Stevie. "We can rehearse right here, can't we?"

"Well, I guess. I'll have to OK it with Jerry Simon."

"Hey look Johnny, we gotta get back to the city. We got some things to take care of. I'll call you tomorrow and you can let us know what's happening," said Danny.

"You got it," said Johnny, "call me tomorrow, and in the meantime, I'll arrange things with Jerry Simon."

Johnny spent the rest of Saturday making arrangements with Jerry and Billy.

SUNDAY MORNING CAME QUICKLY. ROSANNA'S VISIT, LATER THAT AFTERNOON, made him realize how important she really was to him, and how she was beginning to make his life more meaningful. For once, Johnny's life was taking a turn for the better.

15

* * * * * * * * * *

JOHNNY WOKE UP TO A DAMP AND DREARY MONDAY. THE ALARM WENT off like ten crashing cow bells. It was 7:00 A.M. and he didn't feel like moving. He rolled over and hit the alarm clock he had laid on the floor. Johnny crawled out of bed, headed to the bathroom, and washed up. There was an uneasy churning in his stomach. He was thirty miles away from home. "How did I ever end up in a place like this?" he thought. He wondered if he'd ever be a sober and responsible person and be able to be free of the troubles of his past that continued to haunt him. He knew he had a lot of hard work ahead of him, and realized he would have to put his trust in Billy, and believe in himself also. Johnny was beginning to be one determined fellow.

There was a strong rap on the door. Billy walked in. "Here, put these on." Billy handed him some workout sweats. "You'll need these, they'll help you sweat out some of them chemicals you've been putting in your body for so long. I'll be back in half an hour. Be ready, we have a long day ahead of us." Billy made a swift exit.

"What, no breakfast?" Johnny muttered under his breath. Johnny got into his sweats and sat on the end of the bed and meditated for the next fifteen minutes or so.

Billy entered. "OK Covini, let's go to work."

Johnny and Billy headed for the gym. Johnny was finding it hard to keep up with Billy as they walked. Johnny was so out of condition that he was beginning to breathe heavily just walking fast. He knew it was going to be tough keeping up with Billy. "You always walk this fast?" Johnny asked.

"Hey, come on Covini—the day's just begun." Billy replied. "They're two things I want you to keep on your mind all day: hard work and dedication."

Johnny responded, "Hard work and dedication, I'll keep them in mind, but will they do anything for my body?"

"Save the jokes for later Covini. Just follow me." The two men entered the gym. Billy began to check some loose ends on a barbell. "Hey, them sweats don't fit too bad."

"Nah. Not for an out of shape guy like me," Johnny snickered.

Billy laughed. "Don't worry, we'll have you in shape in no time. And you'll be one helluva drummer too. OK, let's get to work. First off, we're gonna do some light weight-training, and then some freehand stuff, and then you'll get your first lesson in self-defense, and then after that, it's road work."

"Road work?" Johnny gasped. "You mean running?"

"I mean running."

"Billy, aren't you forgetting one thing?"

"What?"

"Breakfast."

"Breakfast?"

"Yeah, breakfast. And besides, what's all this got to do with drums and music?"

"You'll find that out tonight. Today we won't eat breakfast, we'll have lunch. Besides, a little self-discipline never hurt anybody."

As Johnny's fitness program began, Billy started him on the weights, and just as he said, he moved him on to freehand exercise and some martial arts training. Johnny had never experienced this type of workout in his life. He was never exposed to any type of hard work or strenuous exercise. Two hours had gone by, and he was exhausted. "Billy, I can't go on any longer. I've had enough."

"You can't quit now, Johnny, we have to do some road work, and then we'll call it a day. Johnny, it's through these workouts and training that you'll get stronger and get rid of a lot of the fears that are holding you down."

"OK, road work and that's it!"

Billy led Johnny to the track. "OK; here it is, this is a quarter mile track. Four laps—one mile."

"Aw come on Billy, I can't do four laps. I think I'm just gonna forget this whole thing. This is crazy!"

"Johnny, when this is over, you're gonna thank me. Don't turn back, just run."

Johnny looked to Billy and felt energized as he sensed Billy's determination. He began to run.

"That's it. Run Johnny! Run! Run!" Billy began to follow Johnny, keeping about twenty yards behind him. Johnny finished his first lap and fell to the ground.

"One more!" Billy shouted. "Get up, Johnny. Get up! You can do it! I know you can do it! You know you can do it!"

Johnny got halfway up and fell again. "I can't do it. I can't go any more."

"Johnny, remember the power, the God of love."

Johnny seemed to have gotten his second wind. Billy's words had given him the strength to stand. Gasping for air, Johnny began to run. He used all his strength—strength he never knew he had. Billy cheered him on. It made him very happy to know he was beginning to instill confidence in Johnny, confidence he knew he would need if he had any hopes of being a professional.

Johnny was now half way around the quarter mile track. He was staggering. He could feel the muscles in his legs begin to cramp. He felt like his heart was about to burst. Billy was now about five feet behind him, "Just a little more, Johnny, just a little more and we're home free!"

Johnny fell a second time. He only had a little more to go. Billy reached down to help him and got him back on his feet. He grabbed Johnny's right arm and put it around his shoulder. Together they walked the last stretch of track.

Johnny walked off the track and fell to the ground. As he lay on his back with his arms stretched out, he felt like his lungs were about to collapse. "I did it Billy! I did it!"

"Yeah, Johnny," Billy stood over Johnny with his hands on his hips and breathing heavily himself, "You did it!"

Billy laid down beside Johnny. They rested in the shaded area for about five minutes, just catching their breath.

Walking back to the gym, Johnny asked, "Billy, do you think I'm ever gonna make it?"

"Johnny, only you can tell that story."

"What do you mean?"

"Do you want to make it?"

"Billy, I want to be honest with you—I'm scared."

"Scared of what?"

"I mean I never told anybody this before—"

"Well, tell me Johnny, now's as good a time as any."

"I'm afraid I'm gonna end up an old factory worker or something like that."

"Well you and I both know that ain't no fun."

"Fun? Just thinking about it gives me the creeps."

"Johnny, what do you want to be?"

"I want to be a success. I mean not just a success, I want to be a professional drummer. I want to be part of a band that's going somewhere with people that are serious and dedicated. The problem is, I've been let down so much, I just keep believing I'm going to stay down."

Billy stopped walking and grabbed Johnny's arm. He looked toward him. "Johnny, the way you believe you're going to stay down, is the way you're going to go if you continue to believe that way. You have to change your way of thinking. You want to be a professional musician? Then that's the way you're going to have to believe. You have to get all that garbage out of your brain. It's been tearing you down for too long. Let it go, man, let it go. If we're going to continue to work together, you're going to have to change your thinking, otherwise it won't work. I'll plant the seed, but you're going to have to grow."

"OK Billy. From now on—it's think positive, 'cause I ain't going into no factory." They laughed.

They entered the building. "Look, why don't you go get cleaned up, and I'll meet you for lunch," said Billy.

"OK—You got it. See you in about a half." Johnny walked back to his room. Upon entering, the phone rang. It was Rosanna.

"Hello Johnny," she said.

"Rosanna, is that you?"

"It's me Johnny, how are you?"

"I'm fine now. I just finished a gruesome workout with Billy."

"Johnny, guess what?" she said excitedly.

"What?"

"Your Uncle Al and my father are good friends."

"What?!"

"Your Uncle was in the store today and he and my father were having wine and cheese at nine o'clock in the morning. They're both in the back room sleeping—they drank too much wine."

"But how could he be? He's in Italy."

"He had to come back right away, something about a problem with the I.R.S."

"Gee I hope it's nothing serious."

"Johnny, who came in with your uncle? They won't leave the store."

"Don't worry Rosanna, they just want to protect my uncle, and they sure won't let anything happen to his friends, so you're in good hands." Johnny knew that his uncle always traveled with body guards because of the type of business he was in—gambling.

"Oh. OK. I feel better knowing that. Johnny, I can come up today."

"Great! What time?"

"I'll be there for dinner. I have to go now, I love you."

"I love you too." Johnny got cleaned up quickly, and wasted no time getting to the cafeteria. He was starved.

JOHNNY AND BILLY SEATED THEMSELVES AT THE TABLE. THE MEAL CONsisted of Johnny's favorite dish: spaghetti and meatballs. He was eating so fast.

"Hey, slow down Covini. You're going to end up choking to death."

"Billy, I'm starving. I told you we should've had breakfast."

"Well you might not be here for dinner if you keep that up. Listen, Jerry reminded me to mention to you you have a group therapy session from two to four."

"Group therapy? Man, I need some rest. You almost killed me this morning."

"Look you finish your lunch, catch about an hour's rest, be at therapy at two. You have to follow the rules, otherwise, Jerry may not let you and your band members use the music room. So let's just keep Jerry happy."

"OK, we'll keep Jerry happy."

"Good. Now listen, after dinner I want you to meet me at the music room—say about 7:30, and that's when you're going to take the endurance test. I probably won't see you at dinner, I have some things to do and I probably won't be back till seven."

"That's OK. I'm expecting Rosanna to have dinner with me."

"Johnny, I don't know if you've been informed, you're not supposed to have visitors here during the week—weekends only."

"Oh man, don't tell me this Billy." Johnny placed his fork down on the table. He rubbed his hand over his face. "You know what? This is really getting frustrating."

"Look Johnny, I don't make the rules."

"Yeah, but she called. She's already gonna come up."

"Hey look Covini, I'm really sorry, you're going to have to see Jerry about this. It's really not my department."

"OK, I'll see Jerry about it." Johnny pulled himself together and began to eat his food again. "Now what's all this stuff about an endurance test?"

"You'll find out tonight."

"What's this—suspense theater?"

"Oh funny Covini, real funny. Look, I don't want to crowd your mind. You're going to have a therapy session this afternoon and I'd like to see you get the most out of it."

"OK, as long as it is not another episode like this morning, 'cause I am beat."

"Don't worry, it won't take long. Hey look, I gotta get going."

"Hey, where you going in such a rush—you didn't finish your meal?"

"I got some session work this afternoon, and I gotta be in Philly by two o'clock."

"Hey, where you recording at?"

"Ever here of Far Out Studios?"

Johnny's hands dropped to the table. "Far Out Studios? You gotta be kidding!" Johnny couldn't forget the experience he had at Far Out Studios.

"You been to Far Out Studios before?"

"Look, you go ahead, I'll tell you about it later... oh, and uh Billy thanks for all your help, man."

"Just stay with the program Covini. See ya tonight."

Johnny finished eating and went back to his room to catch an hour's worth of z's.

JOHNNY ENTERED THE THERAPY ROOM. HE SAW JERRY STANDING LOOKing over some paperwork before the therapy session began. "Hey Jerry."

"Hey Johnny, how'd the workout with Billy go today?"

"I'm too tired to talk about it."

"Well if anybody can get you back in shape, it's Billy."

"Hey Jerry look, I got a problem."

Jerry set his papers down. "What's the trouble?"

"There's no trouble, it's just that I want Rosanna to be able to come up whenever she feels like it—you know, me and Rosanna, we like to be around each other."

"Johnny, look I know how you feel, but the center here, it's got its rules and regulations, and visitors during the week, that's a tough one."

"Look Jerry, Rosanna called today, she may be up for dinner today."

"Look we gotta get this therapy session under way. Rosanna can come up tonight, but that's it. I can make a special arrangement for you, but after that it's gonna have to be phone contact only."

Johnny's expression was not a pleasant one.

"C'mon Johnny, let's get this session under way, it looks like everyone's here."

The two hours Johnny had spent at therapy were very rewarding and helped him clear up a lot of his hang-ups and insecurities. For the first time in years, Johnny knew he was on the road to recovery.

Johnny went back to his room to get cleaned up, and then went out on the grounds to get a breath of fresh air, hoping Rosanna would be there in time to have dinner with him. As Johnny walked along, he noticed a car coming up the driveway. It was Rosanna. Some of the grounds keepers were looking on and whistling at this beautiful woman in a shiny new car. Johnny was smiling. He knew Rosanna was the type who didn't like to be flirted with, and he thought it was humorous. He walked over to the steps of the building and waited patiently for her to park her car. As she approached, Johnny said, "My God, you're beautiful." He held her in his arms. "You know, for the first time in my life, I really feel lucky. Rosanna, as long as I live, no one else will ever have you. I hope you can accept that."

"I already have, Johnny." They kissed.

Everyone on the grounds actually began to applaud. Johnny and Rosanna felt a bit embarrassed. They probably were the two happiest people in the world at that moment. Johnny suggested, "Let's go have dinner."

AS THEY WERE EATING DINNER, JERRY APPROACHED. "JERRY, I WANT YOU to meet someone. This is Rosanna. Rosanna—Jerry Simon. Hey Jerry, have a seat."

"Rosanna, very nice to meet you. Did you travel far to come here?"

"Philadelphia."

"Oh, you and Johnny are from the same neighborhood maybe?"

She smiled at Johnny, "Yes."

"I'll say one thing, you definitely look good together, and from the looks of it, you seem to care for each other very much. I wish you all the best."

"Hey Jerry, listen," said Johnny, "I wanted to know—"

"I know, you want to know when you can use the rehearsal room for your new band."

Rosanna looked to Johnny, "You didn't tell me anything about a new band!"

"I'm sorry, Rosanna. I'll tell you all about it later."

"You can use the rehearsal room Tuesday, Thursday, and Saturday evenings, three hour limit—6:30 to 9:30. They're the hours, and I trust I can depend on you to follow that schedule."

"Oh, no problem, Jerry. You can depend on me." Johnny was excited.

Jerry asked, "What did you have in mind in the way of music?"

"We plan to do our own music."

"Who's going to do the writing?"

"I'm hoping we can all have a little input in the writing."

"Johnny, you know it's a tough business—that much I know from what Billy told me, but he made it, and I think if you stick with him, you can make it too. You're fortunate to have someone like that on your side. Hey Johnny listen, I'll see you tomorrow at therapy. And Rosanna, it's been a pleasure."

"Nice meeting you, Jerry," Rosanna replied.

Johnny looked to Rosanna. "You know, I never knew there were any nice people left in this world. Where the hell have I been?"

"Now you have to concentrate on where you're going, Johnny. You must not look back, you must concentrate on the future and be the success that you were destined to be."

Johnny lifted his glass of milk to make a toast. Rosanna picked up her glass. They paused for a moment. "This is crazy—toasting with milk," said Johnny. They laughed. "Here's to us and the future," he said.

"To us and the future," Rosanna replied.

"Tonight you get to see me take the endurance test, Rosanna."

"What is the endurance test?"

"I don't know, that's all Billy told me."

"Is it some type of exercise?"

"I really wish I knew, I think Billy's trying to play tricks with my brain."

"Well, maybe it will be fun Johnny. Let's just wait and see."

"I don't know, for some reason I got a feeling it's going to be strenuous fun."

BACK AT JOHNNY'S ROOM, ROSANNA AND HE WERE JUST RELAXING ON the bed, watching TV. Johnny had about an hour to kill before meeting with Billy at the rehearsal room. He was glad that Jerry approved of Rosanna being there on a Monday. He needed Rosanna to comfort him. She was just what he needed.

"So, did my uncle and your father ever wake up today?"

"Yes, they woke up, but I had to call my mother to come to the store to help me. My father was in no condition to work after all the wine they drank. Your uncle wasn't feeling too good either. His body guards had to practically carry him out."

"How did you know they were body guards?"

"Well, I put things together after I spoke to you today. How long has your uncle been in that business?"

"What business?"

"Oh c'mon Johnny, my mother told me all about it today."

"Is your father involved in gambling at all with my uncle?"

"No. I think your uncle likes my father too much to let him get involved in that kind of business. You know, it was your uncle who lent my father the money to open up the hoagie shop."

"He's a good guy, my uncle. If it weren't for him, I probably would be in prison right now."

"Yeah, well you're not in prison, you're here, and I think this place will do you a lot of good. And besides, you got me too."

Rosanna's words put Johnny's mind at ease. He leaned towards her and held her tightly. She was beginning to make him feel like a new man. "Hey listen, we have to go meet Billy and see what he's got in store. I can't wait," he said sarcastically, "but first I have to call Danny Rosco. Oh shit! He never gave me his number. What time is it?" He grabbed for his alarm clock on the floor. It was 6:45. "Maybe he got that job at Sigway Shoes. I'll call information."

Johnny got the number and dialed. The phone rang at the other end. "Gee, I hope he got the job and he's working tonight." He wanted to contact Danny as soon as possible. Johnny was anxious to tell him the good news, that they would be able to use the rehearsal hall.

"Hello. Sigway Shoes."

"I need to speak to Danny Rosco."

"Mr. Rosco's with a customer right now. Can I take a message?"

"Look, tell him it's urgent."

"Well I'm sorry sir, but we prefer not to interrupt a salesman when he's with a customer."

"Look pal, it's an emergency. Would you get him to the phone?" Johnny's anxiety was causing him to be very forward.

"OK. Hold on."

"I hate these sales people," Johnny whispered to Rosanna.

"This is Danny Rosco, can I help you?"

"Danny, it's me—Johnny Covini."

"Hey man, what's the emergency?"

"Look I got the OK. We can start rehearsing here Tuesday, Thursday, and Saturday nights—6:30 to 9:30."

"Hey Johnny, that's great. Do we start tomorrow?"

"It looks good. I'll touch base with you tomorrow and let you know what's happening and when we can start."

"Hey man, let me give you my home number, in case you can't reach me here."

"Hey Rosanna, hand me that pencil and paper, will you. OK Danny, let's have it."

"555-7686."

"555-7686—got it."

"Hey Johnny, I gotta go. I have this customer waiting."

"OK. Talk to you tomorrow." Johnny hung up the phone and turned to Rosanna. "OK. C'mon, let's go see Billy."

The room was empty. Billy and his musicians hadn't shown up yet. "Typical musicians," Johnny muttered to Rosanna, "never on time." Johnny sat behind the drums.

"I've never seen you behind a set of drums before. You look

so comfortable—so confident. How can you play so many different things at one time? All those drums—all those cymbals?"

"Well, you don't play them all at one time. You use the bass, snare, and high-hat and create a basic four-four beat."

"What's a four-four beat?"

"You know, it's a timing pattern."

"I'm a little confused."

"Well, when Billy gets back, I think by the sounds of it, the endurance test means I'm going to have to play. I think then you'll be able to understand it a little more clearly."

The musicians and Billy entered the room "Hey Billy," Johnny asked, "how'd the session go?"

"It went well, Johnny. I'm really proud of it. You see, I wrote the music, and I think it's got potential."

"Hey Billy, I want you to meet Rosanna."

"I'll say one thing for you Covini, you sure got good taste in women." Rosanna was embarrassed and blushing. "Glad to meet you, Rosanna. It's a pleasure."

Rosanna smiled. "Glad to meet you too, Billy."

Billy turned to the musicians. "Fellows, I'd like you to meet Johnny Covini. He's a drummer too, one of the smarter musicians."

Johnny shook hands with all the musicians and introduced them to Rosanna. "Billy, I OK'd it with Jerry. He said Rosanna could be here tonight."

"Fine with me," Billy replied. "OK, you ready for the endurance test?"

"I'm ready."

"OK. Here's some drumsticks, go warm up on that drum pad near that guitar amp while the guys get tuned up."

Johnny was practicing some single-stroke roles on the drum pad. He was nervous and felt very uncoordinated. He was beginning to sweat. He looked to Rosanna and frowned. She smiled, but she knew Johnny was nervous. She almost felt sorry for him.

"OK. Johnny. You ready?" Billy asked.

"About as ready as I'll ever be. Let's go to it."

Johnny walked to the drum set and seated himself. His body was shaking from the anxiety. He didn't want to let Billy down. He was determined to give it his best shot.

Billy felt that Johnny was comfortable now. "OK Johnny I'll give you a count of four, then you come out playing. This is a ten-minute jam, a high speed rock'n'roll number that my man Jake here wrote." Billy pointed to the guitar player. "OK, ready gentlemen? 1—2—3," as he shouted four, Johnny hit the snare drum with an accent. They began to rock.

Johnny began with confidence and provided a good beat for the band. Rosanna looked to him and smiled; she was excited. It was her first time watching him play. He was playing the drums with grace, however, Billy was signalling him to play harder—with more volume. They continued to play and five minutes passed.

Sweat was pouring down Johnny's face. His volume and tempo began to decline. He hadn't played rock'n'roll for quite some time, and was out of shape. Billy walked over to Johnny and shouted in his ear, "Pick up the tempo, man. And play louder! You're losing the momentum." His volume dropped even lower. He just couldn't seem to play fast and hard. Billy knew Johnny would have to build a lot of endurance to be able to play rock'n'roll drums in big stadiums. But Johnny had never really played with musicians of this caliber before. Billy and his band-mates were professionals, and very well seasoned.

Eight minutes had passed. Johnny was played out, barely able to hold the sticks in his hands. His tempo and volume were dropping rapidly. The song was reaching its end. Being a musician, Johnny's feel for music told him there would be some breaks and fill-ins at the end of the song.

Billy got Johnny's attention. He was signaling him and going through the motions to play the fills. Johnny played the fills and they were way off. His accuracy had never been worse. He was losing time and barely being heard. He'd had a very trying day, and was exhausted.

The song ended. Johnny wasn't thinking, and ended four bars too late. He stood up and was breathing heavily. His clothes were soaked with sweat. He handed his sticks to Billy. "You put me through a hard day today, man, and this was murder." He took another deep breath. "Let's go, Rosanna. See you tomorrow Billy."

As they left the room, Billy shouted, "Hey Covini—good job." Billy knew Johnny had the determination to succeed and felt happy for him.

Rosanna and Johnny entered his room. Johnny collapsed on the bed. Rosanna got him some water and a towel. He gulped the water down quickly, and took a deep breath. Rosanna began to wipe the sweat off his face.

"Man, I think Billy's a little too pushy."

"He just wanted to see what you can do, Johnny."

"See what I can do? I think he was trying to kill me."

"Don't worry Johnny, pretty soon you will be able to play twenty minutes with lots of strength and energy."

Johnny held Rosanna close to him.

"How 'bout if I fill the tub with hot water," said Rosanna. "You can soak for a while, and then I can rub your back for you".

"Now that's the best thing I've heard all day!"

"Just relax till the tub fills." As Rosanna walked toward the bathroom to prepare Johnny's hot bath, he was excited by her beauty, and couldn't believe he had found someone like her who was willing to put up with his crazy life.

While Johnny was soaking in the tub, Rosanna straightened up his room a bit. The bathroom door was half open. "Rosanna, can you come in here a minute?"

She walked in hesitantly. She found herself getting a bit excited, watching Johnny soak in the tub.

"You know, Rosanna, maybe it wouldn't be a bad idea if…

Rosanna knew what he was about to say and interrupted.

"No Johnny, I don't think I should soak in the tub with you."

"I won't tell anybody."

"I'm sorry Johnny, I can't. Now if you want me to stay and rub your back, get dried off and put your pants on. I'll wait for you in the room."

"OK, OK—I'll be out in a minute." For the next ten minutes, Johnny stayed in the tub. Rosanna propped herself on the bed and watched TV. There was total silence.

Johnny dried off and found a pair of pants hanging on the door, that Rosanna had placed there in the course of straightening up the room. He entered the room and was anxious for her to rub his back. He sat on the edge of the bed. They embraced. He began kissing her with a fierce passion. She had never been handled in this manner before. Rosanna was quite naive, and Johnny's actions were beginning to make her uncomfortable.

"Johnny—wait. You're too hungry. Please stop, I'm not ready for this."

"Rosanna, I can't go on like this much longer. Somewhere along the line we gotta break the ice." He was very frustrated at this point.

"Please, be patient with me." She moved over and asked him to lay on his stomach. She began to rub his back. Johnny's tension was starting to ease. Rosanna's touch made his worries and frustrations begin to dissolve.

"Rosanna, I'm sorry. I get so crazy when I'm around you. It's just that whenever you're around, I just can't help myself. You get me so damn worked up."

"It's OK Johnny, I understand. Just relax and I'll make you feel better." Rosanna knew what Johnny was going through, but because of the traditions and moral upbringing so vital in Italian families, she knew there was no way she could lose her virginity before marriage. And marriage was the furthest thing from Johnny's mind. It was as tough on her as it was on Johnny, but the love they had for one another would keep them together no matter what.

Fifteen minutes had passed and Rosanna had to be leaving. "Johnny, I have to go now. I have a long drive and I want to get home early."

"Hey Rosanna, it's early yet."

"I really better be leaving now. You can call me tomorrow."

He didn't want her to leave. He wished she could stay the night. There was no doubt in his mind, he'd finally met the right woman and knew he would soon have to ask her to marry him. Before Rosanna could get her coat on. Johnny put his arms around her. "Hey, I'll call you tomorrow."

Rosanna smiled, "I'll be waiting."

"I love you, Rosanna."

"I love you too, Johnny." They held each other tightly.

"Good-bye, Johnny."

"Good-bye, Rosanna." She left quickly. He felt sad and was exhausted from the trying day that he'd had. He climbed into bed and fell fast asleep.

TUESDAY MORNING JOHNNY WAS AWAKENED BY A LOUD KNOCK AT the door. He was feeling very groggy and sore all over. "Who's there?" he moaned.

"It's me Johnny, Billy."

"Yeah, hold on Billy." He rose slowly. He was stiff and could barely move. He hobbled over to the door and opened it. "Hey Billy, come on in."

"Hey man, it's eight o'clock, you should be up and ready by now."

"Eight o'clock? I was dead to the world."

"Hey listen man, why don't you get yourself cleaned up and get a good breakfast. I gotta go see a friend of mine who's hurting pretty bad. He's doing drugs and drinking pretty heavily, and I think the only way to get him here is to go see him first. He called me about an hour ago. He couldn't sleep all night, and he's talking about suicide. I gotta go see him Johnny. I'll be back about noon, and then we'll work out."

"Yeah sure, Billy, I understand. I'll see you when you get back. I hope your friend makes it OK." Billy left and the phone rang. Johnny picked it up quickly. "Hello?"

"Hey Johnny, what's happening?" It was Danny.

"Man, what are you doing up so early?"

"Man, I can't sleep in this noisy city."

"What's up?"

"Well, when do we start to rehearse? You said Tuesday, Thursday, and Saturdays, and today's Tuesday."

"OK, I don't see why we can't start tonight."

"OK listen, Stevie and I will be up this evening. Starting next week, we have a full group—Jerry Carvelli and Mike Danella will start working with us then. You know this afternoon, Stevie and I will be in Norristown."

"Hey, that's right down the road from here. What's going on?"

"Stevie's going to be doing some session work for Freddie Bohnner."

"Hey, I heard of him, he's a great guitarist."

"Stevie asked me to go along so he could introduce me to some people, and maybe I can get some session work myself."

"What time are you guys leaving?"

"Stevie's picking me up about ten."

"Hey listen, I wonder if you could do me a favor."

"Sure Johnny, what do you need?"

"Maybe you guys could leave a little early and pick up my drums for me."

"Oh, you mean over at Harry's Bar?"

"No, not them, they belong to Harry. Besides, they're junk.

Listen, where I used to live, you ask for a kid named Joey Cunningham. He lives in the apartment next to mine with his parents. My drums are in old man Johnson's garage. The kid takes care of them for me, and he will take you to them. If there's any problem, just tell him to call me and I'll tell him it's OK."

"OK, Johnny, no problem. We'll be there about 11:30. We'll just load Stevie's van up, and that'll do it."

"OK, see you then."

Johnny took a hot shower, got breakfast, and went back to his room and relaxed till the guys came. About eleven o'clock Johnny decided to wait outside and get a breath of fresh air. Within twenty minutes, Danny and Stevie were coming up the driveway. Johnny was happy to see his friends approaching. They pulled up close to the main entrance, and climbed out of the van slowly. They looked troubled.

"Man what's wrong with you guys? Did somebody die? Why the gloomy faces?"

"Johnny, there's a problem," said Danny.

"What problem? Man, don't tell me somebody stole my drums."

"Look Johnny, take it easy. I got some bad news."

Johnny was beginning to worry. "Look man, where's my drums?"

"They were burned up in a fire. Old man Johnson's garage went up in flames with your drums in it."

Johnny sat down on the step and took a deep breath. He was devastated. His drum set was worth at least five thousand dollars, and little Joey always kept them in good shape for him—he cleaned them practically every day. In return, Johnny allowed him to play them whenever he wished.

As Danny saw his disappointment, he looked to Stevie, wondering if he should tell Johnny the rest of the bad news. "You better tell him Danny," said Stevie.

"Tell me what?" Johnny asked, "You mean it gets worse?"

"Look Johnny. I really regret to have to tell you this, but..."

"Look Rosco, spit it out man! You're really busting my chops, you know that?"

"The little kid Joey was killed in the fire."

"Killed? Killed?! But how?"

"Nobody knows, Johnny. Somehow he got trapped in the garage. They're still investigating."

Johnny looked at the two men. "Burned up. Poor little Joey— burned up in a fire." Tears began to cover his eyes. "Look man, I don't feel too good. Can we forget rehearsal tonight?"

The two men replied, "Yeah, sure Johnny." They felt sorry for him and his little friend Joey. "You just take it easy man, and I'll call you in a couple days," said Danny.

It was a cloudy day and rain began to fall slowly. The grounds looked deserted. Johnny sat still and stared, never before had he felt so alone. Even the thought of Rosanna couldn't ease his mind at that moment. He'd loved Joey like a little brother. Johnny muddled his way back into the building. He walked into the recreation room. He picked up a cue stick and began hitting balls on the pool table. Balls were banging around from rail to rail. He was plagued with anger. He hit the cue ball with great force and sent the eight ball flying off the table, crashing into a lamp that was setting next to the sofa. Fortunately, no one was in the recreation room. The lamp was shattered.

Hearing the noise, Jerry Simon entered the room. "I can see that someone isn't very happy today."

"You see good Jerry—twenty-twenty vision." He hit the cue ball once again with great force to a dead ringer in pocket left.

"I think you better cool it Covini, before someone gets the eight ball between the eyes."

"Look Jerry, I'm shooting pool, it was just a little accident."

"Come on Covini, hang up the stick."

"Look Jerry! I came in here to shoot pool, and that's just what I'm going to do."

"I don't want to have to take the stick from you, Johnny."

Johnny flew into a rage. "Come on, let's see you take it from me, Mr. Rehabilitation! Let's see what you can do!"

Billy had just gotten back from counseling his friend, and heard all the shouting. He entered the room and interrupted, "Put the stick down Johnny, it's all over."

"This is between him and me, Billy."

"Not anymore Johnny. We can end this right now, or things can get pretty messy." Billy was angered.

Johnny was stunned. He stared at Billy. There was fire in his eyes. His hands gripped the cue stick tightly. He threw the stick to the floor and left the room in frustration.

"Man, what the hell happened here?" Billy asked.

"I don't know," said Jerry, "something must have gotten him upset."

"Man, it looks like we got one angry dude on our hands. This guy is scary."

"Billy, don't give up on him. He needs your help, as well as mine."

Billy shook his head. He leaned over the pool table and took a deep breath. He was worried. "Let me go see if I can talk to him."

Johnny rushed back to his room and actually began to pack his clothes. Billy entered Johnny's room. "Man, what's troubling you? And what the hell do you think you're doing?"

"I'm leaving, man. I'm getting the hell out of here. I've had enough of this bull shit. I don't need all this crap. I was better off on the streets."

"Yeah sure, the easy way out."

"That's right, the easy way out!" Johnny shouted.

"Well, there is no easy way out!" Billy shouted back. "Your problem is that stinking attitude of yours. Ain't nobody can tell you nothing! Well let me tell you something, Mr. Covini, your attitude isn't worth anything if you can't deal with the problems of this crazy world—all you'll be is another statistic, another victim of your environment. Look man, can't you see where I'm coming from? There's nothing out there on the streets. Let it go, at least here you have the chance to be somebody. You're a good musician—you can make it. You can do something good with your life if you just give it a chance. Now look, I don't know what's bothering you today, but we can work it out."

Johnny finished packing. He put his duffle bag around his shoulder. "Are you through Billy? Are you through? Because if you're not, that's tough. I'm leaving, man."

Jerry entered the room. "Johnny, what are you doing? If you leave here, you're going to jail."

Billy turned to Jerry. "Forget it, Jerry. It's all over, man. It's all over. This guy doesn't want help."

As Johnny walked down the hall, Jerry shouted to him, "Johnny, I'm going to have to call the police."

"Call whoever you want. Who the hell cares!"

Johnny rushed out of the building and started down the driveway to exit the grounds. Lo and behold, Rosanna was coming up the driveway. Her mother was with her. Her mother had received word that a relative was hospitalized in Allentown and wasn't doing very well. She had asked Rosanna to drive her up there that afternoon while Rosanna's father took care of the hoagie shop. Rosanna had decided to prepare a hoagie and asked her mother if they could go about a half hour out of their way to give Johnny the hoagie. This was a great opportunity for Rosanna to introduce her mother to Johnny.

As she entered the grounds, Rosanna looked on in dismay. She couldn't understand why Johnny was heading for the exit with his duffle bag over his shoulder. She stopped the car. Rolling down the window nervously, she asked, "Johnny, where are you going?"

"Go home, Rosanna, and leave me alone." He continued to walk.

Rosanna quickly put the car in reverse. The car drifted back slowly. "Where are you going—what's wrong?"

"There's nothing wrong. Just go home."

Rosanna's mother was fifty years old and very pretty, like her daughter. She didn't look her age. She was a very pleasant woman, and everyone liked and respected her. However, she was beginning to get very angry. "Rosanna, what are you doing? Stop the car. Why is this man doing this? I think we should leave immediately."

Rosanna was beginning to get angered also. She was fed up with his stubborn attitude. She stopped the car, and jumped out in a rage. She ran toward him. Rosanna's mother put her hands together in a praying fashion and looked up. "What the hell is wrong with you? Why are you so stubborn? Why won't you tell me where you're going?"

"I don't owe you an explanation! I don't owe you anything!" Johnny shouted.

"What do you mean you don't owe me anything? What am I some piece of dirt all of a sudden?"

"Look Rosanna—"

"No. You look, Johnny Covini. Who do you think you are? Do you just think you can turn people's feelings on and off like that?" Rosanna snapped her fingers. "What kind of a man are you anyway?" She began to cry.

"I don't have to listen to this, Rosanna."

"Yes you do, damnit! You do have to listen—that's your trouble, you don't want to listen to anybody."

"Look, I have some problems."

"So you're going to leave? You're going to give up? You know you can't leave here. You know you'll end up in jail. What's the problem that's causing you to do this? For God's sake, grow up, will you! Grow up Johnny, before it's too late."

Johnny just stood and stared. He was shocked. Rosanna looked away, toward the entrance to the grounds. He continued to stare at her. Johnny felt guilty. He dropped his bag to the ground.

She had broken him down. She had managed to bring him to his senses, and calmed the troubled sea within him. He turned her towards him. "I didn't think you had it in you, Rosanna." They smiled at one another. Billy and Jerry and some of the staff looked on.

"Yeah, I guess it's rubbing off."

"You know I didn't mean anything I said. You know I need you more than anything in the world."

Rosanna just nodded. Johnny clutched her in his arms and kissed her. "Johnny, I want you to promise me something. I want you to promise me you will be a success and never give up."

"I promise, I'll never give up."

"Johnny, I have someone I want you to meet."

He looked to the car and noticed the woman. "Who is that in the car?"

"It's my mother."

"Your mother? By the way, how come you're here today?"

"I have to drive her to Allentown to visit my aunt in the hospital. I wanted to bring you a hoagie on the way up and say hello, since it was on our way."

"I don't know, Rosanna, she probably hates me now."

"Come on Johnny, she won't hate you."

"Oh yeah, just how do you know that?"

"Because she knows that her daughter's in love."

Johnny walked toward the car reluctantly. They were holding hands. "Hey, what's your mother's name, anyway?"

"Just call her Mrs. Angelini."

Meeting Rosanna's mother for the first time made him very nervous, especially under these conditions. He couldn't seem to stand still.

"Mother, I want you to meet Johnny Covini." Rosanna's mother extended her hand out the car window and smiled.

Johnny extended his hand and said, "Nice to meet you, Mrs. Angelini."

"It's nice to meet you, too, Johnny," she replied.

Johnny felt embarrassed. "Yeah, well—uh... I better get back in now, Rosanna. I see Jerry looking on, hopefully he hasn't called the police yet." He could not think of any words to say to Rosanna's mother. Johnny and Rosanna kissed quickly. As Johnny began to walk back, Rosanna shouted, "Johnny wait, I have something for you." Rosanna handed him the hoagie. "You better hurry, you don't want to get in trouble. I love you."

"I love you too."

As Rosanna drove off, she and her mother had brief words about Johnny. Her mother was too concerned about Rosanna's aunt in the hospital in Allentown. As Johnny approached the entrance, Jerry was looking on. Johnny felt a bit ashamed of his actions toward Jerry. He stopped suddenly. He could not look Jerry in the eye. He looked to the left and then to the right.

"Hey Jerry, look—uh... there was this little kid, you know, back at the neighborhood." Johnny began to get all choked up. His eyes began to fill with tears. "He was like a little brother to me." He began to cry.

At this point, all Jerry heard was a bit of mumbling. "Johnny, what's wrong? What's troubling you?" He came to Johnny's aid, and placed his arm around Johnny's shoulder. Johnny could barely stand up. Little Joey's death was just too much for him to handle after everything else he had been through. "Come on, Johnny, we'll go in and talk about it. You're going to be OK."

As they walked by the admissions office, Billy had been checking some files. He was quite frustrated and could not understand why Johnny acted the way he did. He heard Johnny crying. He immediately dropped the files and proceeded to see what the problem was.

Mildred Stone was sitting at the admissions desk. "My God, what could be the problem?" Even though she and Johnny had their disagreements, she still felt she had to fill her obligations at the Welsley Center. With the three of them now assisting him, Johnny realized how much he needed their help.

"I'm sorry everybody, I didn't mean to act the way I did."
He was still crying. They began to become very concerned. They
knew from past experience that he could be facing an emotional
crisis and even a nervous breakdown.

Jerry spoke. "Look Billy, why don't you take him to your
office, I think you can calm him down. I'll be in in about fifteen
minutes. At this point I think just one of us needs to be with him
for a little while."

Mildred felt sorry for Johnny, and felt a bit confused. She
really thought Johnny was beginning to get well. They all knew by
now he needed more help than they thought. His nerves were weak.
His withdrawal from drugs and alcohol was taking a drastic effect,
and little Joey's death would be an event he would never forget.
Jerry looked to Mildred. "Let Billy be with him for a while. I'll let
you know how he's doing later."

IT WAS NOW 4:00 P.M. BILLY HAD SPENT THREE HOURS WITH JOHNNY
and had managed to calm him down. Jerry dropped in occasionally. He did not stay for any long period of time. He knew that they
both had a good rapport because of their similarities in the music
business. Billy had explained to him that he could speak to him
about anything, even his most personal inner feelings, and assured
him he could confide in him. He told him that he needed someone
that he could trust one hundred percent. Billy felt a deep responsibility toward Johnny, maybe Billy needed a friend he could trust also.

Johnny felt relieved. He felt like a load was lifted off his
shoulder. From that point on, Billy would be a big part of Johnny's
life.

THE FOLLOWING MORNING JOHNNY WAS PRESSING A 150 POUND BARBELL
on the bench. Billy counted, "Seven, eight..." Johnny was groan-
ing. Halfway through the ninth press, he began to roar. "Come on

Johnny, you can do it—Nine!" With all his might, Johnny pushed harder and made the count of nine. "OK Johnny, One More!" Billy shouted.

Johnny took a deep breath and began to push. The veins in his neck appeared as though they were going to burst, but he was determined. "One more Johnny, just one more. Reach down in your soul, remember the power. Nothing can stop you." As Billy spoke, Johnny was halfway there. He let out a giant roar and completed the tenth press. Billy had just introduced him to some new exercises. The most strenuous was doing push-ups on his fingers with a fifty-pound weight on his back. He could barely do a push-up on his hands, let alone his fingers.

Billy had demonstrated the exercise to him. Johnny had placed a fifty-pound weight on Billy's back. He did twenty push-ups. Johnny was amazed. He took his turn and collapsed on the first try. "We'll start you out with a lighter weight, then you can work your way up," Billy explained, "But remember, your goal is fifty pounds two weeks from now." Johnny felt this exercise was impossible for him to do. Billy saw his discouragement. "Don't get discouraged, just do it."

"OK. Two weeks." Johnny replied. After exercising and weight training, the two walked to the center of the track. Billy began martial arts training.

"Johnny, I want you to know martial arts is not just an exercise, or self-defense, it's a very spiritual and scientific concept. You can use it as a drummer. You'll be able to concentrate, play with better timing, more feeling, and be clearer and more precise. Remember these things when you're playing. A clear mind makes a better drummer. A strong body makes a louder and more powerful drummer, and your speed will be incredible. You'll need all these things if you want to be in the big leagues and play the big auditoriums. A good drummer makes a good band."

AS THE DAYS WENT ON, JOHNNY WAS VISITED BY ROSANNA AND HIS UNCLE Al every weekend. His physical, mental, and most of all, spiritual condition began to improve rapidly. He was probably in the best shape of his life. At the end of the two week period, he reached his goal, and was able to do twenty push-ups on his fingers with a fifty-pound weight on his back. Both he and Billy were impressed with his progress. Johnny's nights were not boring. Billy would work with him on the drums the nights that he wasn't rehearsing with his new band. He proved to be a hard worker. All he needed was to be given a chance. He received a new set of drums at the center from his uncle Al. Al had heard about the fire that destroyed his drums and took little Joey's life. He felt very bad for his nephew and took the time out to go to a local music store and have a salesman give him advise on the best set of drums to buy for Johnny. Now Johnny could use his own drums at the Center and not Billy's.

His weekends were quite occupied also. Rosanna was there every Saturday and Sunday to see him as their relationship became stronger than ever. Occasionally she would bring her mother, but could not convince her father to take the drive up to meet Johnny. Even Uncle Al and his wife were beginning to see more of Johnny. His band members would come up early on Saturdays to play basketball before their Saturday night rehearsals. He was beginning to realize there was more to life than sex, drugs, and rock'n'roll.

For once in his life, Johnny felt that he had some good friends and a purpose for living. Not to mention a wonderful relationship with a beautiful and caring woman. This time he was on the right road—the road to recovery. He felt born again .

Even his friends from the old neighborhood were coming to see him. Some of them he hadn't seen for years. He didn't realize so many people cared about him. Johnny asked many of them if they had seen Lefty around. No one had seen him for quite some time. Johnny was puzzled. He could be dead, he thought.

16

* * * * * * * * * *

EIGHT MONTHS HAD PASSED. BILLY AND JOHNNY WERE RUNNING ALONG the roadside, finishing up their morning road work. It was December and the smell of Christmas was in the air. Billy began to slow up. Johnny was puzzled. Billy had never slowed down like that before. He finally stopped running and began to limp.

"Billy, what's wrong?"

"It's this damn ankle. It's been giving me trouble for a while now."

"It's probably from beating on those damn bass drums too long."

"Yeah, I think you're right. I gotta sit down Covini."

"Yeah, come on man, sit over here. Let me help you." The two men sat on an old tree stump that sat back off the winding back road.

Billy began rubbing his ankle. As both breathed heavily, Johnny asked, "So how am I doing, Billy?"

"You're going to make it, Johnny, but we have to keep working. How's your band doing?"

"Good. We have a rehearsal tonight. We're arranging our last song tonight."

"What do you have planned?"

"Well, we have a name for our band."

"Oh yeah. What's that?"

"Midnight Angel."

"Hey, I like that, man, and then what?"

"Well, then we hit the studio, and hopefully some record company will give us a recording contract."

"Hey Johnny, wait a minute. Don't go so fast. It doesn't happen like that."

"What do you mean?"

"I mean record companies get hundreds of tapes every day from bands. What makes you think your music is more tasteful than the other stuff they receive?"

"Hey, come on Billy. I thought you said keep a positive attitude."

"Yeah, well I just don't want you to think everything comes that easy. I mean, it might, you know I could be wrong, but just the same, you may have a lot of hard work ahead of you. And I think with that in mind, then you and your band will find true success."

"Billy, you're really a talker."

"Yeah, maybe so but right now, you gotta get me back to the center, this ankle is killing me."

Johnny helped his friend up and put Billy's arm over his shoulder. Johnny laughed, "Hey Billy you want to try some of those karate techniques now?"

Billy found Johnny's statement amusing, and the two laughed together despite Billy's ailing ankle.

THE FOLLOWING DAY CAME QUICKLY. IT WAS ANOTHER DAY OF WORKING out, and another day of therapy. Johnny was a different man. It appeared as if he'd never had a bad attitude. The once unhealthy, broken down man was now a man of self-respect and strength.

Billy had gone to the doctor that morning to get his ankle checked. Johnny had no problem working out alone. His worst fears had left him. He had learned to set goals and reach them, and was preparing for the greatest goal of his life. As Johnny curled a barbell, his biceps were reaching their potential. They began to grow and ripple as an amazing change took place in his body. He placed a three-foot long two-by-four across a chair, put his hands on both ends of the board, and began to dip down and up again twenty times. He then placed a rope over his head, onto his shoulders with a twenty-five-pound weight on each end and repeated the exercise twenty more times. He went through his entire routine without Billy that day, and felt very proud. Once again, he felt independent, but with a new outlook.

JOHNNY AND HIS BAND WERE HAPPY TO BRING ON THE NIGHT. THEIR REhearsal was exciting. They were beginning to play with vigor and enthusiasm. His drumming was getting sharper and faster. He sat behind the drums with a black tank top. His hair was now shoulder length, and styled well. His muscles were attractive as sweat began to cover them. He played with grace and power. With his dark hair, and new healthy look, he appeared as the perfect image of the ultimate rock'n'roll drummer.

Danny and Stevie were playing well, as they worked hard to affect the status of the band. Stevie soared along the neck of the guitar, as he let it scream with rock'n'roll sounds and pulsating rhythms. Jerry Carvelli, the lead vocalist, belted out some of the finest high notes ever. Mike Danella, the keyboardist, was sharper than ever. When the band ended its song, the fellas let out a hearty "All right!"

"Hey man, we're really kicking!" said Danny.

"Man this is the best rock'n'roll band I've ever been in," added Stevie. "What do you think, Johnny?"

"Man, I'm glad you fellas talked me into this. Next to Rosanna, this is the best thing that ever happened to me. We're gonna make it fellas, I know we're gonna make it."

ON FRIDAY MORNING, BILLY'S ANKLE WAS BANDAGED AND HE WOULD have to supervise Johnny while on crutches for about a week. Throughout the workout, Billy was astonished at Johnny's accomplishments. After lunch, Johnny assisted Billy in working with some new patients which Johnny found very rewarding. He couldn't believe it—he was actually able to help other people.

Later that night, Johnny spoke briefly with Rosanna on the phone and retired early. Saturday he and Billy took a break from working out. They decided they needed to refrain from physical activity for the weekend. He managed to join in on a therapy session conducted by both Billy and Jerry, and spent a few hours in the afternoon with Rosanna. Saturday night was spent with the guys rehearsing their music.

EARLY SUNDAY MORNING THERE WAS A KNOCK AT JOHNNY'S DOOR. IT was Rosanna. He had left the door unlocked because he knew she would come up some time that morning. He was sound asleep. She entered the room and sat at the edge of the bed and woke him with a kiss. "Good morning, sleepy head," Rosanna whispered as Johnny slowly woke up.

"Yeah, it sure is a good morning with you here." He held her in his arms. "You're here early this morning, aren't you?"

"I couldn't help it, I miss you."

"I miss you, too. I'm really glad you're here—you know that? I'm really glad you're here."

He held her tightly. They began to kiss and caress one another. He put his hand on Rosanna's leg, and began to move it upward. She was wearing a black leather skirt with black lace stockings, black heels, and a bright red blouse. Her coat was fur. It was a present from her mother and father. Their business was doing well. Rosanna had a very shapely figure, and a beautiful face. Her hair was black and styled to perfection. Johnny was overwhelmed by her beauty. He was becoming very excited. He continued moving his hand up her thigh. She began getting excited also. She stopped him. "No, Johnny, we have to wait."

"I'm sorry, Rosanna."

"It's OK I understand, but I promised my family I would wait till I was married."

The phone rang. It was Danny Rosco. "Johnny, I have some good news. We go in the studio tomorrow afternoon."

"How'd we do that?"

"Jerry Carvelli's cousin owns Powerhouse Studios, and he can get us some studio time free."

"How about that, Rosanna—we're going to make a tape! So Danny, is this guy professional?"

"He's the best. He's got the best sound people working for him. We can't miss. Johnny, when he's through with us, the record companies will love it. Things are happening Covini, looks like we're on our way."

"We're gonna make it this time Danny, we're gonna make it."

"OK, I'll pick you up at twelve o'clock tomorrow."

"OK See you tomorrow." Johnny hung up. "This is it Rosanna, I can feel it. I know it's going to work. I love you Rosanna— I love you—I love you—I love you!" Johnny grabbed her and kissed her on the cheek. Rosanna began to laugh and was very happy for him. "Hey, wait a minute—how am I going to get out of here tomorrow?"

"Well I don't know about tomorrow, but I got a pass for you today, and you're coming with me."

"So I see you have pull around here."

"That's right. I spoke to Jerry in his office before I came to your room, and you and I are going to your Uncle Al's for dinner with him, your Aunt and my mother and father."

"Hey, that sounds great, when are we leaving?"

"As soon as you get out of this bed and get cleaned up."

"Hey, I wonder if my Aunt Carmella is going to make some of that homemade pasta? Gee, I can still remember being a kid and going to Aunt Carmella's for dinner. I can still remember that sweet smell of the homemade sauce slowly cooking while she was preparing some homemade bread. She would always get mad at my Uncle Al for giving me wine—man that wine was delicious!"

"Your Uncle Al was at our home last night and said that your aunt will make everything you like, and as a special treat, I made you an Italian love cake."

"What's an Italian love cake?"

"Don't worry about it, when you taste it, you'll love it."

Johnny sat back on the bed just before he went to take a shower. He held Rosanna and looked in her eyes, "Well, I don't need any Italian love cake to make me love you, but I'll take the cake just the same." They both laughed.

"Go take your shower. We have to leave." She slapped him on the butt.

"OK I'm going, I'm going!"

LEAVING THE BUILDING, JOHNNY WAS SURE TO THANK JERRY FOR LETTING him have the afternoon with Rosanna and her family. While riding down the expressway to Philadelphia, Johnny said, "Hey you drive pretty fast for a girl, you know."

"Yes I know, my father told me the same thing. You men. You think you're the only ones who can drive fast. This is 1980, not 1920 Italy."

"Hey, how about letting me drive?"

"No Johnny, not until you get your license back."

"You sound like my mother did."

"Well I'm not your mother. I'm your lover and friend."

Johnny smiled. "I know."

ROSANNA DROVE THROUGH THE BIG BLACK GUARDED GATES. THEY PROceeded up the driveway, and then walked to the big white doors.

Rosanna knocked at the door.

"I hope your father likes me, Rosanna."

"Yeah, I hope so too, Johnny."

"Thanks, Rosanna, I needed that."

Uncle Al answered the door. "Johnny! How are you?"

"I'm OK Uncle Al."

"Rosanna—come right in. Ahh, you have a beautiful woman here, Johnny—you treat her with respect, you understand?" Johnny just smiled. He slapped Johnny lightly on the cheek. "Let me take your coats. Go ahead, go into the dining room, you two." Uncle Al was very happy to have Johnny there, it reminded him of the old days.

Aunt Carmella and Rosanna's mother were in the kitchen. Rosanna's father was in the living room. The two entered the dining room. Uncle Al followed shortly after putting their coats away.

"Johnny," said Uncle Al, "I want you to meet Rosanna's father, Pondolona—he's in the living room."

Rosanna interrupted, "Mr. Mundella, are my mother and Carmella in the kitchen?"

"Yes, Rosanna."

"I'll go help them."

"Uncle Al," Johnny asked, "can I see Aunt Carmella first?"

"No, not yet, Johnny, I want her to see you when you're sitting at the dining table—you know, like when you were a young boy. Come with me."

They entered the living room. "Pondolona, I want you to meet my nephew, Johnny Covini."

Pondolona stood up. "Ahh Johnny, good to meet you." He gave Johnny a hug and patted him on the back. Having lots of respect for Al, and being grateful for financial backing when he was a poor man, Pondolona wanted Al to know that he was proud to have his nephew court his daughter, and would be very happy to give her in marriage if the question was raised. "Johnny, your Uncle Al has always been good to me, and I want you to know that I am very happy for you and Rosanna. Any nephew of Al's is OK with me. I want you to take good care of my daughter. I know how much she cares for you."

"Don't worry Mr. Angelini, I'll take care of your daughter. I promise you."

"I think we should have a drink," said Al.

"Soda for me, Uncle Al."

As he poured the drinks, Al said, "Whiskey for my friend and me, soda for my nephew Johnny." He handed them their drinks. "This is one of the happiest days of my life. My good friend Pondolona's daughter and my nephew going together, that's wonderful. Johnny, I want to make a toast to yours and Rosanna's future. May you always have love, peace, and prosperity—and make lots of babies." The three laughed and toasted. "Let's go to the dining room." They entered and sat at the dining room table.

Aunt Carmella entered with a big dish of pasta while Mrs. Angelini carried the salad. Carmella was a little woman with black hair and a beautiful complexion. She wore a beautiful flowered dress that blended well with her bright smile and brown eyes. Rosanna was holding the sausage and meatballs in a big dish. There was lots of bread and good wine at the table. There was plenty to eat for everybody. Aunt Carmella stopped for a second with the dish in her hands and stared at Johnny. Uncle Al quickly sat up and took the dish from her. She walked around the table to Johnny. Johnny stood up. Everyone looked on and smiled. "Oh Johnny," she said, and hugged him.

"How are you, Aunt Carmella?"

She began to cry. At first she couldn't speak. "I'm fine Johnny."

"Thanks for coming to see me at the Rehabilitation Center."

"You've grown to be a handsome man. You were always such a good boy."

"I'm afraid he's not a boy anymore, Carmella," said Uncle Al.

"I'm so happy to see you. Sit down Johnny, so we can have dinner."

Everyone got seated. Uncle Al poured the wine.

Rosanna and Johnny drank soda. "OK, everyone eat," said Aunt Carmella, "there's plenty of food."

Rosanna looked to her father. He knew they always said grace before they ate at home. Rosanna's father looked across the table to Carmella. "Carmella, wait a minute. I think Rosanna wants to say a prayer."

Rosanna grabbed Johnny's wrist as he was about to bite into a meatball. "What? Why are you holding my wrist?"

"We have to pray first."

"But I'm hungry. We can pray later. Then we can give thanks for a full belly."

She stared at him sternly. "Johnny put the fork down."

"OK, we'll pray."

Rosanna said a beautiful prayer and everyone began to eat. Johnny told Aunt Carmella how good the food was and that she was still the best cook in the world. As everyone ate, Mrs. Angelini began to ask Johnny some questions.

"So Johnny, what kind of work do you plan to do when you leave the center?"

"Well, I'll tell you, right now—"

Rosanna interrupted, "He's a musician, Mother."

"Yeah, I'm a musician," said Johnny.

"A musician. And where will you work?"

Johnny looked to Rosanna. Rosanna looked to her mother.

"He's going to make an album."

"What kind of an album?"

"A record, Mama, a record."

"I know a record, but what kind of music?"

"Pop music," Johnny replied.

"What's pop music?"

"You know, the stuff they play on the radio today."

"You don't mean that loud music, do you?"

"Well yeah, maybe a little loud."

"But I don't understand. What about a job?"

"Mama, that is his job, he's going to be a success."

"Louisa," Pondolona interrupted, "eat, let's not talk about work today, it's Sunday. Let's take it easy and talk about other things."

"Thank you, Father," Rosanna replied.

Johnny spoke up, "No wait, your mother has a right to know what I do. Mrs. Angelini, I'm a drummer, and tomorrow my band and I are going in the studio to make music so record companies can hear us. If it works out, Rosanna and I will be rich and have everything we ever dreamed of."

"And if it doesn't work?"

"Mrs. Angelini, I love Rosanna, and it will work. And we will be together forever and be very happy. That I promise you."

"Louisa," said Pondolona—Al and Carmella looked at each other and frowned. "Rosanna found a good man. Let's toast to Rosanna and Johnny." As the six toasted, Johnny put his arm around Rosanna and kissed her.

"I think your father likes me."

"Yes, I know, I can't figure it out."

"Thanks Rosanna."

LATER IN THE AFTERNOON THE WOMEN WERE CLEANING UP. THE MEN went to the living room. Johnny and Uncle Al began to talk. Pondolona fell asleep and was snoring. Uncle Al just smiled and shook his head. "I think Pondolona drank too much wine, but he's my friend and a good man. You know Johnny, I promised your mother that I would always take care of you, but sometimes things get a little busy. You know the kind of work I do is a rough business, and sometimes I have to be very careful. You know I worry a lot about your aunt, she wants me to quit. She said she wants to live in peace without having to worry anymore. I don't know anymore, Johnny, things just aren't the same, I'm getting tired. Maybe she's right. We have enough money, we have a beautiful home, it's just that I'm afraid that I'll get bored."

Al and Carmella lived in a beautiful home in South Philadelphia about a half-mile from Veteran's Stadium. It sat about a quarter mile from the road. The big black gates and stone wall were elegant. The house had plenty of ground surrounding it.

The winding road between the lawns that led to the house reminded one of a fairy tale castle. Trees stood high in various spots on the lawns. The house was shaded by the weeping willows. The stone mansion was huge with a large double gold and white door. There were plenty of rooms and lots of windows with gold and white trimming. Inside the home, was pure white walls, crystal chandeliers, a spiral staircase, and exotic Italian paintings hung on the walls everywhere. The bright red carpet laid wall-to-wall throughout the entire house. The Victorian furniture, and the rest of the home were spotless.

Al owned a Mercedes and a Jaguar. He had a home and a boat in Florida, where he and his wife would go at least three times a year. They also took a trip to Italy every two years. He had had his home in Philadelphia built to his specifications. Carmella did all the decorating and picked out all the furniture. They both had good taste and the best of clothes. They always helped the less fortunate, and gave money to various religious and fund-raising organizations. They, unfortunately, were never able to have children. There was really no need for Al to work any longer.

"You know Uncle Al," Johnny suggested, "you should think about retiring. You know, kick back, take it easy. You and Aunt Carmella can go visit the old country for a while."

He patted Johnny on the cheek. "I think I'm getting old, Johnny. Too old to worry about it anymore. Maybe you're right, maybe I should retire." Uncle Al took a deep breath, tears filled his eyes. Johnny looked on in pity. He knew Uncle Al's struggle, and how he'd fought his way to the top.

"Drink your wine, Uncle Al—it's good for you."

17

* * * * * * * * * * *

Johnny and his band, Midnight Angel, were at Powerhouse Studios on Monday. He had obtained permission from the center to leave whenever the band had a recording session. They were preparing to lay down tracks for their demo tape to send out to record companies. Johnny was feeling very competent. He approached the drum set. The rest of the band was feeling just as good. They picked up their instruments. The lead vocalist, Jerry Carvelli, sat out so they could just lay down the rhythm track without vocals. Everyone was comfortable. The engineer called out, "You guys ready?"

Johnny let loose with a drum roll. As he warmed up and gave an OK to the engineer.

"Let's do it," Danny shouted "Give us a count, Johnny baby."

Johnny clicked his sticks together to give a count and came down with a snap on the snare drum. The music began. They sounded sharper than ever; each man being confident of the others. They worked together to produce a pulsating sound. Johnny's drumming was solid and crisp. He played with grace and simplicity. He was truly a man enjoying his work. Stevie Roselli was playing the rhythm track with power and energy. He was probably anxious to do his solo track on the next take, but for now, he was just enjoying the rhythm. Danny's work on the bass, along with Johnny's bass drum, sounded like thunder. They provided an excellent bottom for the song structure. Being fortunate to put the right combination of people together, the band seemed to be bound for success.

The song came to a climactic ending. The engineer looked to his assistant. "Not bad, huh."

"Not bad? These guys are great. We can work out something very special for their music. I think we better call Pauli and tell him what we've got. He's been looking for a good band to manage. OK fellas, I want to play that back for you, I think you'll like it just the way it is."

The guys moved to the front of the room to hear the playback speakers. As the rhythm track played, they looked to one another nodding in agreement that the track was excellent. They were amazed. Chills began to run through them. It was their first studio track, and it was great.

The song ended on the playback speakers. "Well fellas, what do you think?" asked Marty, the engineer.

"Man I think it's happening," said Danny.

"Sounds real good to me too," said Stevie.

"Let's go with it," added Mike.

"I think we should move on to the next track," said Johnny.

"OK Stevie," said Marty, "get ready to do your guitar solo, then you're next, Jerry, for the vocals. In the meantime, I think the rest of you guys should go in the next room and start working on some backing vocals."

Stevie retuned his guitar and prepared for his solo while the engineers made adjustments on the mixing board. He placed the headphones on so Marty was able to adjust the sound.

"Is it coming through OK, Stevie?"

Stevie nodded. His guitar was tuned and the rhythm was coming clearly through the headphones.

"Stevie, I'm going to take it from the chorus just before your solo."

Stevie shouted, "Let it roll!"

When the music started, Stevie took a deep breath and started tapping his foot. He appeared very confident and excited. The last chorus ended. He began his solo. His fingers began to move speedily. He played clearly and precisely. Each note was clean and polished. He played with strength and energy. The solo was unique. He knew what the song needed—the power he projected was incredible.

Marty looked to his assistant at the mixing board. "This guy is hot—Pauli is going to love this band!"

Stevie ended his solo with grace and simplicity. He was well-seasoned as a guitarist, and now he was able to project his ability in a professional manner. Marty stopped the tape. "Excellent Stevie, excellent. No need to do it again—that one will do it." Stevie smiled. He was very proud of his work.

Jerry finished his vocal track and the other fellas did their track on backing vocals, and the band called it a day. Their first trip to the studio as a band was a successful one, and it was a happy day for all of them. Marty assured them that he would contact Pauli the following day.

"Well fellas, you finally get to meet my cousin, Pauli Rizzo," said Jerry.

The fellas were hoping that Pauli would be their manager. He had all the connections they would ever need. Could it be Pauli was their miracle?

BACK IN THE GYM TUESDAY MORNING, ANOTHER WORKOUT BEGAN. BILLY laid a fifty-pound weight on Johnny's back and held it in place. Johnny groaned as he did push-ups on his fingers to reach a twenty count. They proceeded to the weight bench.

The barbell contained 250 pounds. Billy saw Johnny's strength increasing and began adding more weight. He was now doing 100 sit-ups on the incline bench with no sweat. He was in the best shape of his life. He felt like nothing could stop him.

As the two did their daily road work, people looked on. They began to race. The two of them were building incredible endurance and speed. At the end of their run, Billy had the lead.

"I'll get you next time, Billy. Next time the race is mine!" As both breathed heavily, they began clowning. They went into a martial arts position and began to throw kicks at one another—right on the side of the highway. They acted like they were hurting one another, however, the people looking on thought it was real.

Suddenly, a police car pulled over. Two officers got out of the car and walked to the two men. "OK you two, break it up!" one officer shouted. Johnny and Billy began to laugh. They laughed so hard it hurt.

"A couple of jokers," the officer said to his partner. They both shook their heads at them. "This job's going to drive me crazy yet!" the partner replied. They jumped in their car and sped away in disgust.

AFTER HIS WORKOUT, JOHNNY GOT CLEANED UP, HAD A GOOD LUNCH, and off he went to the studio. He got permission from Jerry to leave the center that day. Jerry saw Johnny's progress and trusted him. He knew Johnny was a changed man. He felt confident that Johnny could leave the center and return at a proper hour, and most of all, return sober. He took full responsibility for Johnny and believed in him. The rest of the fellas took the day off from their jobs. They were anxious to hit the studio again.

The session went very well and the band finished two songs that afternoon. Marty shouted, "OK fellas, that does it for today. I have some people I want you to meet. Pauli asked me to call them when I informed him of your unique sound. He couldn't make it today, but you will meet him soon enough."

The band members paused for a moment. They stared at one another. They knew there was a surprise in store for them.

"Fellas, did you get that?" Marty saw their anxiety. "Look, just relax and follow me."

Powerhouse Studios had a pretty big meeting room. They did a lot of work for many record companies and were well equipped to entertain executives. As Marty and the band approached the room, there sat two executives from Seko Records. Marty spoke, "Have a seat, guys. I want you to meet Jack Cassenelli and Dave Kominski from Seko Records."

Everyone got acquainted and the negotiations began. Mr. Cassenelli began to speak. He was a stocky man, about 5'10". He had a round face and short black hair, parted on the side and graying at the temples. He wore tortoise shell frame bifocals and a tan three-piece suit with a white shirt and brown tie, and brown leather shoes. "Gentleman, Marty here likes your music, in fact, he spent three hours last night mixing your first tune. We had an opportunity to hear it earlier today, and we like what we heard. Of course, we value Marty's opinion and have lots of respect for his expertise in the music industry. He's brought us a lot of acts which have gone on to be some of our best money makers. He thinks that you have something special, and from hearing the tune you did yesterday, Dave and I feel the same way."

As Jack Cassenelli spoke, the fellas just sat and stared, some with their mouths wide open. They were in shock. They couldn't believe what they were hearing. They knew they were on the verge of a recording contract, a dream come true.

Jack asked, "Which of you is Jerry Carvelli?"

Being excited, Jerry felt like he was in school. He raised his hand. "I'm Jerry Carvelli." The guys laughed. "Sorry," Jerry added, "got a little excited there."

"It's OK Mr. Carvelli, I can understand your excitement. I want you to know that I spoke to your cousin, Pauli, who you obviously know. He has informed me that he fronted the band some studio time. Obviously you gentlemen do not have a bank account for the band due to your short time together, but obviously there is

one thing that you do have, and that's talent, and talent is what
we're looking for. Of course, when we see talent, we invest in it.
So you see, if you were to sign a contract with Seko Records, we
would take care of you financially, and that's why we're here. You
fellas are fortunate, it looks like your years of hard work in this
grueling business have paid off. You caught a break. We're very
happy to hear that Pauli is interested in managing your group, and
most of all, Marty here thinks you guys are special. And there's
one more thing you guys have that's more important than anything, and that's chemistry. You work well together. And when you
work well together, that's 75% of a good band. Any questions so
far?"

Danny spoke, "You mean that's it? You mean you want to
take us on as recording artists?"

"Well, not quite. There's a lot of preparation and lots of papers to sign. And before we do anything, we'll have to meet with
you along with Pauli at Seko Records in New York. I'm sure Pauli
will have a good talk with you fellas and inform you of all the
legalities," said Cassenelli. He then turned the fellows attention to
Mr. Kominski.

Dave Kominski was a medium built 5'9" man about 165 lbs.
His jet black hair was combed back on the sides, and the front of
his hair had a sixties look. His sideburns were long, reminding one
of Elvis. He had an oval face and a slightly pointed nose. He appeared to be only 35 years old. He wore a three-piece light gray
suit, and fancy black leather shoes. His shirt was light blue with a
light maroon tie and a handkerchief in the jacket pocket. "First off,
I want you to know that Seko Records is a very reputable company, as you all well know." The guys looked to one another and
smiled. They knew Seko was big time. "We at Seko Records
strongly believe in every artist that we sign, and we are behind
them 100%. And in return, we ask the same, that you give us 100%.
By that I mean it's music all the way. We're not asking you to play
other people's music in the bars. We're not asking you to play

parties for $50 a man. We're asking for your own music. We're asking for your creativity. We need all the energy and musical knowledge that you have as individuals and as a band. This is a business. It's a multi-billion dollar industry, and if you want to be part of it, and continue to be part of it, you have to give your hard work and dedication every day of your musical life."

Johnny took a deep breath, and began to bite his upper lip. His forehead began to sweat. Danny rubbed his hand through his hair. The rest of the guys became fidgety. They were on the verge of a recording contract and for the first time they were confronted with the serious side of music.

Mr. Kominski continued. "You see fellas, there's music and there's the music business. It's just like the minor leagues and the major leagues, and today when you leave this room, you will know you are professionals. And to be a professional, you have to act like a professional, live like a professional, and be a professional."

As the fellas looked at each other in amazement, they began to realize what lay ahead of them. There was silence for a moment. "Well, what do you think, guys?" said Mr. Cassenelli.

Johnny spoke. "Well, quite frankly, Jack, I'm in shock. I mean I can't believe it all happened this fast."

"Well Mr. Covini, sometimes things are crazy in this business. Some people wait all their lives and the big break never comes. You guys have something that works. I think you guys can go places."

Mr. Kominski took the floor once again. "OK let me explain a little bit about how a recording contract comes about, and how you will be employed by Seko Records. After you have signed on Pauli as your manager—and I hope you do—he will get you a good entertainment lawyer, then we begin. "First off, you will obviously have to leave your present jobs, which for some of you may be a hardship. However, Seko Records will pay you a salary to continue to work on your music at our studios where it will be reproduced. You will continue to draw a salary until your record is in the retail stores. You will obviously have a road crew, and all the other things that go along with a touring rock'n'roll band. Your job is to play music and play it well. Your tour will support your record sales. Your album will most likely hit the stores at the onset of your tour.

One thing we do advise at Seko Records is a clean life—good eating habits, no drugs, no alcohol abuse, and most of all, and probably the hardest thing to resist, is the women. You will meet lots of women. They will probably be your biggest supporters, and the fact that you are a bunch of handsome characters will even enhance the matter. We have seen quite a lot of bands burn out because of sex, drugs, and rock'n'roll. If any of you have a steady girl or a wife, if at all possible, I advise you to take her on tour with you, if you feel she is an understanding person and realizes what life on the road can be like. You will find the music business will be much more rewarding, and you will be a better musician if you take this bit of advice. OK gentlemen, thank you for your time and patience, I believe Jack will take it from here."

"OK. Are there any questions?" Mr. Cassenelli asked. All the fellas signaled no. Mr. Kominski had given them a brief education but a solid one. They knew what they had to do and were prepared to work. "OK, I'd like to leave you with this. Go home, do a lot of thinking about what we have said to you today, get a good night's sleep. I'm sure you will meet with Pauli tomorrow, and he will go over all the details with you. We will wait for his call."

At that point, the fellas had a strong feeling they would be signing with Seko Records with Pauli as their manager.

Jack and Dave shook hands with everyone and thanked Marty and the band for their time.

WALKING TOWARDS THEIR CARS, DANNY ASKED, "SO WHAT ARE YOU guys going to do with all your money when the band makes it big?"

"Well my first project is to get a Jaguar," Jerry replied.

"How about you, Stevie?"

"A brand new home, and a beautiful woman—blonde hair, big blue eyes, personality, and of course she has to have a good body."

"Yeah, got to have a good body," said Mike, as the fellas began to laugh.

"What about you, Covini?" Danny asked.

"Yeah what about you?" the fellas chimed in.

"Rosanna and I will get married and live happily ever after, and make lots of babies and live in paradise."

"Wo, listen to Mr. Family Man over here. I'll believe that when I see it!" said Danny.

Stevie spoke up, "Listen to us, who's to say if our music will even sell?"

Johnny turned to Stevie, "I'm not turning back Stevie, it has to sell, and only we can make it happen. As a matter of fact, let's make a deal right here and now. Let's all put our hands together and believe we will make it." The guys joined hands and made each other promise to never fail.

18

* * * * * * * * * *

On Wednesday the fellas were back at Powerhouse Studios to do more recording. Pauli would not be able to meet the band for another four weeks. He and his family were leaving for Connecticut to spend the holidays with his mother, and would stay until January 20th. Pauli's mother was not well, she had been diagnosed as having bone cancer. Pauli could have used a long vacation anyway. Marty notified Seko Records and Kominski and Cassenelli were informed. Marty suggested the guys continue to record at Powerhouse and finish the album.

On Thursday morning, Johnny was asked to take a part-time job counseling at the Welsley Center. Jerry also told Johnny that he recommended Johnny's parole, and hooked him up with his own apartment near the center. On Thursday afternoon, it was back in the studio. Johnny didn't want to live in Philadelphia at the present time. Now Rosanna could visit him whenever she felt. Danny could drop him off at Rosanna's house after sessions, and she could drive him home and spend a few hours.

Johnny did not feel ready to go back to the neighborhood and visit his friends; the memories still haunted him, but he knew he soon would have to face his friends once again and prove to himself he could enter his old neighborhood and not be overcome by the fear of the past.

Johnny had learned well from Billy that hard labor and dedication were the winning edge. The hard work paid off. The band was producing a sound of its own—unique and polished.

CHRISTMAS WAS GETTING NEARER AND ON FRIDAY AFTERNOON AT 3:00, the band decided to quit early. They'd had a grueling week of recording, and Christmas was just three days away. There was still a lot of work to do in the studio, and now Christmas. Johnny didn't quite know how to act. He hadn't had a fun Christmas since his mother died. He was never married and never had a family of his own. He hadn't had a real relationship since Penny. But this Christmas was different. He had Rosanna, Billy, and Uncle Al, and he certainly valued his friendship with the guys in the band. He was happy and the Christmas spirit filled him. He called Rosanna from the studio and told her he wanted to spend the evening shopping for gifts with the rest of the guys.

ON THE MORNING OF CHRISTMAS EVE ROSANNA PICKED JOHNNY UP AT his apartment. They were going to spend the day at the shopping mall in King of Prussia, a suburb of Philadelphia, just browsing and enjoying the Christmas decorations and displays at the stores. As they entered the mall, Rosanna suggested some lunch.

"That sounds great," said Johnny, "I'm starved!"

"What would you like to have?"

"Well you know since I've been in this training program with Billy, my diet has been a little restricted, and I'm dying to have a big fat cheeseburger—you know, the ones with onions and lettuce and tomato, and those big thick fries."

"I know just the place—Houlihan's."

AS THEY WAITED FOR THE WAITRESS TO BRING THEIR ORDER, JOHNNY WAS thinking of a way to tell Rosanna how she had made this Christmas very special for him. Rosanna was just looking around at the Christmas decorations in the restaurant. She was so full of life and loved the holiday season. "Look at that beautiful tree in the corner. I can't wait till we decorate our tree this evening, it's so much fun decorating on Christmas Eve."

Johnny cared so much about Rosanna and was glad to see her so happy. "Uhhh Rosanna, listen... there's something I want you to know. These last few years haven't been exactly the best ones of my life, and I have to admit, I've had some pretty miserable and lonely Christmas's. I mean I never really had anybody to share them with, but this year is different—I have you, and now I have the music. What more could a guy ask for? A good woman and soon a recording contract with a major label—I just can't believe it. It's just like a dream come true. I just don't know how to show you my appreciation or thank you."

Rosanna took Johnny's hand. Her eyes began to tear. "Johnny, you have to remember one thing, I wasn't exactly fulfilled until you came into my life. You know, working in that hoagie shop day after day isn't my idea of a career, and my father, sometimes I think he thinks I'm a work horse. You know those old Italian men— sometimes I think they have no feelings for women. But now I feel secure, we have a good relationship, and just knowing that you're there makes me happier than I've ever been."

The waitress, a young girl about eighteen or so appearing very anxious, brought their order. Her bleach blond hair was a bit frizzed and she looked very tired. The restaurant was packed for lunch. The girl was very busy and a bit nervous.

Rosanna asked her, "Are you open late this evening?"

"Seven o'clock, and I can't wait. This place has been a mad house for the last two weeks, and I'm beat."

"I know how you feel. I work in my father's restaurant in Philadelphia, and I know how gruelling it can be sometimes for a waitress."

"It's good to meet somebody who understands. Sometimes I think these people are heartless. OK, I'll be back in a bit. Enjoy your lunch."

"Rosanna, this burger looks great. I haven't had one of these for months."

"Yeah, it's definitely a treat for me also—especially after looking at hoagies all the time."

"So what will we do when we leave here?"

"I want to go to the department stores. Macy's and Bloomingdales have such beautiful decorations, and the salespeople are so nice."

Rosanna and Johnny finished all their shopping through the weekend and planned to just enjoy the afternoon and decorate the tree that evening.

"OK. Whatever you want to do today is fine with me."

The two finished their lunch quickly and decided to first walk through Bloomingdales. The place was mobbed. The typical Christmas: people rushing, banging into one another, long lines, shoplifters being pursued by security, stressed out salespeople just waiting for the day to end, but through it all, the Christmas spirit filled the store.

Rosanna and Johnny went to the third floor to see the store's Christmas display. "Hey Rosanna, look at these Christmas balls-they're ten dollars a piece!" Johnny was shocked.

"I take it you've never shopped in Bloomingdales."

"Are you crazy, at these prices?"

A tall woman about five-foot-nine with medium length blond hair and make up very well applied looked at Johnny. She was puzzled. Rosanna and he looked like a very rich couple. She must have wondered why he was complaining about the price. The woman wore a long fur coat and had a Gucci handbag, probably worth about $350. The coat must have been in the thousands.

Johnny was wearing a long gray tweed coat and a black scarf. His coat was open and his scarf undone. Underneath was a purple shirt. He wore gray pleated pants and fancy black shoes. Rosanna was wearing a long black skirt and a white silk blouse. Her shoes were high heel, black suede. Over top she wore a long black leather coat. Her hair and face were beautiful as always. Now and then Rosanna would buy Johnny clothing. Rosanna helped him choose a lot of the clothes he wore.

"Hey Rosanna, I think this lady's flirting with me," Johnny whispered.

"She's not flirting with you, you're in Bloomingdales and you're complaining about prices, and stop being so conceited."

"Aw come on, I'm just kidding." He put his arm around Rosanna and kissed her. They continued to tour the store. There were people with guitars walking through the store singing Christmas carols. The two stopped to listen as the singers gathered in one spot for a moment. This was one of the most exciting days of their lives. After spending two hours at Bloomingdales, it was time to go to Macy's.

As they entered the store, there were various women displaying all sorts of perfumes and colognes. A well-figured woman with red hair approached the two. She asked Johnny if he would like to try a new line of cologne.

"Sure, what kind is it?"

"It's called Purple Dreams."

"Purple Dreams? Sounds pretty wild, don't you think Rosanna. What do you think, take a walk on the wild side, or what!" Rosanna took Johnny's right hand.

"Here, let her spray some on you hand first, and we'll see if it smells good."

"Hey, not bad."

"I like it, Johnny."

"Yeah, spray some of that on my neck. Hey, thanks a lot. What's your name? Maybe someday we'll come in and buy some off of you."

"I'm Lauren, and I'm here every other week. Here's my card."

Johnny handed the card to Rosanna. "Here, maybe you can get it for my birthday."

As they began to walk through the store, Rosanna asked. "Johnny, when is your birthday?"

"February 27th."

"Oh, you're a Pisces."

"Oh, don't tell me you're into that astrology stuff."

"No, I'm not into that astrology stuff, but if there was ever a true Pisces, it's you."

"Oh yeah, and why's that?"

"You're warm, romantic, sensitive, and a dreamer, but sometimes very emotional."

"Oh. So that's how a Pisces acts. So when's your birthday?"

"March fifth."

"March fifth, and what sign are you supposed to be?"

"Well, it's only a few days after yours."

"Wait a minute—don't tell me, you're one of those Pisces too."

"That's right."

"You know, this relationship is getting more and more interesting every day."

The two went down to the bottom level of the store. "Johnny come on, I see the Christmas displays." She was so anxious she began to pull Johnny by the arm. She felt like a little girl.

"Hey Rosanna, take it easy—you're pulling my arm off."

"I'm sorry, it's just that I get so excited." Macy's was no different from Bloomingdales. It was probably even more crowded, and being a commission-basis type store, the salespeople had no complaints, they just had to be careful they didn't kill one another to see who would get the bigger sales.

"Johnny, look at these beautiful Christmas trees! Aw, look at the little stuffed dogs under the tree." She picked a stuffed dog up, and squeezed it. "Oh, he's so soft." She rubbed it on Johnny's face. "Isn't he cute, Johnny?" He was embarrassed. "Johnny, you're blushing!"

"Well, you know, I'm not into stuffed animals too much."

"Will you buy him for me?"

"Well how much is he?"

"He's only fifteen dollars."

"Fifteen dollars! For that thing? Besides, what are you going to do with a stuffed dog?"

Rosanna frowned. Johnny smiled. "OK, OK, I'll buy it for you."

"Oh, thank you Johnny! You can pay for it on the way out of the department. In the meantime, I'll just hold him."

"Hey, Rosanna, at least these Christmas ornaments aren't quite as expensive as the other place—we're down to seven dollars for a Christmas ball."

"Come on, let's go look at the dolls and doll houses."

Johnny must have thought, "Whoever thought I would be looking at doll houses!" He found himself getting just as excited as Rosanna. Falling in love had brought out the best in him.

"Here, hold the stuffed animal for a minute." Two teenage girls standing by looking at the displays looked to Johnny and laughed. He felt so embarrassed holding the dog in his hands. Rosanna was handling the dolls and looking them over.

"I think I'm going to get this doll for my niece."

"Oh don't tell me I have to spend another fifteen dollars!"

"No, I'll buy this one Johnny. You're turning into a real tightwad, you know that."

"You know, I think you've got a lot to learn about money."

"Oh yeah? And when did you become a financial genius?"

"When I met you."

"And what is that supposed to mean?"

"It means if I stay with you long enough, I'm going to go broke."

"Well who says you have to stay with me?"

"Rosanna, I'm getting a little frustrated, you know that."

"No, you're not frustrated, you're just cheap."

"You know, how'd you like to spend Christmas alone?" They both were getting angry—the typical thing in most relationships, arguing over money.

"Good. I'll take you back to your apartment. You can spend Christmas by yourself for all I care." Customers were beginning to look on.

"Well, who said I need you to take me back?"

At that point, singers were walking through the area with their guitars, singing a Christmas carol. They stopped and began singing to Rosanna and Johnny. They were forced to stop arguing. They felt so stupid.

Johnny thought to himself, "I feel like such a jerk." He looked to Rosanna. She looked back. With the stuffed animal in his left hand, he put his right arm around her. As she held the doll in her right hand, she put her other arm around him. They smiled at one another and kissed. Lots of people were looking on and smiling. When the carol finished, the two continued to tour the store and felt closer to one another than they had at the beginning of the day. They felt so bad for the way they'd spoken to one another. They were so in love. They were having such a good time that they hated to leave, but they had to get back to Rosanna's house because her mother and father were expecting them for dinner, and they wanted Rosanna and Johnny to decorate the tree.

PULLING INTO THE DRIVEWAY, JOHNNY SAID, "WHO DID THE CHRISTMAS decorations? This place is incredible."

"My mother and I." The shrubbery running the length of the house was covered with red, green, and white lights. On the front door was a big wreath lined with red and green lights and displaying red and white Christmas balls. Each window of the house was outlined in red lighting. Johnny was fascinated. He hadn't seen a house decorated quite like this one in a long time. He was so excited he just kept rambling on about its appearance as they approached the front door.

Rosanna unlocked the front door and they entered. The house was very warm and Johnny felt comfortable. "Here, give me your coat." Rosanna placed their coats in the closet and asked Johnny if he would like a sandwich.

"Sounds good—what do you have?"

"I know my mother made some fish. She always makes fish on Christmas Eve. She also made some sausage and meatballs, and plenty of cookies. How 'bout some sausage and meatballs and some bread on the side? OK, and then we have to get the tree decorated."

As they entered the kitchen, Rosanna found a note. Her parents had to leave a little early, and they would be back at nine or ten. They had lots of visiting to do. When she told Johnny, he smiled. "You mean we have this big house to ourselves?"

Rosanna laughed. "Don't get any ideas, Mr. Covini. You eat, and then we decorate the tree."

"Yeah, but I don't know how to decorate a tree."

"You can learn, and besides, it's lots of fun."

As they ate, Johnny began asking questions "Did you always live here, Rosanna?"

"No, I was born in New York."

"Where in New York?"

"Brooklyn."

"Brooklyn? Pretty tough place, isn't it."

"Oh, it's not that bad once you get to know everybody."

"Why did you move to South Philadelphia?"

"A friend of my father's was selling the hoagie shop and wanted to go back to Italy. My father always wanted his own business, and this one was well established. So he decided to move to Philadelphia."

"By the looks of this house, he's done pretty well for himself."

"Yeah, it's a good business and he's a hard worker. But I'm getting tired of it all. I don't want to work in that hoagie shop anymore."

"What do you want to do?"

"I want to get married and I want to have children and have a beautiful home just like this one."

"You mean you don't want to be one of those career women?"

"Taking care of a home, children, and a husband is enough of a career for me."

Johnny stopped eating for a moment. As Rosanna was about to take a bite of food, he stopped her. He pulled his chair close to hers and looked at her. "How did I ever get so lucky?"

"What do you mean?"

"They don't make girls like you anymore, they're few and far between."

"Stop it. You're embarrassing me!"

"Don't be embarrassed, it's true." Johnny thought to himself. He knew he soon would have to ask Rosanna to marry him. He loved her so much and he wanted her to have everything she dreamed of. "Look Rosanna, if it weren't for you, I think I would still be a washed out musician. I mean the rehabilitation center, Billy, my Uncle Al, sure they've all been a big help to me, but I realize now, I needed someone to share my life with. Someone who could understand me—someone who really cared about me. I want you to know one thing, I'm never going to give you up. I'm with you for life."

Tears began to fill Rosanna's eyes. She picked up her napkin and put it to her nose. She placed the napkin on the table and then held Johnny tight. Johnny put his arms around her. "Oh Johnny, I'm so happy."

IN THE LIVING ROOM THE FIREPLACE DISTRIBUTED A WARM, COMFORTABLE atmosphere from its consistent flame. Johnny had carried the Christmas tree in from the garage. Rosanna's father had picked it up earlier in the day. They both worked together to put the tree on its stand. They went to the basement and gathered all the decorations and began to decorate together. As they decorated, they laughed and joked and were able to be more open with one another than ever before. Johnny told Rosanna his innermost feelings. He told her about his childhood and how he began playing drums. He told her how he began drinking and taking drugs. Rosanna listened patiently. He continued on about the deaths of Tom Cat and little Joey. He even told her about his relationship with Penny. For the first time, Johnny was able to tell someone about his whole life and knew they really cared. Rosanna's mother was a very understanding woman. She must have taught Rosanna well how to understand men.

"OK, looks like we're ready to light the tree," said Rosanna. Johnny placed the plug in the socket and turned the switch on. The lighting was beautiful. The tree was lined with all sorts of colored lights. Tinsel was hanging everywhere. Garland surrounded the tree and was displayed beautifully. The tree was covered with Christmas balls and little figures. The balls were blue, red, and gold. The tree stood about seven feet and had a well-displayed star at the top with an angel in the center.

Rosanna and Johnny were like two little kids. They were amazed. "It's beautiful!" Rosanna exclaimed.

"Did I really help to do that?" asked Johnny.

"I told you you would learn."

"I can't believe it. This is the best decorated tree I've ever seen."

"How about if I make us some tea and we can sit in front of the fireplace and admire our work."

Johnny laughed, "Now that's a good idea." As Rosanna headed for the kitchen, Johnny grabbed her. "Hey wait." He began to kiss her passionately. The two caressed one another and couldn't seem to let go. Their emotions were growing stronger and stronger toward one another. Johnny must have thought, oh God, how much longer can I go on? I want to make love to her so bad. But he wanted to be understanding and respect Rosanna's wishes. He knew she wanted to stay a virgin until they were married. He was burning for her.

Johnny began kissing her on her neck. He quickly undid the top button of her blouse and then the next button. He took his left hand and pushed the top of her blouse over her shoulder. He then pushed the strap of her bra over her shoulder and began to kiss her all over. He undid another button and then pushed the right side of her blouse and bra over her shoulder. Her skin was so smooth, he thought. She was so pure. He began to kiss her breasts. Together they slowly moved to the floor. As Johnny kissed her breasts, he began to run his hand up the side of her thigh. Their hearts were pounding. Rosanna began to realize she could no longer help herself, and was about to do something she would regret. "Johnny, please, don't do this. We can wait."

"I can't wait any longer, I'm burning inside. I've got to have you."

"I can't Johnny, I can't. Please don't do this. And besides, my parents could walk in any moment now."

Johnny got a hold of himself and realized Rosanna was right. If her parents walked in, it would destroy everything they had. He backed off and took a deep breath. "I'm sorry Rosanna, I just get so crazy inside for you."

"It's OK Johnny, I understand. I feel the same way, but I just don't want to make a mistake. All these years I've been told girls should remain pure until their wedding night. It's the only way I know."

Johnny grinned. "Well, there's one thing I know for sure, it will be worth the wait."

She kissed him on his cheek. "Let me go make our tea now."

As she began to pull her bra straps and blouse back over her shoulders, Johnny said, "Here wait, let me do that for you."

Rosanna made them tea, and they were able to sit in front of the tree together for a half hour before her parents arrived. It was their first Christmas together, and would probably be the most romantic Christmas they would ever spend. Her parents arrived a little late—about eleven o'clock. Rosanna's father and mother were kind enough to ask Johnny to stay the night (in a separate room, of course), so they wouldn't have to drive all the way back to Jeffersonville.

CHRISTMAS MORNING THE FOUR HAD BREAKFAST AND THEN ROSANNA drove Johnny back to his apartment for a change of clothes, and to pick up the presents that Johnny had purchased for her, her parents, and his Uncle Al and Aunt Carmella. The six would be having dinner together at Rosanna's house and there they would exchange their gifts.

It was a beautiful Christmas for everyone. They had dinner at two, and then opened their gifts. Johnny and Rosanna had gotten each other a few gifts. Johnny had purchased a fur coat for Rosanna which would be her last gift to open. Uncle Al had given him $3,000 to buy Christmas gifts. The other gifts he had bought her made her happy enough, but now, what could be in this big box, she thought.

Everyone was looking on. Her mother was so happy for her, she knew how much Johnny loved her daughter. Her father couldn't believe his little daughter grew up and was now a woman in love. Uncle Al and Aunt Carmella were certainly happy for Johnny. They knew Johnny was finally happy and secure and had a good woman who would stick by him the rest of his life. Rosanna opened the gift slowly. "Oh my God," she said, "what can it be?" She got the paper off and placed the box on the table. She lifted the top off and pulled away the paper that covered the fur. "Oh my God—I can't believe it! Johnny, it's beautiful!" He helped her pull it out of the box and get it on her. Rosanna looked beautiful, the coat was perfect. She couldn't stop thanking him. Everyone was commenting how beautiful the coat was. Rosanna regained her composure, "OK Johnny, now you have to open your big gift."

Sitting in the center of the living room was a large box wrapped in shiny red paper with gold ribbon around it and a large green bow at the top. It must have been four feet high and four feet wide. "Well, this is the largest Christmas present I've ever gotten." He lifted the side a little bit. "Man, what do you have in here—it's heavy."

"Just open it up, you'll find out soon enough."

He began tearing through the paper and couldn't wait to get the box opened. He tore the last piece of paper off and opened the top of the box. He lifted off the Styrofoam and opened the plastic that surrounded the gift. He couldn't believe it—electronic drums. He had mentioned to Rosanna that someday he would get electronic drums for special effects and just to have fun with. "Rosanna, I don't believe it, this is just the brand I wanted. How did you know where to get them?"

"Oh, I listen to everything you tell me about drums and where you buy equipment sometimes. So I talked to a qualified salesman and we were able to get you just what you wanted."

"Rosanna, these are beautiful." He began lifting them out of the box. Taped to the side of one of the drums was a pair of ProMark hickory drumsticks, size 2-B—just the right size that Johnny used. "And what is this?"

"Drumsticks."

"And how did you know I used this size?"

"Johnny remember, I'm in love with a drummer."

Engraved on the drumsticks was Johnny's name. "Rosanna, I can't believe you—you even got my name engraved on them. Thank you Rosanna, I'll never forget this." The two kissed and the family members all clapped and made a toast to Johnny and Rosanna—a love affair that would last for eternity.

19

* * * * * * * * * *

JOHNNY AND ROSANNA HAD SPENT A QUIET NEW YEAR'S EVE AT Rosanna's house, and three weeks later, on January 21st, the last day of recording had arrived. The band members were seated in the lounge just talking, cracking jokes, and having some fun. A small, thin, almost undernourished looking man with brownish-blond thinning hair and hazel eyes entered the lounge. It was Marty. He needed a shave and looked beat. "Hey look, you guys have to pardon my appearance, I just came out of an all-night recording session. It had to get done. Just let me get some coffee and we can get started. I'm going to call out for some sandwiches, do you guys want anything?"

"No, we just want to get to work Marty," Danny replied.

"OK, as you all know, this is the last day of recording. All we need is a little more drum work and some vocal parts, and then we finish the mastering. I want to congratulate you fellows on an excellent job, I think Seko Records has a winner here."

Marty got his coffee, ordered some sandwiches and everyone entered the studio. "OK Johnny, what I need is your best drum solo yet—you know, for the one you wrote, 'Cry Of The Drummer.'" Johnny approached the drums with his sticks in his hand. He made a few adjustments and sat on the throne. The other fellows just took a seat in the studio and looked on. Marty positioned himself behind the controls. The studio door opened slowly. A medium height chubby fellow entered the room. His black hair was almost to his shoulders. His hair was dry and stringy and he was balding in the center of his head. He wore a waist-length leather coat with a fur collar. His coat was black and so was his shirt which was buttoned to the top. His wool pants were gray, and his high heel boots were black. He was dressed well. It was Jerry Carvelli's cousin Pauli, the owner of Powerhouse Studios and now Midnight Angel's manager.

"Hey Pauli, how you doin'?" said Jerry. "How's Aunt Milly?"

"Not so good Jerry, but how about you?"

"I'm OK Pauli, I'm OK. I'll keep Aunt Milly in my prayers."

"How's everybody doing today?"

"Good Pauli, good," everyone said.

"How's the recording coming along? I hear Seko Records was here talking with you guys," Pauli said.

Jerry introduced the guys in the band to his cousin. "Pauli this is Danny Rosco, Stevie Roselli, and Mike Danella." Pauli and the guys shook hands. The fellas couldn't thank Pauli enough for the free studio time and managing them.

Pauli was impressed by the looks of the four. He knew the record industry was big on first impressions and that having a good-looking band was fifty percent of a saleable product. There stood Danny Rosco: blond, curly hair, shoulder length, the sides covering his ears. He was thirty years old and looked twenty-five. His eyes were blue. He had a fair complexion. His teeth were well-structured, pure white. He stood about 5'11". That day he wore a red shirt, black pants, and gray and white alligator skin boots. He was a looker and had the personality to go with it.

Mike Danella had long black hair. He always kept his hair well-styled and groomed. He probably had the nicest hair out of the whole group. It was jet-black down to his shoulders and it covered his ears. It was layered well, and short on the top. No wonder his hair looked the best, his sister was a hair stylist. His eyes were dark brown. He had dark skin. He was six feet tall and built well. He worked out at the spa faithfully. He also had the reputation for being one of the toughest musicians in the Philadelphia area. Mike wasn't afraid of anyone. Standing there in his white shoes, black leather pants, and purple shirt, he appeared particularly impressive to Pauli.

Jerry Carvelli had the long, sleek look. He stood about six-foot-two, very trim, and was the perfect singer. His hair was long and curly. It was blond, but natural. His eyes were blue and mysterious. His skin was pure white. Jerry and Danny were both Polish on their mothers' side. He had a smile that was enough to shake any girl's mind. Jerry was very intelligent and had a personality that wouldn't quit. He had a reputation for being a lady's man throughout his musical years. No one knew just how many women he'd had relations with, but the count was supposedly in the hundreds. But now it was time to get serious. Supposedly, he had been seeing one girl for the last year and a half.

Stevie Roselli was a wizard on the guitar. His solos were outstanding and original. He spent most of his years practicing two to three hours a day perfecting his talent. He was ready for the big time. He was confident and he knew he was good. He earned that right. Stevie was always a one woman man. He'd have a girlfriend for a year and then move to another. He was always faithful to the girl that he was involved with. He never cheated, but he definitely was a man of change. He also had the look that a rock'n'roll musician needed to succeed. Stevie stood about five-foot-nine, brown hair—a little shorter than most of the guys in the band-but still had a well-styled, long look. His eyes were brown and mysterious. When you looked at him, he would give you a feeling of peace, and that he was—a peaceful man just wanting to play his guitar and have some fun. Off stage, he would generally dress very casually—jeans, sneakers, leather jacket. On stage, he was a monster, bursting with flashing clothes and all types of movements which dazzled audiences. And now he had his chance to dazzle the world as the band would prepare for its first major tour.

"Eh Pauli, I'll introduce you to Johnny later, he's about ready to do a drum track right now," said Jerry.

"Great, I think I'll stay and listen, this ought to be exciting!" Pauli sat beside Marty. "Eh, you look tired Marty."

"Yeah I know, I had to finish up some recording with the group Paradise."

"Listen, try to get home early today and get some rest, I don't want you getting sick on me. We got a lot of work to do for a lot of record companies."

As Johnny sat behind the studio's big black drumset, you could see the excitement in his eyes as he prepared for his solo. He got warmed up using triplets on the double bass drums, followed by triplets on the tom toms. He was producing a solid, thunder-like sound. As Johnny's blood began to warm up and circulate, he began to play with precision and speed. Marty called through the microphone, "Johnny, it sounds like you're ready."

"I'm ready."

"You need a click track to keep time?"

"No, I'm OK."

"Johnny, you know the solo in this song needs to be fast, but tasteful. Every note and every beat must be heard. It has to be strong and positive, with tons of energy."

Johnny thought to himself. He suddenly realized his strength and endurance were to be tested. This drum solo would probably have to be his best yet.

Marty gave the cue and Johnny began to play. He began with a hard-driving riff on the snare drum. His right foot was moving constantly on the bass drum pedal. His left foot kept the high hat cymbals clashing. The drum rolls that he was playing were fast, solid, and clean. Marty was smiling and giving him a thumbs-up sign. He was playing just what Marty wanted to hear—every note clearly. Marty was impressed.

As he continued to wail on the snare, Johnny began to incorporate the tom toms mounted on the bass. As he played the toms, his foot would speed up on the bass pedal, and then back to the snare. It sounded like thunder. Jerry's cousin Pauli was amazed at this guy's speed.

Danny just stood and stared, "I never get tired of hearing this guy play. He's definitely a different drummer." He whispered to himself, "Keep on rockin' Johnny, you're the greatest man, you're the greatest."

Stevie Roselli barely heard him as he looked on in amazement. Mike and Jerry were spellbound. They had seen Johnny play before, but never like this.

Johnny came off the snare, moved his left foot to the left bass drum. He was now playing two bass drums. His feet were flying. The sound from the big twenty-six-inch bass drums was earth-shaking. His solo was now concentrating on the bass drums and tom toms. His hands flew across the drums. He began playing cross-overs from the floor toms to the mounted toms. You could barely see his hands moving. He rolled on the small tom and then quickly moved to the large tom. He was going back and forth with speeded repetition. His coordination wasn't thrown a bit. His feet just kept a fast steady pace. He quickly returned to the snare, and gave one last fast roll around the whole drum set and came to a sudden stop. Next would come the climax of his solo.

He began playing very lightly on the snare and would occasionally give a thunder-like roll from the bass drums.

He seemed to be using everything he had ever learned. His concentration couldn't be broken. It was all drums and nothing else. He was incredible.

As he continued to play the snare he began to pick up volume and speed, and then began adding more rolls on the bass drums. He started using the cymbals. The studio set was surrounded by cymbals, set up just the way he liked it. The drumsticks seemed to be flying through the air, rushing from one cymbal to the other. One would wonder how he was able to continue to play on the drums and yet crash the cymbals at the same time. His style was one of a kind. His strength and endurance was never better. Billy had trained him well. It seemed he didn't want to stop playing. His feet now went into a steady pattern on the bass drums. His hands played all the drums. Every cymbal was hit with precision.

This would truly be an award-winning solo on the band's first album, and there was no doubt that the audience would go crazy when the band hit the concert halls. It would be a drum solo they wouldn't forget. With both hands rolling on the twenty-inch crash cymbals, and his feet pounding out the big bass drums, Johnny ended his solo.

Pauli looked to Marty. "If the rest of the band plays like this guy, they're going to rock the world. This drummer's the best to come along in years. His speed and energy are incredible. Where's he from, anyway?"

"Right over the bridge—South Philly. They say Billy Curry's been working with him."

"No wonder he's so good. But it looks to me it's a case of the student outshining the teacher."

"Yeah, he certainly is one of a kind. I've recorded a lot of drummers, but never like this one. This guy's a killer."

The band members walked to the back of the studio to shake Johnny's hand and congratulate him on an outstanding job.

"Johnny, that was great man!" said Danny.

"Johnny, excellent job," said. Stevie.

Mike and Jerry were joking around. "Eh Mike not bad for an old guy, huh," said Jerry.

Mike chimed in, "Whoever said rock'n'roll was only for teen-agers? Good job, Johnny. You're going to kill them when we hit the stage."

Johnny was laughing as he wiped the sweat from his face with his towel. As Pauli looked on, he must have thought, this band is going to go places, they have something that very few bands have: chemistry, they definitely have chemistry, I finally found the band I was looking for.

Johnny climbed off the drum throne. His jet black hair was beginning to get much longer. His face looked more youthful. He always kept his hair styled well. He hooked up with a good stylist in Philadelphia who was experienced at cutting hair for a lot of rock'n'roll musicians in the area, and would sometimes cut hair for professional artists who were on tour when they played Philadelphia. Johnny's face was no longer pale and drawn. His shoulders were no longer slumped. The good looks that he possessed naturally had come back to him. His big brown eyes shone and expressed joy. The physical training that he had continued with Billy had given him a new body. He looked strong and very healthy. He was one handsome character. With his black tank top, faded jeans, and black alligator boots, he looked like a top-ranked rock'n'roll drummer. Pauli was once again very impressed with the looks and personality of this band.

Located in Cherry Hill, New Jersey, Powerhouse Studios was founded by Pauli Rizzo. He was forty years old and had actually started in the business as a rock'n'roll guitar player at the age of twenty. He had played the nightclub circuit in the tri-state area and New York for five years with a band called Blue Mountain. After being turned down by a record company for a job with a major recording artist, he became very frustrated and quit the business. He took a job with a construction company where he would get some fresh air and live a better lifestyle.

After two years, he realized he had to get back in the business, but felt it was too late to continue as a musician. He had gotten married and wanted to live a more settled life. That's when he thought a recording studio would be the perfect outlet for his musical interests. He had a knack for business, and acquired a vacant building and convinced a local bank to lend him the money for his business. The knowledge he had acquired in the construction business had been a big help in the remodeling of the building. Also, being part of the music business for a long time, he knew a lot about professional recording equipment. This knowledge helped him save a lot of time and money.

The outside of the building was white. There was a big fluorescent sign with purple lettering displaying the Powerhouse emblem. It was a fairly large building with plenty of parking. It had a nice sized lounge, four rehearsal rooms, and a beautiful office. The recording room was equipped with a forty-eight track system. The equipment was the best. When Pauli went into the business he knew what he needed to be professional, he also had a good staff and hired a cleaning person who kept the place spotless. The inside of the building was a totally professional atmosphere. Pauli had a reputation for being a kind and honest man, but he also was firm and constantly stressed hard work and dedication to his employees.

Pauli had seen a lot of bands in the twelve years at Powerhouse Studios, and knew that this band had what it took. He walked over to the band members.

"Hey Johnny, I want you to meet my cousin Pauli," said Jerry. "Pauli, meet Johnny Covini."

After shaking hands, Pauli said, "You play well Johnny."

"Oh thanks Pauli." Johnny was still breathing heavily and sweating as he continued to wipe his face with the towel.

"You know, we can use you around here sometimes. We get a lot of singers who need studio musicians. If you ever want to do some side work, let me know."

"Well thanks Pauli, but right now I just want to concentrate on the band. I think we're going to New York soon to talk to some people at Seko Records about our tour, aren't we? Oh and by the way Pauli, thanks for being our manager."

"Well, by the sound of Marty's voice on the phone last month, it was too good to pass up. And now that I see you guys in person, it's greater than I imagined. Marty sent me a tape of your first five songs—it's fantastic! You must be excited."

"I don't know if I'm excited or in shock."

"What do you mean?"

"I've never played in a recording band before. I never went on tour—I mean I can't believe this is happening."

"Don't worry Johnny, once you get out there on the road, you'll believe it's happening. When you see twenty thousand people screaming their heads off, you'll believe it after they give you a headache." Johnny and Pauli laughed.

"Eh Pauli listen, I can't begin to tell you how grateful I am for letting the band use the studio. If it wasn't for that, Seko Records may have never known we existed."

"It's OK Johnny, any friends of my cousin Jerry are my friends too, and besides, we're all Italians, right?" Marty approached. "Except for this guy, I don't know what he is!" Pauli joked.

"Thanks Pauli, I can always depend on you to make my day," said Marty. "Johnny, great job—I liked the solo, it's a winner."

"Thanks Marty."

"OK guys," said Pauli, "I will see you in my office in 15 minutes, then you can come back and finish your vocal tracks." Pauli spoke with the band members for about an hour and gave them a total rundown of his background and how he could be an asset to them as their manager. Now they would have to go to New York to meet representatives from Seko Records. Pauli assured them they would have the best entertainment lawyers and would keep them informed of all money matters. Pauli had a reputation for being an honest guy. The band was fortunate to have someone like him.

After the meeting, the vocal session went better than expected and the fellas called it a day.

20

* * * * * * * * * *

ON WEDNESDAY MORNING, JOHNNY WAS RUNNING A BIT LATE. HE JUMPED out of the shower and quickly dried himself off. He gave his hair a quick blow-dry, and then began to get dressed. He had to be at the center at 9:15 to help Jerry with a group therapy session. The phone rang. Johnny picked it up quickly, "Hello."

"Johnny, is that you?" The voice sounded distant, kind of sickly.

"Yeah this is Johnny, who's this?"

"Johnny, it's me, Lefty," Lefty began to cough.

Johnny was confused, he couldn't understand the voice. "Who is this?"

"It's me kid, Lefty."

"Lefty, what's wrong? Where you been? You sound awful. How'd you know where to locate me?"

"Don't have time for all that now, kid. Look, I'm dying. They gave me six months, and I feel like I'm going to die right now."

Johnny was in shock. He hadn't heard of nor seen Lefty in almost a year. Lefty was in the hospital dying of cancer. Johnny must have figured that much out. He felt so bad for the old man. Guilt began to overcome him. He never tried to contact Lefty. He was so concerned about getting his life together he forgot all about his old friend Lefty.

"Lefty, where you at, I'll come and see you."

"I'm at St. Stan's Medical Center—Center City."

"Lefty, I'll be there soon as I can, just hold on!" Johnny hung up the phone quickly and called the center immediately. Billy had told him he would be going into the city some time that week and had asked Johnny if he would like to come along. Billy would be going to the music center on Eighth street to order some new drums. Billy had decided to hit the road again with a new band he had formed. Johnny dialed directly to Billy's office. Billy picked up the phone.

"Welsley Center, Billy Curry speaking."

"Billy this is Johnny."

"Johnny, how'd the session go yesterday?"

"I'll tell you later, but right now I need a favor."

"Johnny, what's wrong? You sound upset."

"Billy, I just got word that a friend of mine's dying in the hospital. He needs me there. I know that you said you were going into the city this week and thought maybe you could make it today."

"Sure Johnny, all I have to do is make a few phone calls—you know, cancellations, and I'll pick you up at your apartment in about a half an hour."

"Eh thanks Billy, can't tell you how much I appreciate this."

"Hey, no problem Johnny, your friend needs you. See you in a bit."

Within 35 minutes Billy picked Johnny up, and they drove off.

AS THEY DROVE DOWN THE EXPRESSWAY BILLY SAID, "JOHNNY, I'M really sorry to hear about your friend."

"Yeah, me too Billy. I just feel so damn bad I never tried to contact him."

"Well, don't worry about that Johnny, the important thing is that he needs you now, and you're going to be there for him. Laying guilt on yourself isn't going to help matters."

"Oh shit, I forgot to call Rosanna this morning! I didn't even call Jerry—he was expecting me to work with him in a group therapy session."

"Don't worry about it Johnny, I saw Jerry this morning and told him what was happening."

"Thanks Billy. I gotta calm down. If Lefty should die before I get to the hospital, I'll never forgive myself."

"Johnny, chill out. We'll be there in no time."

"So Billy, why you buying new drums—what's going on?"

"I'm going on tour again Johnny, and I'd like to have some new drums."

"Don't tell me—Billy Curry back on the road again?"

"That's right man, I miss it. We signed some papers and made arrangements yesterday. You gotta hear the band, we're really sounding good. I mean we're ready."

"I can't believe it, Billy Curry in concert again."

"How'd your band do yesterday at the studio?"

"Everything went fine Billy. We're ready, the master tape will get done sometime this week, and then we're going to Seko Records in New York City."

"Johnny, I'm proud of you man. You've come a long way."

"Eh Billy, if it wasn't for you, none of this may have happened."

"Yeah, but just remember one thing Johnny, I planted the seed, but you made it grow. You worked hard and now you'll reap the rewards."

Billy drove quickly to Philadelphia. In no time they were pulling into the medical center's parking garage. Billy could see Johnny's anxiety, and tried to park quickly. After parking they ran toward the hospital doors. As they ran, Johnny said, "Damn, I forgot to ask Lefty what room he's in."

"It's OK Johnny, we can ask at the front desk."

"Oh yeah, I forgot about that."

"Calm down man before you end up in the hospital." After the two ran up the steps almost knocking a few people over, they reached the front desk. Johnny looked a wreck by now. Sitting there was an elderly woman who must have been in her sixties, very thin, and her hair gray and barely combed. One may have thought she was a patient by the looks of her.

Before she could say a word, Johnny asked nervously, "Can you tell me where Lefty is?"

"Please sir, calm down."

"Look lady, my friend Lefty is in here somewhere, and I have to see him."

"Well first of all, who's Lefty?"

Billy interrupted, "Johnny what's his name—his real name?"

"Gee, I'm sorry lady, I think his name is Vincent Gambini."

"Well that's better, let me check." As she looked on the computer, Johnny was biting his upper lip and breathing heavily through his nose. Billy's arms were folded around his chest as he looked around the hospital lobby.

"Yes, here we are," the woman began, "Vincent Gambini-"

"That's him! That's him!" Johnny shouted.

"Room 331," she said, "the elevator is down the hallway to your left."

"Come on Billy, let's go."

They rushed toward the elevator. In no time they were on the third floor. Fortunately things were not too busy that morning and the elevator did not have to make any stops for others. As they exited the elevator, a narrow sign read "Rooms 325 to 331." They walked quickly down the hall.

"This is it Billy." Suddenly Johnny stopped. The number on the half-open door read 331.

Billy looked to him. He wondered why Johnny stopped. "Johnny, what's wrong?"

"I don't know Billy. I haven't seen him in so long, what will we talk about?"

"Johnny don't worry about that, the main thing is Lefty needs you just to be here, otherwise he would have never called you."

"Yeah, I guess you're right." Johnny had told Billy a little about Lefty when they were driving to the hospital.

As Johnny entered the room, Billy asked, "Do you want me to wait out here? I mean, maybe you want to talk to your friend in private."

"No, I want you to come in with me. Lefty will enjoy the company."

"OK, let's go in," Billy replied.

There was Lefty, just lying there helpless. He was asleep. The covers were pulled up to his chin. His mouth was half-open and he needed a shave. His beard was gray, and his face drawn. His head was totally bald, probably from chemotherapy. His arms were outside of the covers lying straight by his side. They looked like toothpicks. Johnny was terrified. He never thought he would have to see his friend in this condition. Billy felt so bad for his friend Johnny. He knew how close Johnny was to Lefty. Tears began to fill Billy's eyes.

Johnny walked to the side of the bed. He spoke quietly, "Hey Lefty." Lefty's eyes opened slowly and his mouth closed.

Johnny's eyes began to tear as he thought of the past—how Lefty had taught him many things. Lefty's head turned to the right. He looked to Johnny with drawn eyes. He almost looked scary. It looked like the cloud of death was over him. "Hey Johnny, my buddy, how you doin' kid?" he mumbled, "I'm glad you came to see me."

"Yeah, I'm glad too, Lefty, it's good to see you."

"No it's not. I'm an old, ugly man."

"Nah, you still look like the same ol' Lefty to me."

"Bullshit, but thanks anyway."

Johnny snickered and then wiped the tears from his right eye with the palm of his hand.

"Don't crumble on me now, kid, let's have some laughs before I die."

"Yeah sure, Lefty, let's have some laughs."

Billy had taken a seat on a chair that set against the wall about three feet from the bed, just in back of where Johnny was standing. "Hey Lefty, I want you to meet a good friend of mine." Billy stood up and came to the side of the bed. "Lefty, this is Billy."

Lefty could barely extend his hand. Billy took Lefty's hand and shook it lightly. "Billy, it's good to meet you."

"Good to meet you too Lefty, Johnny's told me a lot about you."

"Probably all bad, huh." Lefty began to cough. With his condition, he would get coughing spells off and on. Johnny poured some water into a glass which sat on a table beside the bed. He held the glass and straw to Lefty's mouth. He could barely sip it because of all the coughing, but he managed to get all the water in him and the cough subsided. "Sorry fellas, in my condition that happens."

"It's OK. Lefty, we understand."

"Billy, have a seat. You can turn the TV on. I have to talk to Johnny."

"Lefty, Billy's OK."

"It's OK. Johnny, I'll be right here." Billy sat back in the chair.

"Johnny, it's killing me kid—I can't take the pain. I want to die Johnny. I can't live in this pain anymore. They gave me six months to live, but I want to die now."

"The pain will stop, Lefty. Besides, pain never stopped you."

Lefty smiled. "Hey Johnny, you remember I fixed you up with your first girl?"

"Yeah I remember Lefty, I was scared to death, but I have to admit, she was beautiful."

"She better have been, she cost me $200."

"$200? Man you never told me that!"

"It was your birthday, wasn't it?" They both grinned. "Yeah, we were living kid. We had it all—wine, women, and money. You still booking numbers?"

"No, I gave that all up, Lefty."

"Good for you kid, it's a rotten business. Look kid, before I die, I want you to know, I have $150,000 in the bank; it's yours." Lefty was fading.

"Hey Lefty, what about your family?"

"Family? You're my only family kid, you're the only one who ever showed me respect."

"Look Lefty, you just can't go giving money away like that, that's your life savings. And besides, how do you know when you're going to die?"

"Look, just go see Joe Lorenzo the lawyer. You know where he's at."

"Look Lefty, calm down. Before you know it, you'll be out of here. It'll be like old times, just me and you Lefty." Johnny was fantasizing. He felt so bad for Lefty, he just wanted him to feel comfortable. He knew there was no hope for his friend. He just looked too old and weak.

"Look Johnny, just do what I asked you. Everything's set and the papers are signed. Just make sure Joe Lorenzo doesn't get more than he's supposed to. I think he's getting five grand for handling everything. I don't know, sometimes I just don't trust that guy."

"OK Lefty, when you die, I'll take care of everything. I want you to die in peace."

"Johnny, I do need one big favor when you get the money."

"Sure Lefty, what is it?"

"See that I get a good burial. You know, the works. I want to go out in style."

"I'll take care of it Lefty, don't worry about anything."

"Thanks kid. I'll never forget you."

Johnny looked behind him to Billy. Billy was speechless as

he looked at Johnny's sad face.

Lefty took a deep breath and his head rolled to the left of the pillow. Lefty died. Lefty must have known his life would end that day. He must have sensed it when he called Johnny.

Johnny turned his head to Lefty again. Fear gripped Johnny's face when he saw Lefty's head hanging helplessly on the pillow. "Lefty! Lefty! What's wrong?"

Billy jumped up and rushed to the side of the bed. Johnny was getting frantic. "Johnny take it easy, I'll get the nurse."

Johnny began shaking Lefty. "Lefty come on—you said six months, not today! Come on Lefty—wake up!"

Billy had gotten a nurse. A young Korean woman who had been with the hospital for quite some time had been taking care of Lefty. When she and Billy reached the bed, they had to pull Johnny away from Lefty. Johnny was getting out of control. He couldn't face Lefty's death.

The nurse tried to remain calm as Billy held Johnny. She placed the stethoscope on Lefty's chest and got absolutely no response. She then felt for his pulse at his wrist and once again got no response. "I'm sorry, your friend is gone." The nurse had tears in her eyes. Lefty was diagnosed as "no code," and there was no need to call a doctor right away.

"But he told me he had six months to live."

"Your friend probably didn't want to alarm you. He wanted you to think he had a lot of time left."

Johnny began to cry. Billy guided him to the chair. The nurse gave Johnny some tissues. Johnny sat there and leaned his head on his hands as his elbows rested on his knees.

The nurse suggested to Billy to let Johnny sit and cry for about five minutes and then get him to leave the hospital. Lefty's body would have to be picked up by a funeral home.

Five minutes had gone by and Billy told Johnny that they should be leaving. "Come on Johnny, I'll take you home."

"No Billy, I'm OK. I want to go to the music store like we

planned. I'll just let the hospital know on the way out that I'll be taking care of Lefty's funeral and burial. I'll call them tomorrow. I will also make arrangements with Santino's Funeral Home in South Philly. But today, let's just do what we planned to do. I think Lefty would like it that way."

JOHNNY AND BILLY ENTERED CENTER CITY MUSIC ON EIGHTH STREET. The store was one of the biggest music stores in Philadelphia. A lot of the professionals shopped for equipment there. There were guitar amplifiers all over. There must have been 500 guitars hanging from the racks in all different shapes, sizes, and colors. There were drums and cymbals all along the wall covering the whole length of the store. Pianos and organs flooded the floor, and tons of accessories covered the wall in back of the display cases. The cases displayed all sorts of microphones—gold, black, and silver. There was a separate room for all the P.A. equipment. Johnny had been there before, but never really noticed just how much stuff was there. Now that he was off the drugs and booze, he was able to be more observant.

"Billy, this place is incredible. I've been here once before, but I never realized they had so much equipment."

"That's because they expanded the store and did some renovating."

"Man, I thought there was something different."

The two approached the sales counter and a young man addressed them. As he was about to ask them how he could help them, he recognized Billy. "Aren't you Billy Curry?"

"Yeah, that's me."

"Man, I caught you down at the Spectrum and really enjoyed the show. What are you doing these days?"

"I just put a new band together and we'll be hitting the road soon."

"Yeah, I heard about the old group splitting up."

"Yeah well, all good things must come to an end."

The young man must have only been twenty years old and had shoulder-length black hair. His big brown eyes were opened wide by Billy Curry's presence. He was a drummer himself and was very excited about meeting Billy in person. "You know Billy, I've listened to a lot of your music on records. Your drumming has taught me a helluva lot and for that I want to thank you."

"Hey, no problem. I'm glad you like the music. I want you to meet a friend of mine, Johnny Covini."

"Eh man, I heard about you—you're with Midnight Angel. You guys just finished up at Powerhouse Studios."

"Gee, the word gets out fast, doesn't it Billy?"

"Hey Johnny, Center City Music knows everything that's happening."

"Man I heard about the exciting drum solo you did—can't wait to hear it on tape. When are you guys starting your tour?"

"We'll be going to New York soon to make the arrangements. I couldn't tell you exactly when we tour." Johnny was grateful that the young man acknowledged him, but he still felt saddened about Lefty's death. "Hey Billy, go ahead and order your drums, I want to check out the display sets on the floor."

The store was fairly crowded for a Wednesday morning. There were all types of musicians shopping around, some with long hair, some with short hair, some with just plain wild hairdos. For the most part, they wore leather jackets, high heel boots and faded jeans. Some looked burned out, while others were full of energy. As Johnny looked around, he was grateful to God to be part of the recording industry, and most of all to be free of drugs and alcohol and have a woman as wonderful as Rosanna, and now he would have $150,000, but he would never forget Lefty.

The young salesman showed Billy all the display drum sets before Billy made his final decision on color and name brand. Johnny just continued to tour the whole store. Billy finally placed his order. Johnny returned to the counter where Billy and the salesman were closing the deal.

"So Billy, what'd you order?"

"Nine piece set of Tama's."

"What type of cymbals you using?"

"I went with the Sabians, got seven of them."

"What color are the drums?"

"I went all out this time Johnny—black with gold hardware."

"Hey, not bad." Johnny looked to the salesman. "Every good drummer should have good looking drums."

"You got that right. He's the best."

Billy signed his name to the order form. "Well, that should do it, Billy," the salesman said.

"OK, how long do you figure before they get here?"

"I'll put a rush on it for you, Billy. Figure about four to six weeks."

"OK man, I'll be waiting for your call. You ready Johnny?"

"I'm ready if you are Billy."

"Oh—one more thing," said the salesman, "can I get your autographs?"

Billy signed his name to the little booklet the salesman gave him. The salesman tore off the top piece and gave it to Johnny. Johnny scratched his head with the pencil in his hand. Billy laughed. "What's the matter Johnny?"

"Well I never signed an autograph before."

"Just do it big and fast." Johnny did just as Billy said and signed his first autograph. Johnny was beginning to feel a little better.

"Hey, thanks a lot fellas, I'll be looking for you at the Spectrum."

They said good-bye and exited the store. Johnny and Billy walked to the side street where Billy's car was parked. Billy had just purchased a new Jaguar. It was jet black, very clean and shiny. The interior was tan with highly polished wood trim. It had a very expensive stereo system and a telephone. Billy made good money as a musician. Johnny was very impressed and was glad to be a protege of Billy. As they walked toward the car, Johnny said, "Billy I didn't get a chance to tell you how much I like the new Jag. You know, I was too concerned about Lefty."

"Hey Johnny, I understand."

"Anyway, it's one beautiful machine."

"Keep playing those drums, Johnny, someday you'll get one too."

"Yeah, but first I have to get my license back."

Billy climbed into the car. As Johnny waited for him to unlock the passenger side, a big black Mercedes pulled alongside the Jaguar. Two men were seated in the front. Both had shiny black hair, dark complexions, sporting black sunglasses, and they were big. They looked mean. There was also a man seated in the back. He wasn't as big, but he looked mean also. His hair was also black, combed back, and very clean-cut. He was a bit pale and unshaven. His long, pointed nose looked even longer because of the sunglasses he wore. They were small, black and round. They all wore open collar shirts with gold chains and black cashmere coats. It was a bitter January day. They looked like guys from the Mob. The man that sat in the rear told the driver to let the window down from the push-button panel. It was Frankie Benelli and his bodyguards.

Billy unlocked the passenger side of the Jag and before Johnny could get in, he heard a shout. "Hey Covini, I've been looking for you man." Johnny couldn't believe it, of all people it had to be Frankie Benelli.

"Yeah, well I haven't been looking for you, so why don't you just ask your bozos to move the car and let us out."

The two guys just laughed at Johnny's remark. They weren't moving unless their boss gave the OK. And Frankie wasn't about to move at that point.

Frankie shouted, "Hey Johnny, remember Tony (The Horse) DiJavante?"

"Yeah, he used to bet pretty heavy with me."

"Yeah well he told me you have some money that belongs to me."

"Tony (The Horse) is lying, man. He blew twenty grand on horse bets and couldn't pay me off, and now he's trying to lay it on me."

"Look Covini, I don't know who's trying to lay what on who, all I know is I'm missing twenty thousand dollars in bets from someone."

Billy began to get impatient. He hit the button and let his window down. "Hey man, you going to let us out? We have to go."

Frankie looked to the bodyguard behind the steering wheel. "Go quiet him down, will you." Frankie was getting angry.

The man got out of the car and shouted across to Billy, "You got a problem nigger boy?"

Billy froze. He just sat and stared for a moment at the man. He looked furious. He couldn't jump out of his side of the car because Frankie's Mercedes was parked too close to it. Suddenly Billy lifted himself across the center panel to the passenger side and got out of the car.

"Billy, wait." Johnny tried to stop him. "It's not worth it Billy, these guys are crumbs. Let me just talk to Benelli, maybe I can straighten the whole thing out."

"Get out of my way Johnny." Billy jumped on the hood of his new car.

The man walked from the door to the front of the Mercedes.

Frankie looked to the man seated in the front, "What's this guy doing?"

"Don't worry about it Boss, Pete will take care of it."

Suddenly Billy jumped into the air with both legs in front of him. The man standing didn't know what was happening. As Billy flew toward him, both feet smashed into the man's face. Billy was a patient man, but nobody was going to call him a nigger boy and get away with it. The man fell to the ground instantly, and it looked like he wasn't getting back up.

The other man jumped out of the car. Johnny remembered what they had done to him—how he almost lost his life, and he wasn't about to let his friend Billy fight these guys alone. Billy had trained Johnny well in martial arts, and Johnny knew just how he was going to fight before he approached the man. As usual, Fankie just sat in the car and let his men do the dirty work—that's what they were paid for. Billy had already punched the other man twice in the jaw just to make sure he had finished him off. Johnny ran to the street to meet him. By now traffic was held up, and there were many spectators. The man attempted to throw a right-hand punch to Johnny's face. Johnny threw his left hand up and blocked it gracefully. He threw a straight-arm blow to the man's right jaw, and then a right-hand chop to his Adam's Apple. The man was stunned instantly. Johnny stepped back and threw a straight kick from his right leg, smashing the man's mouth and nose. The man fell to the ground helplessly. Johnny looked to Billy. Billy had picked the other man up and threw him back in the car. He looked to Johnny, "It appears as though I taught you well Covini."

Johnny just smiled. Billy walked toward the man on the ground. "Johnny I'll help you get him in the car."

"Wait a minute Billy, just one more thing."

Johnny climbed into the car and grabbed Frankie by the shirt. Johnny dragged him outside of the car. He threw him up against the back fender of the car and looked him straight in the eyes. "If you ever say another word to me again, I'm going to split you right down the middle Benelli. You got that?"

Frankie was so scared he couldn't speak. Johnny shook him and asked again, "You got that Benelli?"

Frankie replied, "I got it—I got it."

Johnny threw him in the back seat. Billy picked the other man up and threw him in the back seat. "OK Billy, let's get out of here."

Billy shouted to the man behind the steering wheel, "OK man, move it." The man could barely move.

"Billy, neither of these guys are in a condition to drive."

Billy opened the door and pushed the man to the passenger side. He looked to Frankie in the back seat. "You get up here and drive this car out of here!"

Frankie wasted no time. He climbed over the man in the back seat and jumped to the front of the car. The two men were pretty busted up. They were both bleeding from the mouth and nose. Both their jaws were black and blue. Frankie looked as though he had seen a ghost. Frankie drove off and didn't say a word. The crowd dispersed and the two jumped in the Jaguar and drove away just in time. The police were just arriving.

21

* * * * * * * * * *

Back at the apartment the phone rang. Johnny had just finished his shower. It was seven in the evening and he figured it must be Rosanna. Johnny picked up the phone quickly, "Hello?"

"Johnny, where have you been?" It was Danny Rosco. "I've been trying to get you all afternoon.

"I was in the city. What's up?"

"Johnny I just got word, we start touring next week."

"Next week?"

"That's right, we'll be fronting for a band called The Missiles."

"The Missiles? Those guys are great!"

"So are we Johnny, so are we."

"Geez, it's so sudden. What am I going to tell Rosanna? And besides, I thought Seko Records wanted us to record at their studios first."

"It so happens they're happy with what Marty mastered so far. They're sending it to the factory as is. Look Johnny, we're going on tour and we're not going without you. This is it man, we're on our way."

"OK, what's the next move?" Johnny knew Danny was right. Their career was very important and this was the beginning.

"We have to be in New York tomorrow at 10:00 A.M. to sign

some papers and make all the necessary arrangements. We will also be introduced to a Mr. Sacks, the tour director for Seko Records. I'll pick you up at 6:00 A.M. sharp. We have to leave early because we'll be hitting a lot of traffic."

"What about the other guys?"

"They'll meet us there along with Pauli and a lawyer he's appointed."

"OK, I'll be ready."

"OK, see you tomorrow."

Johnny put the receiver down. He took a deep breath and picked it up again and dialed Rosanna's number. He was already worrying about the fact that he and Rosanna would have to be apart, but he knew he couldn't let anything interfere with his music. It was the break he had been waiting for most of his life.

Rosanna answered. "Hello—"

"Rosanna—"

"Johnny, I've been trying to call you all day. Where have you been?"

"Billy and I were in Philadelphia. He had to order new drums for his upcoming tour."

"I miss you so much when I'm not with you, Johnny."

"I miss you too, Rosanna. Look Rosanna, I have to see you tonight. I mean I'm sorry for such short notice, but I really have to see you."

"Is anything wrong Johnny?"

"I just have to see you, it's very important."

"OK, I'll be there about 8:30."

"OK, I'll see you later."

"I love you Johnny."

"I love you too." Johnny's voice was distant. Rosanna hung up the phone. She felt confused. She knew something was happening.

Johnny hung up. There was a knock at the door. It was Billy.

"Billy, what's up? Come on in man. Come on in the kitchen, I'll make us some coffee."

"Johnny I can't stay."

"Why? What's the problem?"

"Johnny, I came to say good-bye."

"Good-bye? Where are you going all of a sudden?"

"I got a call about five o'clock. I have to go to Florida to-morrow to do some recording before the tour."

Johnny was saddened. "Yeah, but I thought you weren't going on tour for another two months?"

"I'm not. You see, we were supposed to do some recording and pre-tour rehearsing right here in Philly, but there was a problem with management and the plans were changed."

"Wow. This is kind of hard to take, Billy. I mean it's so sudden." Johnny's eyes began to fill with tears. "Man, I'm going to miss you Billy. You're a good friend and a good teacher."

"Yeah. I'm going to miss you too, Covini."

"You know Billy, I want you to know that... uh... well, what I'm trying to say is—"

"Look Covini, it's OK. You don't have to thank me."

"Look Billy, nobody ever helped me the way you did, I mean you didn't owe me anything."

"Look Johnny, I want you to remember something—freely I give, freely I receive. You do the same thing, give of your talent on stage and off. And remember, show love to everyone. Love is the key man, love is the key. The training is over and now the mission begins. You're a drummer. Go out there and play like you've never played before. Remember Johnny, serve God and live for God. Stay young, stay healthy, play drums, and be happy—that's your mission in life."

Johnny was astonished at Billy's wisdom. Billy made Johnny realize his purpose. He felt like a weight was lifted off his shoulders. Instantly, he believed in himself like never before. Billy was a true friend. Johnny would never forget him. He approached Billy and hugged him and patted him on the back. Billy reciprocated.

Billy urged, "Now go out there and do it. Do it. So long

Covini." Billy walked out and closed the door slowly.

Johnny murmured to himself, "Yeah, see ya Billy," and wiped the tears from his eyes with the palms of his hands. Johnny decided to take a short nap until Rosanna came to the apartment.

IT WAS NOW TWENTY MINUTES TILL NINE AND ROSANNA WAS KNOCKING. Johnny woke out of his nap. He had an old black t-shirt on and faded jeans. His hair was all out of place. He ran to the mirror in the bathroom and combed his hair quickly. He wanted to look decent for Rosanna. Johnny ran quickly to the door and opened it. Rosanna stood there smiling. She was so happy to see him. Johnny reached out his hand to Rosanna's and gently led her into the apartment, closing the door behind her. "How are you doing?" he asked. He put his arms around her.

"I'm fine Johnny, how are you?"

"OK, except I need to see you more often."

"I'm sorry Johnny, but I can't get up here too much because of the store and with you not being able to drive, it's hard for us to see each other enough."

"Hey listen, there's a great little Italian restaurant up the road in Phoenixville. How about if we have a late spaghetti dinner?"

"That sounds great. I really didn't have time to eat dinner at home, and I'm starved."

Johnny got dressed quickly and Rosanna and he got on their way to the restaurant. While driving to the restaurant, Rosanna asked Johnny why it was so important that he see her that evening. She was very anxious.

"Don't worry, we'll get to that. Let's just get to the restaurant—I'm starved. When I get my license back I want to drive this car, it's beautiful."

Rosanna's father had bought her a brand new BMW for her twenty-fifth birthday. He had borrowed the money from Johnny's Uncle Al and was able to pay him back in low monthly payments without interest. The color of the car was forest green with a tan leather interior. Johnny was just itching to drive it, but Rosanna was very strict about certain things and wasn't about to let Johnny drive without a license.

The two pulled into the parking lot of the restaurant. As they got out of the car, Johnny said, "Wait till you taste the spaghetti and calamari in this place—it's out of this world."

"Better than Aunt Carmella's?"

"Hey Rosanna, Aunt Carmella's got a style of her own."

The two entered the restaurant. The hostess, a young woman about twenty-eight years old with brown hair approached them. "Table for two?"

"Yes," replied Rosanna.

She seated Johnny and Rosanna and gave them a menu.

"Johnny, this place is very nice."

"I knew you would like it. I've been wanting to take you here for quite some time now." The walls of the restaurant were covered with red and white wallpaper with little diamond designs. The ceiling was bright white. The lights were dim and the place had a very peaceful atmosphere. Italian music was playing at a low volume. The booth that they sat at was covered with red velvet and the table was a dark stained wood and a lighted candle sat between the two of them.

"I wasn't planning on such a romantic evening, this is an unexpected surprise."

"For you, only the best!"

A very young girl about eighteen with black curly hair and brown eyes walked energetically to the table. She appeared a bit pale and tired. She was very thin and stood about five-foot-five. "Good evening, my name is Sharon, and I will be your waitress this evening." She placed two glasses of water on the table. "Would you like to order now?"

"Yes. Spaghetti and calamari for two, and lots of bread and salad."

Rosanna snickered.

"Oh, that was easy enough," the waitress said, "and what can I get you to drink?"

"I'll have a Coke," replied Rosanna.

"Yeah, me too," said Johnny.

The girl took the menus and the two thanked her.

"OK Rosanna, I know you're anxious to know why I asked you up here tonight, so I'm going to get right to the point. I'm going on the road next week."

"Road? But I don't understand."

"The record company has asked the band to start touring next week."

"You mean you're leaving?"

"Yes Rosanna, we have no choice."

"But how will I see you Johnny?" Rosanna was getting a bit nervous.

"Rosanna, take it easy. You knew this would be part of it."

"Yes, but so soon? I mean, we hardly see one another now."

"Rosanna we will be alright. I will come home every month to see you while we are touring."

"Every month?" She reached in her pocketbook for a tissue. She patted her eyes with the tissue. "I'm sorry, it's just that I love you so much, and I couldn't stand not seeing you for a month at a time."

"Hey Rosanna, it's not going to be easy for me either, you know."

"I know Johnny, I know. I'm sorry. You're right, we'll work it out. Exactly what day will you be leaving?"

"I'm not sure, we have to go to New York tomorrow for some last minute instructions and arrangements."

"I'm sorry, I didn't mean to get so emotional. I know I have to be patient and understanding about your career."

The two continued talking about the tour, and after twenty minutes, the waitress approached the table with their dinner.

"Doesn't this look great?"

"Yes, I can't wait to taste it," said Rosanna. She sprinkled some cheese on her spaghetti and began to eat. "Johnny—it's delicious!"

"I'm glad you like it, and I'm glad we came here. And most of all, I'm glad to be with you. Now, how about a smile?"

Rosanna now felt more at ease and smiled, and the two enjoyed their dinner.

BACK AT THE APARTMENT, THE TWO WERE LYING IN JOHNNY'S BED JUST holding one another and enjoying each other's company. They were both thinking of how it would be when Johnny went on the road. They knew how much they would miss one another. Johnny was gently stroking Rosanna's hair. "So what will you be doing now that we won't be seeing each other too much?" he asked.

"Oh, probably working—you know, doing more paper work, more cleaning, helping my father make his wine."

"You make wine?"

"I'll have you know, Mr. Covini, I've been making wine with my father since I was six years old."

"Well I'll believe that when I see it—you stepping on grapes," he laughed.

"That's not how we make wine! You think I step on grapes like they did in the Old Country?"

"Well, isn't that the way you do it?"

"No. We have an electric grape crusher. Johnny you're funny, you know that? So tell me, how was your day in the city?"

"You wouldn't believe it."

"Come on tell me—I'm curious."

"Well, first of all, I went to see an old friend of mine in the hospital, and he died right in front of me."

"Are you serious?"

"Yes I'm serious."

"Who was your friend?"

"His name was Lefty, well his real name was Vincent Gambini."

"Was he a musician?"

"No, he was some old guy that used to hang out in Harry's Bar."

"How did you become friends with him?"

"One time I was hanging out in this pool room and this old guy walked in and saw me shooting a game of pool. I was no great pool player—you know what I mean? So the old guy just asked if he could teach me a little bit about the game-you know, the guy took a liking to me. You know, he was kind of like a second father."

"And how long did you know this guy Lefty?"

"Oh, I guess about fifteen years."

"Gee, I'm sorry Johnny. Why didn't you tell me earlier?"

"Now wait a minute, I'm not done yet."

"Why? What else happened?"

"I ran into this guy I used to work for—some bum named Frankie Benelli."

"Frankie Benelli! Johnny, you mean you used to take bets?"

"You know Frankie Benelli?"

"Everybody knows Frankie Benelli. He's not a very good person to work for."

"Yeah I know, I found that out. Those two animals that work for him almost killed me."

"Johnny are you the guy that was beat up and taken for dead at Harry's Bar?"

"Don't tell me you heard all about that?"

"Yes. The man that delivers rolls to the hoagie shop was telling my father all about it the morning after, and I overheard him."

"Gee, I feel embarrassed. Now you know how much of a bum I was."

"What you were or what you think you were doesn't change anything between you and me, I love you just the same."

"Look, don't tell your father, or anyone for that matter, you know, about me being the dead guy and being mixed up with Benelli. It might get back to my Uncle Al, and that could cause a war. I just want to forget about it."

"I promise. Not a word."

Johnny held Rosanna closer, her head laid against his chest. There was silence for a few minutes then Rosanna asked, "Johnny were you really dead?"

"I don't know. I mean, I was in a body bag."

"I hear these stories about people seeing a bright light or going through a tunnel, or some people see themselves lying on an operating table. I'm sorry, I shouldn't be asking you all these questions, you probably don't even want to think about it."

Johnny took a deep breath. "Rosanna, I know you are going to think I'm nuts, but I did see them taking my body away in the ambulance. But just the same, I'm really not ready to talk about it. I'm sorry."

"It's OK. If you ever feel like talking about it I'm here for you."

Rosanna looked at him with curiosity. Johnny and Rosanna began to kiss and caress one another. They fell deeper and deeper in love as Johnny's departure drew nearer. Johnny's desire to make love to Rosanna was a burning one. He hoped this was the night he could make love to her. The day that he had spent in Philadelphia was like a nightmare and all he wanted was to feel Rosanna's warmth.

As they continued to kiss one another passionately Johnny began to unbutton her blouse. Rosanna was not putting up a defense. It seemed as though she wanted to let herself go. Johnny lifted her gently and reached his hands around her back and undid her bra. He patiently slid her top down her arms. He grabbed the straps of her bra and gently pulled them over her shoulders. By now the two were burning with desire for one another's love.

Johnny began kissing Rosanna all over her neck and her breasts. His hand quickly unsnapped the top of her jeans and he began pulling her zipper down. As Johnny's hand began to go into her panties, a bell seemed to go off in Rosanna's head. She heard her mother's voice telling her to stay pure and wait until her wedding night. Rosanna grabbed his hand, "No Johnny, no."

"Rosanna, don't do this to me. I need you desperately."

"I can't Johnny, I just can't, please don't make me do this."

"Rosanna, we're in love. Nobody's going to know anything but me and you."

"Johnny please, don't make me feel guilty. I can't do this."

"Why?"

"Because it's just not right "

Johnny was burning up inside. He became enraged. "What the hell is with you and this virginity thing anyway? You're twenty-five years old, I'm thirty-one years old—we're supposed to be mature adults." Johnny became more frustrated and sat on the edge of the bed. Rosanna just began to put her clothing back on. Johnny got up and walked to the dresser and leaned on it. "What the hell am I supposed to do? I'm only human, you know."

"So am I!" Rosanna shouted. "You think I don't have any feelings? I want you as much as you want me, but I have to wait."

Johnny shouted, "Why do you have to wait?"

"Because that's the way it is! That's the way I was taught. If I give in now, I may never be the same. Johnny, I was never like the other girls that you knew. When it comes to sex, you and I just don't think the same."

"Well that's for damn sure!"

"Johnny, please understand."

"Understand? Understand what—that I can't have sex with my girlfriend?"

"I'm going home," she shouted, "I thought you would want someone decent after you've been with all those one night stands!"

Johnny turned to Rosanna and gave her a dirty look. "Go home Rosanna, I want to get some sleep."

"When will I see you again?"

"I'll give you a call."

Rosanna grabbed her coat and pocketbook off the chair beside the bed and ran through the kitchen and rushed out, banging the door behind her.

Johnny was so frustrated by now he started pacing toward the bathroom and punched the door. He paced back to the bedroom and sat on the edge of the bed. He couldn't help but think how much he loved Rosanna. He quickly picked himself up off the bed and ran for the door, he didn't even grab his coat. He ran out the door and saw Rosanna backing the car up, about ready to pull away. Rain was falling very heavily, and in no time, Johnny was drenched.

Before she could pull away, Johnny reached the car and began banging on the driver's side window. He was so sorry for the way he spoke to Rosanna. Rosanna looked to Johnny and hit the brake. She felt sorry for him as the rain poured down his face.

"Rosanna! Rosanna—wait! I'm sorry, I love you! Don't go. Please, I have to talk to you!"

She put the car in park and opened the door. She got out of the car and immediately fell into Johnny's arms. They began to kiss and then tell each other how much they were sorry.

"I'm sorry Johnny, please forgive me."

"It was my fault Rosanna. I should have had more respect for you."

"Johnny, I don't ever want to fight with you again. That really scared me." She began to cry. Johnny held her tight.

"I'll never talk to you like that again Rosanna, I promise. Never again."

The rain continued to pour and the two were soaking wet. They were so consumed in love, they didn't even realize the effect of the pouring rain.

22

★ ★ ★ ★ ★ ★ ★ ★ ★ ★

5:30 A.M. CAME QUICKLY AND THE PHONE RANG. JOHNNY HAD HAD A very restless night, all he could think about was Rosanna and how much he wanted and needed her. He couldn't wait any longer. He knew he would have to marry her very soon. She was the woman he wanted to be with the rest of his life. He picked up the phone. "Hello..."

"Hello Johnny. It's me, Danny."

Johnny looked at his clock. "Man what the hell you doin' calling me this early in the morning—are you crazy?"

"Man, don't tell me you forgot about this morning already!?"

"Forgot about what?"

"Johnny, we're going to New York this morning to make arrangements for our tour. Man get it together."

"Oh yeah, I forgot about that. What time you gonna be here?"

"I'm running a little late, I should be there by 6:30. And please Johnny, don't go back to sleep—just be ready at 6:30."

"OK, I'll be ready."

"Johnny, you OK.?"

"Yeah, I just had a bad night, didn't sleep too well."

"Yeah, well maybe on the way to New York we can talk about it."

"Yeah, maybe we can talk about it, Danny. See you in an

hour." Johnny hung up the phone and sat on the edge of the bed and ran his hand through his hair. He then put his hand on the back of his neck and rolled his head around. He felt all tensed from the sleepless night. He wondered how he was going to make it through the day. He slowly raised himself up and went to the kitchen to put some tea on.

The apartment had only two rooms and a bath. The kitchen was about twelve by twelve and was equipped with refrigerator and stove. There was very little cabinet space. Rosanna had helped Johnny pick out dinnerware and flatware, and also taught him how to keep food in a refrigerator. The floor was green tile and the walls and ceiling were white. The stove and the sink were a bit old, but Johnny managed to keep them clean with Rosanna's help.

The bedroom had a blue rug. It looked pretty new, but anyone could tell it was not laid down professionally. The landlord probably cut it out from an old, larger rug and just laid it down. The apartment was furnished with old tan furniture. The bed was brown and the mattress was in fairly good condition. The bathroom looked like it had just been remodeled with white tile and a new sink. Overall, the apartment was old, but clean.

Johnny poured himself some cereal. He ate fast and then drank some tea. He barely finished it. He took a quick shower and began to get dressed. He wanted to look good for the record company executives. He slipped on some new jeans and his tan high heel alligator boots. He then put on a black shirt and buttoned it all the way to the top. He spent about ten minutes on his hair. He made sure he combed it well and then ran some mousse through it, and finished it off with some hair-spray. He walked to the closet and took out his brand new waist-length leather jacket with the fur collar.

Despite his sleepless night, Johnny looked good. He felt good. He definitely looked like a rock'n'roll musician. By now his hair was getting very long and the back was resting on the fur of the jacket. He heard a horn beeping and looked to the clock. It was

6:20 A.M. It must be Danny Rosco he thought.

Johnny ran out the door quickly. There was Danny waiting in his white 1970 Buick. The car was dirty and the chrome rusted. When Johnny looked at the car he became worried. He walked to the driver's side window and motioned for Danny to roll the window down.

"Johnny come on, get in the car—we gotta go."

"Are you sure this car is going to make it to New York?"

Danny just took his hands off the steering wheel and raised them slightly. He looked at the ceiling of the car and said, "This guy—now he's going to worry about the car! Johnny get in the car. We'll make it. Don't worry, it's a Buick"

Johnny walked to the passenger side and got in the car reluctantly. He kept thinking about Rosanna. He just couldn't wait to ask her to marry him. "Listen Danny, we have to go to South Philly first."

"South Philly? What are you, crazy? We have to go to New York! It's bad enough with all the traffic, we might not make it in time as it is."

"Look, this won't take long."

"Johnny, don't do this to me man."

"Look Danny, just do what I ask. I promise it won't take long."

Danny looked up and made the sign of the cross and sped off. "Johnny, would you mind telling me one thing?"

"What?"

"Why are we going to South Philly?"

"I gotta see Rosanna."

"This early in the morning? Johnny, you got it bad!"

"Got what?"

"I didn't know it was this deep."

"It's deeper than you think, Danny."

"Johnny, can't you just call her from New York? Besides, she's probably not even awake this early in the morning."

"So, I'll wake her up."

"Well what's the big deal? Why do you have to see her this morning?"

"I'm going to ask her to marry me."

"Well I've heard it all—a proposal at seven o'clock in the morning! We're on the verge of a nationwide tour and this guy's thinking about marriage."

DANNY SLOWLY DROVE THE CAR IN FRONT OF ROSANNA'S HOUSE. JOHNNY jumped out of the car, ran up the long pathway and quickly climbed the steps. He began to knock on the door. By now it was 7:10 A.M., apparently no one was up yet. He continued to knock. Danny slumped over the steering wheel in frustration.

Rosanna finally looked out the window from her second floor bedroom. She was very surprised to see it was Johnny. She couldn't believe it, she felt so happy. She opened the window. She spoke quietly. "Johnny, what are you doing here so early in the morning?" she laughed. He looked like a little lost boy, she thought.

"Rosanna I don't have much time—will you marry me?"

Rosanna's mother and father woke up and wondered what was going on. Her father opened the window. "Johnny, what are you doing here so early in the morning? What's going on?"

Johnny looked to her parents, "I'm sorry Mr. and Mrs. Angelini," he said, and then looked back up to Rosanna. "Come on Rosanna, I need an answer, and it better be yes."

"But why do you want to get married all of a sudden?" she asked.

"Because I love you and I want to be with you all of the time."

"Johnny I love you too, and I want to be with you too. And I will marry you."

"You mean it? You mean you'll really marry me?"

"Yes. But first you will have to get my father's blessing."

"Your father's blessing? He's not a priest."

"No Johnny, I mean you'll have to get his OK."

"Oh boy, here we go." He looked back up at her mother and father.

Danny was in the car praying, "Please God, don't let us be late. Please Lord, I've been waiting for this chance all my life. I know you won't let us be late."

"Mr. Angelini, I want to marry your daughter."

Mr. Angelini looked to his wife. "What's this guy doing? All of a sudden at seven o'clock in the morning he wants to marry my daughter."

"You'd better go talk to her," his wife said.

Mr. Angelini walked to Rosanna's room and his wife followed behind him. As he entered the room, Rosanna said, "I'm sorry Father."

"You don't have to be sorry," said Mrs. Angelini, "you're our daughter and we understand."

Rosanna's father looked at his daughter and smiled. "Your mother's right, you're our daughter—you don't have to be sorry. This man that wants to marry you, do you love him?"

"Yes Father."

"Do you want to marry this man?"

"Yes Father."

"Then you have my blessing."

Rosanna walked forward and gave her mother and father a big hug. "Thank you both for being so good to me. I love you Mom and Dad." Rosanna walked to the window as Johnny waited impatiently. By now Danny was out of the car smoking a cigarette while he paced back and forth. She stood at the window and waited for her father to come forth.

The man walked to the window and shouted to Johnny, "Johnny, you have my blessing. You may marry my daughter. Now why don't I come down and let you in so we all can have some coffee and breakfast."

Danny heard Mr. Angelini's invitation. "Oh no!" he said to himself, "no way!" He ran up the pathway, climbed the steps and grabbed Johnny's arm. He shouted up to Rosanna, "OK. Rosanna, he will see you tonight, don't worry!"

"Danny, what are you doing man?"

"You made your proposal, now let's go. We gotta get to New York."

Johnny shouted up, "Thank you Rosanna. Thank you Mr. and Mrs. Angelini, I love you all. I'll see you tonight, Rosanna!"

"I love you Johnny!" she replied.

THE TWO MEN WERE NOW ENTERING NEW YORK CITY. DANNY WAS VERY relieved and happy it was 9:30 and they had a half an hour to get to Seko Records. He spoke with joy, "New York City—my kind of town! This is it Johnny Covini, the big time—Midnight Angel, the greatest rock band in the world." He extended the palm of his right hand to Johnny. Johnny reciprocated and slapped his hand. As they got into the heart of New York City, Danny said, "Man I love this big city, and to think Johnny, we're gonna play the Garden-Madison Square Garden!"

"Yeah, I know, I just can't believe it! I really feel like I'm dreaming."

"This is no dream Johnny, this is as real as it gets." Danny spotted a parking garage and quickly parked the car. They had to walk about a block to Seko Records. As they walked down 42nd Street, there were mobs of people all over the place. "Johnny, would you check out all the babes," said Danny, "there's enough girls on this block alone to last you a lifetime."

"Man, I can see you haven't changed much!"

"Who wants to change? You change and you get old. I want to stay young and happy."

"Yeah, well I gotta be careful. I just asked Rosanna to marry me, but what the hell, who said I can't flirt around a little bit."

"Now that's the Johnny Covini I know."

The two reached the building where Seko Records was located. "Well here it is Johnny," said Danny, "Seko Records. I can't believe it. Imagine—us getting signed by Seko Records!"

"Well, what are we waiting for?" said Johnny.

"Yeah, what are we waiting for? Let's do it."

The two entered the building and approached the receptionist. A girl with long brown hair, fair complected, brown eyes and round black eyeglasses greeted them. "May I help you?"

"Yeah, I'm Johnny Covini and this is Danny Rosco. We're with Midnight Angel and we're here to see Mr. Sacks." Johnny turned to Danny. "That is his name, isn't it Danny?"

"Hey, you know I forgot."

Johnny frowned at Danny and then looked at the receptionist. "That's his name—Mr. Sacks." He looked to Danny once more. "You're so overcome by New York City and all the girls you forgot the guy's name!"

"Mr. Sacks is on the third floor. Just take the elevator to your right. Room 318."

"Thank you," replied Johnny.

Danny looked to the receptionist, "Hey, can I see you with your glasses off?"

"Man, would you come on Rosco and quit flirting."

"OK, OK."

The two walked to the elevator. The receptionist just shook her head and mumbled to herself, "Musicians—they're all the same."

The two men took the elevator to the third floor and walked to Room 318. As the two walked into the front of the office, the secretary greeted them. She was blond, young, and very attractive. Johnny looked to Danny, "Now don't get carried away." The girl just snickered. "We're here to see Mr. Sacks."

"Oh, you must be Mr. Covini and Mr. Rosco. Just step into the next room and have a seat, the rest of the band is waiting for you."

"Thank you," the two replied. They walked into the next room. It was 10:15. The rest of the band was waiting impatiently.

"Man, where have you guys been?" said Mike Danella. "You're late."

Danny looked at his watch. "Man, what's this guy saying Johnny, we're only fifteen minutes late." The guys started getting a bit rowdy. A few seconds later, in came Pauli and Jimmy Malone, the band's entertainment lawyer.

"Hey, why don't you guys cool it," said Pauli, "I want to introduce you to your entertainment lawyer, Jimmy Malone." Jimmy Malone had been an entertainment lawyer for over ten years. He was good-looking, smart, and had a great personality. He and Pauli were friends for over five years.

In no time Mr. Sacks, the tour director for Seko Records, entered. Mr. Sacks stood six-foot-tall, medium build, about forty-five years old. He sported a gray pin-striped suit with a vest, white shirt, and a burgundy tie. He was fair complected with medium-length black hair, parted on the side. He looked about ten years younger than his age. He must have loved his work.

"Good morning gentlemen, I'm Mr. Sacks, tour director for Seko Records." The guys introduced themselves. "First of all, I want to thank you for attending on such short notice. We feel that your band is very good, and we don't want to waste any time getting you promoted, so the sooner your tour begins, the better."

Danny interrupted with excitement, "Yeah, the sooner we tour, the better." The guys just laughed, and so did Mr. Sacks.

"Now, I'm sorry to inform you that Mr. Cassenelli and Mr. Kominski will be delayed a few hours. They probably won't be here till about one." The guys sighed.

"What are we going to do till one o'clock?" Jerry asked.

"Well what I'd like to do for you gentlemen is rent you a limousine so you can have a good tour of New York City—you know, it will give you a feel for touring and facing the big cities.

We should have a limo here for you in about forty-five minutes. While you're waiting, I'll have some coffee and Danish sent in."

"What do you think about that—a limousine!" said Danny.

"Wow, my first limo ride," said Stevie. The fellows began to get very excited; all of a sudden they felt like kings.

"Hold on one minute," said Pauli, "I'm not riding around New York City with these guys, Jimmy, how 'bout we go have some brunch and go over some business. We'll see you guys later."

The guys shouted, "Ah, you party-poopers!"

Danny spoke, "What do you think about that, Johnny Covini? A '70 dirty Buick to a big white limo."

"Anything's better than that heap!"

"It got us to New York, didn't it?"

"Yeah, I got a sore rear end from that broken spring."

"Oh yeah, how would you like to take a cab back home?" Everyone laughed. This was a day they would never forget. Mr. Sacks was certainly a nice fellow, he wanted the guys to feel as comfortable as possible.

"OK fellows, I'll see you back here at 1:00, and my secretary will bring you coffee and Danish. The limo driver will come up to get you."

All the fellows thanked Mr. Sacks for his kindness. He made them feel very at ease. After Mr. Sacks left the room, the guys started whispering to one another about being chauffeured around and how they couldn't believe being at a major record company, ready to prepare for a tour. It was a dream of a lifetime.

A woman with a leather skirt and a red top walked into the room. Her permed black hair and pretty face were very appealing to the guys. She brought in the coffee and Danish and introduced herself, "My name is Nancy—Mr. Sacks' secretary. I hope you enjoy your coffee and Danish, and if you need anything before the limo gets here, let me know."

"Hey, why don't you go for a ride with us?" said Rosco.

"Hey listen to this guy over here—" said the men, "he even

has to flirt with the executive's secretary."

"Well, actually I'd love to, but I just have too much work to do," replied the secretary.

"Wo. Shot him down!" said Jerry. The guys laughed. The guys ate most of the Danish, and just joked around for the next forty-five minutes. The chauffeur arrived. He spoke in broken English, "Hello, my name is Raoul, and I will be your chauffeur for the next couple of hours." The fellows introduced themselves and off they went.

When they got down to the limo, it was more than they expected. There it was: a long white Lincoln Continental stretch limo with tinted glass. Raoul opened the door to let the fellows in. They barely acknowledged him while fussing over the big car. Finally everyone got into the limo and they were off.

As they drove along, they could feel all the excitement of the big city. They continually laughed and had a ball. Raoul showed them some of the best sites of the city: Times Square, Fifth Avenue, Greenwich Village, and some of the tallest buildings in the city. As they rode by Madison Square Garden, Johnny said, "I can't wait till we play that place!"

"Yeah, just think of it," said Danny, "playing for New York City. Now I know how the Beatles felt. We did it fellas!" he shouted, and then looked at Johnny Covini. "Ladies and Gentlemen, Johnny Covini—the greatest drummer in the world!"

Johnny laughed and the rest of the fellows laughed with him. The tour of New York City was just what the guys needed. They were glad the two executives were late, otherwise they may have never had such fun.

BACK AT SEKO RECORDS IN A CONFERENCE ROOM WITH MR. SACKS, THE fellows were listening to some success stories of other well-known bands. Suddenly two men walked in; it was Mr. Cassenelli and Mr. Kominski. A couple minutes later Pauli and the band's lawyer,

Jimmy Malone, walked in. Cassenelli and Kominski shook hands with Pauli and Jimmy and greeted them.

"Sorry we're late gentlemen," said Mr. Cassenelli, "You know how the music business is—never on time. We do want to thank you for getting here on such short notice, however, I'm sure Mr. Sacks has already thanked you." The two gentlemen took a seat. "I realize all of this happened kind of suddenly, but we will go over the dos and don'ts of a nationwide tour. Mr. Sacks here will tell you all about it in just a few minutes.

First I'd like to speak a bit about why you're here and why we want to sign you with Seko Records. We believe you are one of the hottest new bands to come along in quite a while. I mean we know we have a good product and that makes us very happy. We generally don't sign bands this quickly, but Mr. Kominski and I know talent when we see it, and we didn't want to have another company snatch you guys up. We want to get you started right away. In the next couple of days you'll be introduced to your set up men, tour manager, transportation manager, costume manager, and so on. All the equipment—drums, amplifiers, and whatever else—will be picked up for you and ready for the road. You will play your first concert at the Philadelphia Spectrum, and then you will hit New York—Madison Square Garden, and keep on moving from there. You will tour for eight weeks and then have a two-week break. I suggest you get some rehearsal time in on the two-week layoff—we don't want you to get stale. I would like Mr. Sacks to take the floor now, to tell you just how important this tour is."

"Gentlemen, I've been tour director for Seko Records for ten years now, and believe me, I've seen a lot of bands come and go. Longevity depends on the band, its members. You can enjoy the benefits of long-lasting success if you play the game right, in reality it's called business. I've seen bands destroyed by drugs, alcohol, women, and interpersonal conflicts. I've also seen bands destroyed by jealousy, egotism, and just plain bad attitudes. Don't let this, and I quote, 'happen to you.' It's a fun business, and it's a business where you can become a millionaire in no time. Be professional. Have respect for one another, and don't look for individual recognition. There are five of you, you are a group, so work as a group. You are like one big machine and that machine will run efficiently only if all its parts are working together.

Life on the road is never easy. You play a concert, you may get to bed late. Sometimes it takes a few hours before you unwind. I suggest you get to bed as early as possible, and very little partying. Now when I say partying, I mean good clean fun—no drugs, no alcohol. I suggest a little workout routine every morning before showering and heading for the next city. Use good eating habits, and most of all, be extremely careful about sexual relationships on the road. This is the age of devastating diseases. It could end your career instantly. This is not a big party, this is a business. You're up early, you're on a plane, and you hit your next city. You do radio interviews and then you hit the stadium for a sound check. You eat a light dinner, and then you go to the stadium. And the next day, it starts all over again."

The fellows were exhausted just listening to him. They weren't young rock stars. They were in their late twenties and early thirties. They knew life on the road wouldn't be easy for them, but their determination was stronger than ever.

Pauli and Malone sat by listening carefully, they wanted the guys to be well-informed.

"I don't mean to discourage anyone," continued Mr. Sacks, "I just want you to know what it's like out there. OK, are there any questions?"

Johnny looked to his friends. They looked back at him. They all looked to one another. Johnny spoke, "We're ready."

"OK, on that note," said Mr. Sacks, "let's get the necessary papers signed with Pauli and Mr. Malone, and that should just about wrap things up."

After all the legalities were taken care of, everyone stood up and exchanged handshakes, and there were thank you's and congratulations. Mr. Kominski quieted everyone down. "There will be a party Saturday night in your honor, right here in New York at the Hilton. Mr. Sacks will give you the details before you leave. We will invite a lot of guests, and I'm sure you will have a good time. And gentlemen, good luck!"

After signing some papers and taking care of some last minute details, the fellows didn't leave Seko Records until 3:00 P.M.

JOHNNY AND DANNY RETURNED TO THE HOAGIE SHOP IN SOUTH PHILLY. Johnny couldn't wait to tell Rosanna the wedding date. He thought about all the wedding arrangements while driving from New York. He barely spoke to Danny. Danny quickly parked the car, and the two entered the store.

Johnny saw Rosanna's father at the register. It was 5:30, and the store would be closing in an hour. He didn't see Rosanna. "Mr. Angelini, where's Rosanna?" he shouted.

"Johnny! How you doin'? You and your friend, are you hungry? Let me make you a sandwich."

"Hey, that sounds good Johnny," said Danny.

"Hey, that sounds good Mr. Angelini, but where's Rosanna?"

"She's in the back cutting lunch meat for tomorrow."

"Danny have a seat, I'll be right out." Johnny walked into the back room quietly. He wanted to surprise her. Rosanna was about to put a pile of meat into the refrigerator when Johnny gently grabbed her around the waist and kissed her on the neck. Rosanna smiled. "I missed you," said Johnny.

"Well, you won't have to miss me any longer."

"What do you mean?"

"We're getting married, aren't we?"

"Yes, and it's all set. The band will have a two-week break after we tour for eight, and that's when we get married."

As Johnny and Rosanna spoke, Uncle Al and his men walked

into the store. "Hey Alphonse!"

"My friend Pondolona, how are you today?"

"I'm good. You and your friends sit down. I will make you something to eat."

Danny wondered who these men were. They looked scary. There were five other people in the store and they all greeted Al. Despite his illegal doings, he helped a lot of people in the neighborhood, and they had lots of respect for him. They took a seat in a booth.

Mr. Angelini shouted over the counter, "I want you to meet Johnny's friend. Hey, what's your name, Johnny's friend? He didn't introduce me to you."

"I'm Danny—you know, the guy that was waiting for Johnny this morning."

"Oh, that was you! Al, I want you and your friends to meet Danny."

Danny got off the stool and walked to Al and his friends and shook hands. Meanwhile, Johnny and Rosanna were in the back room holding and kissing one another. Al had asked where Johnny was.

"He's in the back, talking to Rosanna," said Danny.

"They're getting married, you know," said Mr. Angelini.

"Getting married?! My nephew's getting married to my best friend's daughter? This calls for a drink, Pondolona!" Al looked to his bodyguard as he reached in his pocket for money. Al's bodyguards stood six-foot-two and they were built. They worked out daily. They weren't your average looking bodyguards. They had good personalities, they were good-looking characters, and they had class. They were always dressed well with well-styled black hair. They made good money working for Al. Al had bought them both new cars, and would take them out occasionally and buy them new clothing. Al never had any children of his own. The two men were with him for ten years. They were like sons to him. They started working with him when they were twenty-one. They liked

Al a lot, and had a lot of respect for him. Although they were gentlemen, they would turn into human wrecking machines to protect Al. Their names were Antonio and Benny.

Al looked to Antonio. "Antonio," he said, "I'd like you to run down to the state store and get a bottle of Royal Crown. We have to make a toast!"

"Sure Al, I'll be right back." Al handed him the money, and he was off.

Rosanna asked Johnny what day their wedding would be. Johnny looked to the calendar hanging on the wall. "Well, let me see, the tour starts next week… here we are—how about Saturday, March 28th?"

"I hope we have enough time to arrange everything."

"Arrange what? You just get married and that's it."

"Oh Johnny, no. That's not the way it's going to be."

"What do you mean?"

"We have to have a big wedding—you know, my relatives, your relatives—we have to invite them all. I'm sure my mother and father already spoke about it this morning."

"But Rosanna, I'm going to be on tour for the next eight weeks."

"They have phones on the road, don't they?"

"Rosanna, we can't just arrange a wedding over the phone."

"Just leave it to me, I'll know what to do. I have four cousins who I want to be in my wedding—they're all girls, and you have four good friends in your band. They will walk with them. So we have that settled right now. All I want you to do is get the measurements for their tuxedos, and I will pick them out. So you see, when you come back from your tour, all that will be arranged."

"Man, it's a good thing Lefty left me that money 'cause I don't know how we would pay for all this."

"Johnny, the bride's father always pays for the wedding."

"I can't let your father do that."

"Johnny, don't argue with me, it's tradition. You can call

who you want to invite to the wedding while you're on your tour. Then you can call me and give me the names and addresses over the phone, and I will get the invitations out for you. My mother and I will arrange all the other things, such as my wedding gown, the caterers, the photographer, the wedding cake and so forth. I will ask my father to rent a limousine. And, before you go on tour, we will pick out our rings. Johnny we're going to have a beautiful wedding."

"You know, you're a good arranger. You should start arranging music for the band."

"You take care of the music, I will take care of the wedding. Now, let's go out and tell my father." As they walked to the front of the store, Johnny was surprised to see Uncle Al in the booth.

"Uncle Al, when did you come in?"

"Hey Johnny, I just heard the good news." Uncle Al and his bodyguard, Benny, stood up. He gave Johnny a hug. He then shook Johnny's hand and congratulated him. "I'm very proud of you, Johnny."

"Thanks Uncle Al."

Al then turned to Rosanna and said. "You're a beautiful woman Rosanna." Johnny smiled and looked at Rosanna. Rosanna blushed and looked to Johnny.

"Congratulations Johnny," said Benny and then congratulated Rosanna and kissed her on the cheek.

Danny congratulated Johnny and Rosanna and kissed Rosanna. The door opened and Antonio came in with the bottle of Royal Crown.

"Oh, here's Antonio," said Al, "Pondolona, get us some glasses." Al turned to the five other customers in the store and asked them all to have a drink with him and his friend Pondolona to celebrate the couple's plans for marriage.

Antonio handed the bottle to Al. Pondolona placed the glasses on the counter and Al poured the drinks. As he poured, he asked Johnny what the date would be.

"Saturday, March 28th, Uncle Al."

Al smiled. "Ah, it's going to be a beautiful day. You're going to be a beautiful bride, Rosanna. Your mother will be proud of you. And Johnny, wait till your Aunt Carmella hears the news, I can see her now—crying like a baby." Al looked to Antonio. "Antonio, my nephew and best friend's daughter are getting married. Give them both a big hug and congratulate them. Everyone come to the counter so we can make a toast," said Al.

Al gave a glass to everyone. "Did I miss anybody? I would like to make an announcement. The daughter of my good friend Pondolona and my nephew, Johnny Covini, are going to be married. I wish them the best that life has to offer."

Everyone drank their shot of whiskey, set their glasses down, and clapped for the couple. They all gathered around Johnny and Rosanna and exchanged congratulations. Everyone felt happy, especially Uncle Al and his friend Pondolona. Johnny and Rosanna looked at one another and kissed. Everyone cheered them on.

23

* * * * * * * * * * *

SATURDAY NIGHT HAD COME QUICKLY AND THE BAND WAS AT THE PARTY held by the record company in their honor. Johnny and Rosanna appeared to be the perfect couple. Many of the guests were looking on, especially the women admiring the band members which Rosanna was not accustomed to. A woman with a black leather outfit on and pitch black hair approached Johnny. Her make up was applied heavily and she had the brightest red lipstick ever. The girl really was cute and Rosanna resented her.

"Hey, aren't you the drummer for Midnight Angel?" the girl asked.

"Yes I am. Who are you?"

"I'm Lisa. I've heard a lot about your band."

"Well thank you, Lisa," Johnny replied. "Where are you from?"

Rosanna interrupted, "Johnny, I think I'd like to get some fresh air. Would you mind excusing us, Lisa?" Rosanna pulled Johnny away. She was obviously jealous. Lisa looked on in dismay, she saw the anger and jealousy in Rosanna and wondered how Johnny would survive as a rock star with her attitude.

The two walked out of the hotel to get some air. Not a word was exchanged. Johnny was pissed off, however, he thought it proper to honor Rosanna's request. He did not want to cause a scene at the party. When they got outside, Johnny asked, "Why did you do that?"

"Because I was getting sick of that girl getting too personal with you."

"Personal? Rosanna listen, this stuff goes on all the time. People are curious, you know, they want to talk."

"Well I didn't like her."

"Look Rosanna, when you work in the hoagie shop, don't men come in and make conversation sometimes?"

"Well, not exactly conversation, but they sometimes ask certain questions—tell me their troubles, you know it's all in the business."

"Well this is a business too. A big business. So please don't act like that, Rosanna, it upsets me. I've come a long way and I don't need this kind of stuff going on."

Suddenly there was silence for a few minutes. Rosanna must have thought to herself that Johnny was right. She looked to him. "I'm sorry Johnny, I'm really sorry. I guess there's a lot I have to learn about this rock'n'roll business."

"Rosanna listen, no matter how many women I talk to, there's only one who will ever be able to turn me on, and that's you." Rosanna smiled. "It's true Rosanna—only you, you're all I need to get by."

"Johnny, I'll be with you always no matter what," said Rosanna.

Johnny explained to her, "And when we get married, you can be with me on the road. And maybe we can make a baby on the way."

The two hugged and expressed their love for each other. "Let's go inside," said Johnny, "they'll probably be calling for the band members soon."

As the two rejoined the party, Mr. Sacks was about to speak at the microphone. "Ladies and gentlemen, can I have your attention..." The party suddenly quieted down. "Wednesday night at the Philadelphia Spectrum there will be an all-new and may I add very exciting rock group, Midnight Angel. As you all know, they are here with us tonight, as this party is in their honor. Seko Records honors drummer Johnny Covini, bass man Danny Rosco, on guitar—Stevie Roselli, Mike Danella—keyboards, and Jerry Carvelli—lead vocals. Ladies and gentlemen, from South Philadelphia, U.S.A., truly an American band, with all Italian names of course, ladies and gentlemen, Midnight Angel!"

The people began to applaud the band and the band members took a bow. Mr. Sacks spoke again, "Gentlemen, please come up to the stage and say a few words."

The fellows were so excited they didn't know quite how to act; a party in their honor, and a major concert tour about to begin. As they walked to the stage, people were making all types of good comments. They were patting the fellows on the back and congratulating them. There were people from other bands who Seko Records had signed, record company executives, producers, managers, and lots of people who were friends of people in the business.

When the guys reached the stage, they looked at one another. Mr. Sacks asked who would like to speak first. As usual, they all looked to Johnny. "Looks like you're first Johnny."

Johnny looked at the guys and grinned. He took the mic from Mr. Sacks. "Well, I don't know why I'm always elected to speak first, but just the same, here I am. And here we are. First of all, I want to thank Seko Records for signing us to a recording contract, and I also want to thank Pauli Rizzo for being our manager." Pauli just waved and smiled with his left arm around his wife's shoulder. "For me, at least, it's definitely a dream come true, and I really think I speak for the rest of the band when I say that." The other guys shook their heads in agreement.

"Just about a year ago I was sentenced by a judge to spend time in a rehabilitation center for drug and alcohol abuse, and I must admit, I was a mess. I felt like a real loser. I mean, I thought my life was coming to a definite end. I was broke, busted, and beat. I didn't even want to play drums anymore. And then one of the best people I will ever know in this life said, let's give it one more shot." Johnny looked at Danny. Both of their eyes began to tear. "I told him he was crazy, that I didn't even want to think of playing music again, let alone recording an album. But I have to admit, Danny Rosco is a talker. Now, he didn't have to ask me to play drums—there's plenty of good drummers out there who are sober and have a clear mind, but Danny believed in me. He seemed to know I would get better. Danny and I go back a long way, and I can honestly say that I found a real friend." Johnny turned to Danny and thanked him personally. He shook his hand and patted him on the back. Danny reciprocated.

"Now, as for the rest of the fellows, they probably don't even care about me," Johnny was joking. All the people laughed. "Only kidding, guys. No, seriously, as for the rest of the fellows, they are truly the best group of musicians I've ever worked with. And I mean that guys. I hope we have a long and healthy friendship, and I hope Midnight Angel will never fade out. Now there's two other people who I must thank: one is Billy Curry, one of the greatest drummers in the world who you all know." The crowd applauded. "Billy has truly been a big inspiration, and he's more than just a drummer, he's a kind and considerate person, and a true friend. I just wish he could have been here tonight, but as most of you may know, Billy will be back on the road soon and had other commitments to fulfill. And last, but not least, the greatest thing that has ever happened to me, and she's here at the party tonight. Rosanna, I'd like you to come to the stage for a moment."

Rosanna was embarrassed. She walked slowly to the stage. Everyone applauded. Johnny pulled her close to him. "Not too long ago, in a hoagie shop in South Philadelphia, I met this beautiful woman standing next to me. Ever since that time, I haven't been the same. It's amazing what love can do to a man, especially when you're in love with someone like Rosanna. Rosanna has changed my life considerably. She has taught me to be confident and responsible. She has truly made my life worth living." Johnny looked to Rosanna. "Rosanna" he said, "Thank you for letting me in your life. I will love you forever. Once again, I want to thank all of you. I'll see you at the Spectrum."

Johnny received some of the biggest applause of his life. He walked to the band members as he held Rosanna's hand. They all joined hands and held them above their heads. The crowd continued to applaud and cheer.

ON FRIDAY JOHNNY HAD MADE ARRANGEMENTS FOR LEFTY'S FUNERAL on Sunday night and burial Monday morning. It was a sad day for Johnny. He wished that Lefty could have enjoyed success with him. He knew Lefty would have been proud of him. Lefty was someone Johnny would never forget. He gave him many good memories of his teen years.

After leaving the burial site with Rosanna, he went to Lefty's lawyer and took care of the will that Lefty had made out to him.

AT 8:00 P.M. TUESDAY NIGHT, JOHNNY WAS GETTING SOME THINGS TO-gether. He would be leaving to go to a hotel in Philadelphia with the rest of the band not far from the Spectrum. He heard a horn beep. It was Rosanna to pick him up and drive him into the city. Johnny hoped he would have gotten his license back by now, but there really was no need at this point anyway. There would be no need for him to drive while on tour.

Rosanna drove Johnny to the rehabilitation center before heading to Philadelphia so he could say good-bye to everyone who had been a big support to him. He especially thanked Jerry Simon. Even Mildred Stone wished him the best of luck. He could only spare ten minutes, and off they went to the city.

Johnny was very anxious as they drove down the expressway. "Rosanna, I hope I have everything I need."

"Don't worry Johnny, if there's anything you need, I will get it for you tomorrow. Tonight you will have to relax. You have to get a good night's sleep. Tomorrow will be the biggest night of your life."

"You're right, Rosanna, I have to relax. I just can't believe this-we're opening for the Missiles. That place is going to be packed—20,000 people. I've never played in front of that many people."

"Johnny, don't worry. Your band is well rehearsed. You guys are good musicians, and you work well together. You will be great!"

"Thank you Rosanna, you always make things better."

WHEN THEY GOT TO THE HOTEL JOHNNY AND ROSANNA WERE GREETED by Mr. Sacks. "Johnny, how are you?"

"I'm good—a little nervous, but good."

"It's nothing Johnny. When you hit the stage tomorrow night, you will feel great."

"Mr. Sacks, I want you to meet my fiance, Rosanna."

Mr. Sacks extended his hand, "Nice to meet you Rosanna."

Rosanna shook his hand, "Nice meeting you also Mr. Sacks."

"I guess I'll have to get to the Spectrum early tomorrow to set up my drums," Johnny assumed.

Mr. Sacks laughed. "Johnny take it easy, you're forgetting something."

"What?"

"We've hired road people. There's a qualified man setting your drums up. The band will be going to the Spectrum tomorrow afternoon about one o'clock. All the equipment will be set up. All you will have to do is show him how to situate your drumset, and from then on, he will know just what to do. This is the recording business Johnny, not the nightclubs."

"I'm sorry Mr. Sacks, I keep forgetting about that."

"Come on, let's go to a conference room we reserved—the rest of the band is waiting."

They entered the room, and there the band members were, laughing and joking around as usual. Mr. Sacks would introduce them to their tour manager Joe Houston as soon as he arrived. Joe Houston had been a tour manager for a long time, and managed tours for some of the biggest names in the business. Mr. Sacks spoke a few words as the band members settled down and greeted Johnny and Rosanna.

There was a quick knock on the door. Mr. Sacks opened it and in walked Joe Houston. Joe was six-foot-two-inches, and must have weighed about 280 pounds. His faded jeans seemed to have been falling as his belly hung over his belt.

He had on a t-shirt which read "Midnight Angel—the greatest" and a black leather jacket which was unzipped. His face was very rugged looking and round. His hair was long and stringy and dry. The top of his head was balding. Underneath, was one of the sweetest guys in the world, but when it came time to get tough, Joe was a killer. The man could definitely fight. Nobody pushed him around. His crew respected him because he was a good leader and made the job lots of fun for everybody.

Mr. Sacks spoke. "Gentlemen I want you to meet your tour manager, Joe Houston."

Joe shook everyone's hand. "How's everyone doing tonight?" he asked.

"Fine," they said.

"I don't know, you sound a little nervous to me," he laughed. The guys just smiled, they knew he was right.

Joe continued, "OK here it is, tomorrow there will be a limo to pick you guys up here at the hotel. That will be at 1:00. You will be driven to the Spectrum to make adjustments on your instruments, meet the road crew, and everyone else in your tour." He looked to Rosanna. "Oh, and by the way, this beautiful woman—is she part of the band?"

Everyone laughed. "She's my fiance," said Johnny.

"Lucky you", said Joe. "After you get introduced to everybody, you will get a good solid sound check and a trial run. You will probably play your whole set. That will probably last about an hour and a half, so while you rehearse, play like there's an audience. Just imagine there's twenty thousand people out there. Now, obviously we won't do this before every concert, this is just to get you used to playing in big concert halls. After the Spectrum we hit the Garden. It will be a sound check only. No more rehearsals after Philadelphia— strictly playing for the crowd. And remember, you won't have to make any adjustments on your amplifiers, we will take care of that. And Johnny, just play the drums hard and solid. We will take care of the volume. Are there any questions?"

There were no questions from the fellows. They just wanted to listen and absorb all the information. Joe was a very serious man and held their attention well. "OK after the rehearsal, you will go back to the hotel, shower up and eat a very light dinner. Try to get an hours sleep, or just an hour of relaxation. The limo driver will pick you up at 5:00. You will go on stage at 8:00. OK, that's it. It'll be good working with you guys." Everyone stood and shook Joe's hand and thanked him. "OK gentlemen, see you tomorrow at 1:00."

The fellows decided to go directly to their hotel rooms and just spend some quiet time alone. Johnny wanted Rosanna by his side.

JOHNNY AND ROSANNA WERE LYING SIDE BY SIDE IN BED WATCHING TV. The TV was on very low volume and they weren't saying much. They were both thinking of Johnny's opening night. Suddenly Johnny spoke. "Rosanna, I'm scared."

"You're worrying about tomorrow night, aren't you?"

"Yes."

"But why?"

"Rosanna, that place will be sold out. We're talking twenty thousand people. I've never played in front of twenty thousand people. They're going to expect a lot from us—I don't know if we can do it. I mean, we're good, but not as good as the Missiles."

"Johnny, you have to remember one thing: you're not going to be there to be like the Missiles, you're going to be there to be the drummer for Midnight Angel, and Midnight Angel has to work together as a whole. You know, like a machine and everybody is a part of that machine. Like you told me the other night, you've come along way, and now you must make the final mile. All you have to do is be yourself, Johnny, and they will love you and your band, because Midnight Angel is good, and you're a good drummer."

"How do you know all that?" he asked.

"I'm in love with the drummer." Rosanna looked at the clock by the bed. It was 9:30. "Johnny, I'm going to leave now."

"Why can't you stay a little longer?"

"I think it would be best if you spent some time alone before you get to sleep."

"But why?"

"It will get you used to being alone when you're on tour. We won't be married for two months, and you will have to be alone at nights for that length of time. I know you will be able to call me every night, but there will be periods of loneliness until we can be together. For now, I want you to depend on your friends in the band and your friends on the road crew for support. And make sure you get to bed early at night, I've heard a lot of crazy stories about bands on the road."

Johnny laughed. "I'll be good Rosanna, I promise." The two held on to one another for a few minutes.

"Johnny, I have to go. I will call you tomorrow. I love you."

"I love you too."

Rosanna had gone. Suddenly Johnny felt very alone. He began to think about Billy. He remembered how Billy had told him about a God of love and power. Johnny then remembered the Bible he had picked up in the room at the rehabilitation center. He thought to himself, there must be one in the drawer of the night table beside the bed—all hotels have them. He quickly opened the drawer of the night table, and sure enough there was a Bible staring him in the face. He remembered vaguely where the particular verse was that he was looking for. Suddenly it came to him like a flash of lightning, the Book of Isaiah, he thought.

He turned to chapter forty and there it was at verse thirty-one: "But they that wait upon the Lord shall renew their strength, they shall mount up with wings as eagles. They shall run and not be weary. They shall walk and not faint." Suddenly he felt rejuvenated. He didn't feel alone or scared. "Thank you Lord," he said, "for a friend like Billy. If it wasn't for him, I may have never known you." Johnny set the book down and in no time, he was fast asleep.

Wednesday morning came quickly. Johnny was up at 8:00. He laid in bed till 8:30 and then showered. He left the room at 9:15 and met the fellows for breakfast downstairs. At 11:00, they went back to their rooms to get organized before the limo arrived at 1:00 to take them to the Spectrum for a sound check.

The phone rang in Johnny's room. He picked up the receiver quickly. "Hello…"

"Johnny, it's me."

"Rosanna, how are you this morning?"

"I'm a little busy—you know lunch time at the hoagie shop. Johnny, your cousin Cosmo's here. He wants me to tell you that he wishes you the best and good luck."

"Ask him if he's coming to the concert tonight."

"He said he can't make it tonight, but he'll listen to it on the radio. He won't be home in time to watch it on TV."

"Radio? TV.? Nobody told me about any radio or TV broadcast. Ask Cosmo where he heard that."

"Cosmo, where did you hear about the broadcasts?"

"Somebody had that rock 'n' roll station on in the meat house this morning, you know, WYSP. And they said it would be aired on TV also."

"Cosmo said he heard it would be aired on TV and WYSP. He said they mentioned it was rare that a major concert would be televised live. It sounds like the whole tri-state area will be watching Midnight Angel tonight."

"Why are they treating us like royalty?"

"You are good—you deserve to be treated well."

"Well, I won't complain. Rosanna, I want you to come to the hotel about five o'clock. You can ride to the Spectrum with me and the rest of the band in the limo."

"OK, I'll be there at five."

"OK, I have to leave now, we're going to the Spectrum soon for some rehearsing before the show."

"Good luck Johnny, I'll say a prayer for you."

"Thanks, I think I'll need it. I love you."

"I love you."

THE REHEARSAL AT THE SPECTRUM WENT BETTER THAN EXPECTED. THE guys were familiarized with all the technicalities of the equipment and were introduced to all the technicians and lighting people. The road crew did an excellent job setting up equipment and the guys were more than pleased. Everyone treated them with the utmost respect. They made the band feel very comfortable and eased much of their opening night jitters. The afternoon went quickly and the pressures of opening night were building.

BACK AT THE HOTEL AT 4:45 P.M. JOHNNY WAS ALL READY TO LEAVE. HE placed his duffle bag over his shoulder which contained twenty pair of drumsticks and three towels. He wore an old pair of faded jeans, sneakers, and a black sweatshirt with a leather jacket over top. His casual dress made him feel more comfortable and at ease. He would have to dress in specifically designed clothing for the stage before the concert. He looked at his clock; it was 4:55. Rosanna hadn't shown up yet. The phone rang and he picked up the receiver quickly.

"Hello?"

"Hey Johnny, what's happening?"

"What do you mean what's happening? Who's this?"

"This is Joe, the tour manager. The limo's here and it's five o'clock. Everybody's waiting for you in the lobby. Is there a problem?"

"Did you see Rosanna come in the door?"

"Johnny, there's a lot of people walking through down here— I don't know, I might have missed her. Look, we'll leave word with the guy at the desk. If she comes in he will tell her where to go to get into the Spectrum."

"OK, I'm on my way down." Suddenly Johnny was saddened and then angry. Where the hell could she be? He thought to himself, of all nights to be late. Johnny got himself together and rushed down to the lobby to meet the rest of the band, and off they went to the Spectrum.

Johnny was quiet on the ride over. All he could think about was Rosanna. Where could she be? He thought. The rest of the guys were joking and laughing. They tried to cheer him up and assured him Rosanna just got held up and would meet him later.

BY SIX O'CLOCK, THE BAND WAS BACKSTAGE IN THE DRESSING ROOM. They began getting into their stage clothes and then would have their hair teased and sprayed a bit. At 6:30 the doors opened, and people began flooding in. They were very excited about seeing The Missiles and now an added treat, a band from their own hometown. The concert was sold-out—Twenty-thousand strong.

The excitement started to build. The band could hear the crowds rushing in. The adrenaline started pumping. By seven o'clock, the band was dressed and their hair styled. The other band, The Missiles, had arrived and the two bands introduced themselves. The Missiles wished Midnight Angel the best of luck on their opening night and went to a separate dressing room.

Stevie Roselli paced the floor with the guitar in his hands, warming up for the show. "Just think;" he said, "in one hour—just sixty minutes—we will be out there on stage before twenty-thousand people."

"Hey cool it Stevie! You're making me nervous," said Johnny. Johnny looked at his watch. It was three minutes after seven. "Where the hell is Rosanna?"

"Oh boy, opening night and we gotta worry about Rosanna!" said Danny sitting off to the side and warming up on his bass.

"Hey Rosco, how'd you like a drumstick in your eye?" Johnny was about to begin warming up on his drum pad.

"Hey Johnny, don't get crazy—just kiddin'."

"Yeah, well don't bust my chops."

"Well why don't you give her a call?"

"I'm so freakin' worried, I didn't even think of it." Johnny ran to the phone in the backstage hallway. He called the hoagie shop and Rosanna's house. There was no answer. Rosanna's mother and father had gone to Johnny's Uncle Al's to watch the concert on TV, but where was Rosanna? Johnny slammed the phone and rushed back to the dressing room. He sat down and began playing single stroke rolls as fast as he could on his portable drum pad to get loosened up .

By now, all the fellows were warming up on their instruments. Jerry Carvelli was doing breathing exercises and shouting out high notes. Mike Danella was playing on his portable keyboard. By 7:30, Johnny was sweating and very pissed off. He looked to Danny. "Danny, where the hell could she be? She may have gotten in an accident for all I know-she could be in the hospital!"

"Don't worry Johnny, she'll be here—she wouldn't miss it for the world."

"I hope you're right—we've only got about twenty-five minutes."

At twenty minutes to eight, the crowd was getting restless and began to chant, "We want Angel! We want Angel!"

"Wow, listen to them!" said Stevie Roselli as he continued to pace the floor with guitar in hand. Mr. Sacks entered the dressing room with Mr. Cassenelli and Mr. Kominski. They wished the guys the best of luck, and exchanged a few words with the band members. It was now ten minutes to show time and there was no Rosanna. The phone rang in the back stage hallway. A security guard picked up the receiver.

"Hello, this is Jack."

"Jack, this is Ronny. I'm at the band entrance. There's a girl here trying to get in, she says she's the drummers girlfriend."

"Ask her her name."

"What's your name honey?"

"Rosanna."

"She says her name is Rosanna."

"OK, hold on." The guard went to the dressing room. "Hey, there's a girl at the private entrance says she's the drummer's girlfriend. Said her name's Rosanna."

Johnny jumped out of his seat. With his drumsticks in hand, he ran off. It was just five minutes to show time. The Spectrum was filled to capacity, and once again the crowd started to chant.

Danny shouted, "Johnny, where the hell you going? We only have about five minutes!"

The fellows began to complain to one another. Suddenly they began to get a bit disgusted with Johnny. Joe the tour manager entered. "OK guys, you ready?"

Jerry grunted, "Ready? We don't even have a drummer."

"What are you talking about? What the hell is going on here?"

"His girlfriend just arrived and he went to meet her at the

band entrance."

"What the hell's the matter with him! Doesn't he know we've got a concert to play?"

Danny raised his hands in the air as the strap of the bass guitar hung around his neck. "I knew it! Opening night, and he runs the other way."

The assistant tour manager entered the room. "OK fellas, warm-ups are over. It's time to get it together-it's show time."

"There's no show without a time keeper," said Joe. "My mother was right, I should have been a school teacher!"

"You mean you're missing your drummer?"

"Hey he caught on fellas," replied Jerry.

"Man, you guys have to be off stage by 9:30 and it's five minutes after eight now. It's your first night. You want to get all the playing in you can. Now where the hell's your drummer? We got a show to do."

The crowd became more demanding and began to chant louder and stronger. The band was feeling the pressure. Johnny reached the band entrance.

"Johnny!" Rosanna shouted.

"Rosanna come on, I have to go on!"

"Hey wait a minute," said the guard.

"It's OK, she's with me." The two began to run to the dressing room. They were inseparable and excited, as though together they could conquer the world. Taking deep breaths, Johnny asked, "Rosanna, where the hell have you been, I've been going nuts."

"Johnny, I'm so sorry. I got to the hotel late. The man at the desk gave me directions that he received from Joe. Traffic's bad at 5:30 and I got stuck in it. By the time I got outside, it was 7:15 and it took forever to find a parking space."

They reached the dressing room gasping for air. "Covini, what are you doing!" asked Joe.

"I'm sorry Joe—I'm sorry fellas. I'm ready." Johnny turned to Anita the costume girl, "Anita, can Rosanna stay with you? Will you direct her to stage-side so she can watch us play?"

"Sure Johnny, no problem. She can stay with me."

Johnny kissed Rosanna and told her he loved her.

"I love you too. Play good Johnny!"

The stage was dark as the fans continued to chant. The excitement was incredible. The fellows began their walk to the stage where they would experience the biggest night of their life. They were excited but also nervous, happy but worried. Worried that they would not come off as good as they hoped. Johnny thought of Billy, how he had counseled him, about how he was a musician and that's what he does best. As each thought and phrase entered Johnny's mind, he began to get stronger and more fearless.

Just before they entered the stage, Johnny stopped and looked to his buddies. "Fellas, let's do what we do best. We are musicians, so let's play to the fullest. Let's make music!"

"You got it Johnny!" said Danny. They all acknowledged Johnny's strength and they all joined hands.

"Let's do it!" said Johnny.

The fellas went out on stage being guided by the stage hands with flashlights in their hands. The stage was still dark. The fans began to shout when they saw the flashlights shining. They knew the band was about to begin. The Spectrum was bursting with energy, and with the concert being televised and broadcasted on radio, the whole population of Philadelphia and its suburbs could feel the excitement.

The fellas took their places on stage and Johnny took his place behind the big black drumset. Johnny hit the foot pedal of the right bass drum twice. The crowd began screaming. They were ready for a night of hard driving rock'n'roll. He then rolled across the tom-toms to get comfortable with the set, and the crowd screamed even louder. They began shouting "Angel! Angel! Angel!"

Jerry Carvelli adjusted his microphone. Danny Rosco and Stevie Roselli were being advised to turn the volume on their guitars to the proper level. Mike Danella was making last-minute adjustments on his multi-keyboard setup. The screaming crowd knew that in just a few minutes a band from their own hometown would soon be making music as they saw glimpses of the band members on the dark stage.

The tour manager walked to the side of the stage to a microphone. He began to address the crowd, "Ladies and Gentleman, I would like to introduce the hottest new band in the world…" Before he could get another word in, the crowd began to scream.

Rosanna was looking on from the side of the stage, clapping and cheering. "Give it all you've got Johnny," she said. The crowd settled momentarily.

Joe began to speak again, "From your hometown, Philadelphia, Pennsylvania…" Once again the crowd interrupted, cheering for their hometown heroes. Joe couldn't seem to get another word in. The fellows were taking deep breaths and trying not to be overcome by the fans' cheering. Once again the crowd settled, and Joe spoke through the mike for the last time. "Ladies and Gentlemen, I give you Midnight Angel!"

The crowd screamed to its fullest. Johnny began with a fantastic quick syncopated drumbeat, then went on into a drum roll from the snare to the very last tom-tom to start their first song.

The band came in with a roaring sound full of rock'n'roll power. Jerry Carvelli began to sing his first verse with power and energy, as the other musicians played with grace and vigor. Johnny was rocking steady and held down a solid and steady beat. He seemed to be the picture perfect drummer. Jerry came out of his first verse, and Stevie Roselli came in with a tasteful lick on the guitar. And the crowd screamed to the top of their lungs.

Jerry began the second verse. He seemed relaxed and collected. He sang like he'd never sung before. He approached the middle of the verse and the band accented.

Johnny came in with a thundering double bass drum fill that shook the stage. His strength and energy was incredible. The years that the fellas had spent in the music business had finally payed off. The group was totally polished and professional, as though they'd been playing concerts for years.

Stevie Roselli took an awesome lead on the guitar, and the crowd stood up and cheered him on. His guitar solo vibrated the Spectrum with excitement. Danny Rosco and Jerry were looking at each other. Jerry pretended to have a guitar in his hand, imitating Danny Rosco as Stevie Roselli continued his guitar solo. He played with grace and fluidity. He was throwing kicks into the air as he played his sparkling purple guitar. He was dressed in a purple satin outfit with white shoes, and his hair was styled to perfection. The band began to prove to their fans that they were showmen also.

As Johnny twirled his sticks, incorporating his showmanship into his playing, he wore a black satin top with no sleeves and opened from his chest up. He had black leather wrist bands on his wrists. His pants were blue satin and he wore pure white sneakers. His black hair shone. It was half way over his ears, and down to his collar in the back. It stood a bit short on the top and feathered all around.

The band came to a climactic ending with lights blinking, smoke bombs going off, and sparks shooting into the air. The special effects crew was doing a fantastic job. The crowd gave them a standing ovation for their first song. Rosanna was clapping and cheering, saying "Good job, Johnny   you're the best, you're the best!"

Jerry Carvelli thanked the excited crowd. "Good evening," he said, "and hello Philadelphia!" The crowd responded with a cheer. "We want to do a song that the drummer and I wrote. Let's hear it for the drummer, Johnny Covini, ladies and gentlemen." Johnny stood and took a bow, and the crowd cheered him on. He then looked to the side of the stage and winked at Rosanna. She smiled and threw him a kiss. Jerry continued, "The name of the song is 'No Turning Back.'"

The band began its second song with grace and simplicity, showing courage and aggressiveness. Johnny continued to play with rock'n'roll power and a back beat that was second to none. They definitely were one of the best new bands to hit the concert halls, and were earning the respect of everyone in the Spectrum. Girls were screaming, some with tears in their eyes. Banners were held up all over the Spectrum. Some said, "I love drummers,' others said, "I love guitar players," and so on. One banner said, "Johnny Covini, We Love You." Others said, "Jerry I Love You."

At home Uncle Al, his wife, and Rosanna's parents were all together at Al's house watching the concert on TV. They were all tapping their feet and very excited. Al poured wine for himself and Pondolona, and they toasted to Rosanna and Johnny.

Back at Harry's Bar, everyone was watching and cheering the band on. The bar was mobbed. Harry was jumping up and down. The elderly man had never been quite that excited. "Johnny, Johnny Covini," he said, "I can't believe it! He made it on TV." Suddenly at Harry's Bar, a beautiful well-built brunette about five-foot-five entered the bar. It was Penny Delulla. She had flown in from L.A. to see some of her family and thought she might find Johnny at Harry's Bar to say hello. She couldn't understand what all the commotion was about. She managed to squeeze through the crowded bar and asked Harry for a drink.

"What will it be?" Harry asked.

"Rum and coke."

Harry made Penny's drink and brought it to her. "You know honey, you look familiar."

"Yeah, I was here about a year ago. I'm Johnny Covini's friend."

"Oh yeah, now I remember."

"What's all the excitement on the TV? And by the way, has Johnny been around?"

"Yeah, he's around. He's down at the Spectrum."

"What's he doing down at the Spectrum?"

"He's playing drums for his new band."

"His new band?"

"Yeah, take a look for yourself, he's right up there on the TV screen."

A patron held up his glass of beer for a toast. "Let's here it for Johnny Covini—our man from South Philly." The bar full of people cheered and toasted.

Penny spoke to herself, "You did it Johnny, you finally did it." She took a sip of her drink and then said, "I knew you could do it Johnny," as tears filled her eyes.

Back at the Spectrum, the band was playing their hearts out, making rock 'n roll history. It seemed as though never before had all these sizzling elements been displayed by a rock 'n roll band like Midnight Angel. They continued to play through their repertoire and one hour and 15 minutes had passed. Finally they came to the song that included Johnny's drum solo, titled "Cry Of The Drummer."

"Thank you Philadelphia," said Jerry. The crowd clapped and cheered, and cheered and clapped. Jerry looked back at the band members and smiled. He could feel his heart pounding with joy and excitement. He couldn't believe how the crowd was continually cheering them on. This was a night the guys would never forget. Jerry addressed the crowd, "This song was written by our bass player, Danny Rosco, and once again, our drummer, Johnny Covini." The crowd roared. Jerry turned to Danny, and said, "Take it Rosco."

Danny began the song with a rock 'n roll jazz riff on the bass. After he played for about thirty seconds, Johnny came in with a crescendo on the snare and floor tom. He crashed the cymbal and came in with a hard-driving, straight ahead rock 'n roll beat that cut like a knife.

Jerry, in his black leather vest and pants and white snake skin boots, belted out the first verse with grace, power, and energy. His blond hair was a big mass of curls down to his shoulders. The band sounded great, and was rocking steady.

Johnny was playing with precision and concentration, knowing that his solo was fast approaching. Jerry finished his first verse and Stevie came in with a spellbinding guitar solo. He played with speed, accuracy, and clarity. He soon came out of his solo, and quickly began playing rhythm. The band was holding a steady rhythm, and suddenly came to a strong, accented stop.

Johnny began his solo. The rest of the fellas walked off and Johnny took the stage alone. He began his solo with a rudimentary type sound on the snare. He played at a medium tempo with a very tasteful touch that sounded like a cross between an African rhythm and a jazz feel. Individual cheers were coming from all over the Spectrum. He continued to play the snare, and quieted down. He played paradiddles quietly on the snare, and then suddenly he played powerfully in very loud triplets using the tom-toms and the right bass drum. Almost as suddenly as he had stopped, Johnny resumed the paradiddle pattern. His accuracy and clarity were astounding.

Rosanna shouted from the stage side, "Go for it, Johnny! Show 'em what you got!"

He began to play louder, staying on the snare drum, and then began to use the smaller tom-toms mounted on the bass drums. Suddenly he stopped. His feet began to roll the bass drums with lightning speed; it sounded like thunder. The crowd was hysterical. It sounded like twenty thousand people all screaming at the same time.

As he continued to pound the pedals, he began to play the whole set at a medium tempo. The crowd back at Harry's Bar listened intently and watched the TV screen in amazement. Penny spoke quietly to herself, "I always told you you were the best, Johnny."

All over the city streets people were riding in their cars tuned in to the concert on radio, as they listened to one of their hometown heroes play his astounding drum solo. Horns were beeping all over the streets of South Philadelphia, celebrating the band's maiden voyage.

Johnny began to pick up tempo, and began to play at full speed. Cymbals were crashing, and new drum rolls were being created. Johnny was doing drum work he never knew before. He was amazing himself. He brought the volume and tempo down and went to the snare drum. The crowd gave its biggest applause of the night.

Johnny started picking up tempo and volume once again. Working a tricky beat going from the snare drum to the high hat cymbals, his speed and fluidity were amazing.

Joe, the tour manager, looked to his assistant. "This drum solo's going to make rock'n'roll history—this guy is incredible."

He began to play the whole set again as fast as his mind, heart and body could go, as the other musicians walked back on stage. Mike Danella, in his shiny satin burgundy outfit, and Danny Rosco in his black leather pants, black alligator boots, and pink satin sleeveless top, smiled to one another. "Johnny's never played like this!" shouted Rosco to Mike.

The guys positioned themselves and were ready to play as Johnny's solo was coming to a climax. He suddenly came to a pounding stop. He then did a hard-driving simplistic roll on the snare drum and the other musicians came in forcefully to finish out the song with Johnny. The Spectrum was shaking with excitement. Every human being in the place stood and gave Johnny a standing ovation, as the band played on.

The band continued to play, and the crowd stood on their feet. The band came to an outstanding and dramatic ending. They stopped suddenly, and Johnny played for thirty seconds. He rolled around the whole drumset speedily and then did some triplet rolls on the bass drums, and the band joined in for a truly awesome ending.

The crowd was screaming, and the guys were advised to walk to the front of the stage and take a bow together, the tour manager motioned them on. As they approached the stage front, they put their arms around one another's shoulders. Girls were trying to climb up on stage, as security people were working forcefully to hold them back.

Rosanna was clapping her hands at stage left, and shouted, "I love you, Johnny Covini!" Johnny could vaguely hear her, and turned to her. "I love you too, Rosanna!"

The people back at Harry's Bar were cheering them on as they shouted, "Encore!" The fans at the Spectrum shouted the same. Uncle Al, Aunt Carmella, and Rosanna's parents were applauding at home.

Johnny looked up and said, "Thank you sweet Jesus, and thank you Billy, wherever you are!"

John Michael Austin, formerly a full-time nightclub musician, now works as an actor in Philadelphia based movie productions. Also the founder, writer and drummer for his music group, *Hereafter*, Mr. Austin lives in a small township near Valley Forge where he is at work on a new novel.